ORWELL

THE WAR
COMMENTARIES

ORWELL

THE WAR
COMMENTARIES

EDITED WITH AN INTRODUCTION BY W. J. WEST

PANTHEON BOOKS NEW YORK

Library of Congress
Cataloging-in-Publication Data

Orwell, George, 1903-1950.
Orwell, the war commentaries.
Includes index.
I. West, W. J. (William J.)   II. Title.
III. Title: War commentaries.
PR6029.R8A6   1986   940.53   86-5057
ISBN 0-394-55701-8

Manufactured in the United States of America

First American Edition

For R.F. and R.S.

C O N T E N T S

M   A   P   S

Reproduced from volumes 5, 6 and 7 of J.F. Horrabin, *An Atlas-History of the Second Great War*, Thomas Nelson & Sons Ltd., London, 1942 & 1943.

Publisher's Note: *Orwell: The War Broadcasts*, also edited by W.J. West, was published in the United States in 1985 by Arbor House, New York, as *Orwell: The Lost Writings*.

P R E F A C E

Some eighteen months ago I had the good fortune to discover a large number of writings by George Orwell which he produced while working full-time at the BBC from August 1941 to November 1943. They fall into two broad categories. There are those he spoke into the microphone himself, which were mainly literary. They were published earlier this year in *Orwell: the War Broadcasts*. In the Introduction to that volume I gave an account of Orwell's days at the BBC; and the book concluded with a selection of letters to contributors revealing links between the worlds of Radio and Letters at that crucial time.

Secondly, there are the weekly news talks written by Orwell on the progress of the war from the end of 1941 to early 1943, which he did not for the most part broadcast himself. They make up this second book. Each book can be read quite independently. (Readers of the first volume, incidentally, should note that the title of this one, listed there provisionally as 'Through Eastern Eyes: Orwell's War Commentaries', has been changed. I discovered that the series 'Through Eastern Eyes' in which the commentaries were broadcast also included other programmes, not by Orwell. The present, simpler title *Orwell: the War Commentaries* seemed therefore more suitable.)

The Introduction which follows gives in some detail the political framework, established by censorship, within which Orwell worked. The texts themselves are followed by a selection of broadcasts, mostly on India, put out by enemy radio stations. Together they give a unique picture of an actual propoganda war, broadcast over public address systems in offices and canteens, and from radio sets in homes and villages, throughout an entire sub-continent. It was exactly this kind of war that was to form the background of Orwell's totalitarian vision of the future in his most famous novel *Nineteen Eighty-Four*.

All the scripts printed here are in the BBC Written Archives Centre (WAC) at Caversham Park Reading. I take this opportunity to thank the staff at the Centre for making my work there, and the search for materials whose very existence was at times in doubt, so great a pleasure. I am also deeply grateful once again to my originating publishers, Duckworth, whose close interest in the book has helped it in innumerable ways.

Exeter, July 1985   W.J.W.

INTRODUCTION

The coming of radio early this century gave the ancient art of propaganda an entirely new dimension, one that was to prove particularly useful in time of war. Even a victory won by the enemy in the heat of battle could be made to seem a defeat if convincing false news could be disseminated immediately by radio and the enemy given the task of refuting it. Propaganda talks could be aimed at selected countries and at specific sections of their population, and real damage could be caused where no army could reach even in a long campaign. Ample experience had been gained of this new theatre of war in the Spanish Civil War and during the German encroachments in Europe in the thirties. By the outbreak of the Second World War there had grown up what Churchill was to describe as 'battles for the Empires of the mind'.[1]

Britain found herself vulnerable to this type of warfare. Her home radio service had developed rapidly and was regarded all over the world as a model of public service broadcasting, but the range of her overseas programmes was small. The Empire, exposed in every quarter of the globe but still intact, was an obvious target, and if the 'jewel in the crown' of this Empire was India it was a jewel, as all could see, that was loosely fixed. Britain's Axis enemies had pioneered the new radio propaganda techniques before the war and, knowing of her difficulties in India and of the large number of Indian troops fighting for her, had set up radio stations aimed at India. They inaugurated a campaign to dislodge the jewel entirely, hoping to bring to an end the mighty British Raj itself by fomenting civil unrest and supporting any movement for Indian independence.

The only possible answer to a campaign of this kind was to create a team of professional propagandists who could counter the lies and misrepresentations coming from the Axis stations as quickly as possible after they were broadcast. This task was given to the British Broadcasting Corporation. Through the Indian section of its Eastern Service the BBC was soon putting out a great variety of programmes,[2]

---

[1] In a speech at Harvard University, September 1943.

[2] For examples of these programmes see W.J. West (ed.), *Orwell: The War Broadcasts* (1985), Appendix B and elsewhere.

the cornerstone of which was a series of weekly news commentaries. Although they were spoken by Indians and seemed to the listener to be an account of the war literally as seen 'through eastern eyes' – the title of the series – they were actually written by an Englishman.

The choice of George Orwell to write them was, on the face of it, an odd one. Orwell was, as he himself said in a letter at the time,[3] an agin'-the-government-man who believed passionately that India ought to be given her freedom at the earliest possible moment. But he also saw clearly that there were far greater dangers for the Indian people in domination by a non-English-speaking totalitarian power than in the mere continuation of British rule for a few more years, or even until the war ended. And he was reassured in this view by close friends of his from India, such as Mulk Raj Anand, who both knew the Indian Congress leaders well and had experience of the reality of Axis rule in Europe.

Although the talks were put out anonymously, or as the work of the people reading them, Orwell was prepared to stand by their contents. Towards the end of 1942 it was suggested by the Indian Intelligence Officer Laurence Brander that Orwell should step forward from the shadows, put his name to the talks and even read them out himself. Orwell agreed, and it is due to this decision that his authorship of these commentaries has become known at all.[4] We can regard them both as a fortunate survival of a propaganda war and as an example of how a great writer saw and understood the war as it was progressing week by week.

To know the enemy he was fighting all Orwell had to do was to turn on a radio set and tune in to any one of a dozen Axis stations, such as 'Lord Haw-Haw' and the 'Workers Challenge'[5] aimed at Britain or 'Radio Himalaya' and 'Free India Radio' aimed at India. But he did not even have to resort to his own set, for he was provided every day by the BBC Monitoring Service with printed transcriptions of all propaganda broadcasts, translated into English where necessary. This extraordinary publishing enterprise is one of the great unacknow-ledged triumphs of war propaganda research. Within twenty-four hours or less the BBC's monitors transcribed all the material from

[3] See *OWB*, p.43.

[4] For an account of how the scripts were found in detail, see *OWB*, p.7ff.

[5] 'Lord Haw-Haw' was an English nickname for William Joyce, who was hanged as a traitor after the war. The talks he gave were in his own name, but the BBC monitors referred to him as 'William Joyce, otherwise known as Lord Haw-Haw'. For a typical example of his numerous talks, see below, Appendix no. 17. 'Workers Challenge' was a station in Europe which purported to be a revolutionary socialist outpost located somewhere in England.

radio stations in Allied, Axis and neutral countries. This material was typed out, printed and circulated to the Ministry of Information and all Government departments, supplying invaluable information to military men, politicians and their propagandists.

When Orwell came to write the scripts of his war commentaries he therefore had before him all that the enemy had said the previous week, a substantial book in itself. He also had the press releases from the MOI giving the Allied version of events, and an echo of these in the daily press and news broadcasts put out by the BBC's home service – which, of course, also drew their material from the MOI. Out of this vast chaos of words he had to condense a view of the war which would be comprehensible to the average educated Indian listener and counter what he judged to be the spirit of the Axis talks. This latter task was made easier for him by the appearance on the air-waves of a radio news service in Berlin, 'Azad Hind' ('Free India'), which was run by Indians. It transmitted its manifesto on 19 January 1942 and may well have been intended as an answer to Orwell's department's work. The manifesto makes the position of the service and its founder, Subhas Chandra Bose, crystal clear:

> Azad Hind radio service is organised by Azad Hind, an organisation embracing all Indians living abroad. It is only after extreme effort that it has become possible for us to bring into existence such an organisation. In these politically disturbed times it is absolutely necessary, at home as well as abroad, that we must stand together, and keep in touch with one another. We decided it was our duty to provide a political platform on which all Indians living abroad can work hand in hand, before we spoke to you. We had to wait long but it was not in vain. We are filled with unlimited joy that we can speak to you today, in the same name of all Indians living outside India, who are still free from British and foreign control, and can express their political opinions.
>
> Azad Hind will be operating in many parts of the world. Its activities are manifold and widely-spread, and radio service is its latest enterprise. We attach great importance to it for it is the only way open to us of bringing to your ears our voice and feelings. We are free from British propaganda and control, and can view world affairs from a purely nationalist point of view. We know there are people in India not so fortunate, and we think it our moral duty to acquaint you with the trend of world events, and to win your confidence in our activities to achieve freedom for our dear Motherland. Let it become a medium for cooperation between those outside and those inside India. The distinguishing feature will be that our transmission will be by Indians and for Indians. To most of the Indian public the only channel of information is British, and thus they imbibe unconsciously the British propaganda, and live in an unreal world. Some of you might listen to

other foreign radio stations to learn the so-called 'other side of the picture', but this in no way compensates for the absence of a national radio. People who listen to foreign stations do not take advantage of the news and comments because of their deep suspicion of false propaganda, and such a prejudicial state of mind prevents them from distinguishing the truth. Therefore many listeners get an altogether false picture of the international situation. The right way to know world affairs is to listen to sources on which you can rely, and that will be the special duty of our transmitter. We want to prepare India for a fight for full national independence. The time has come to act. If we want our freedom we must pursue a logical but bold policy.

Bose was a man of considerable ability. Educated in India and at Cambridge, he did brilliantly in the Civil Service examinations but resigned from the Service shortly afterwards, the first Indian to do so, to work with the leaders of the nationalist Indian Congress party. He was well known during the inter-war years, and his book *The Indian Struggle 1920-1934* (1935), banned in India, gained him an international reputation second only to Gandhi's and Nehru's. In 1938 he was elected President of Congress.[6] On 2 July 1940 he was arrested on a charge of sedition, and later confined to his house to await trial, but he escaped and made his way to Germany through Afghanistan and Russia, flying from Moscow to Berlin on 28 March 1941. The setting up of Azad Hind was the first important outcome of his stay in Berlin. Later he left Germany. He travelled by submarine from Kiel to Sumatra, an immense distance, and then by air to Tokyo, where he arrived on 13 June 1943. He led the Indian National Army and died finally from injuries received in a plane crash in Formosa on 18 August 1945.

Azad Hind's programmes were not without a humorous note – the BBC was regularly referred to as the 'Bluff and Bluster Corporation' – but for the most part they echoed Bose's own speeches: tirades against the British in India which totally simplified the situation there and skirted round the actual role Bose saw for himself in an India free from British rule but part of the new Japanese 'Co-Prosperity Sphere'. Orwell never once mentions Bose by name and only rarely makes a direct allusion to him and his colleagues, but his broadcasts are often a direct answer to Bose.

There were other broadcasts to India from Japan and from stations

---

[6] When elected President Bose was drawn in the Presidential car by fifty-one bullocks through fifty-one gates of honour in commemoration of the fifty-first Indian Congress. The facts about Bose which follow are largely drawn from Hugh Toye, *Subhas Chandra Bose, the Springing Tiger: A Study of a Revolution* (1959).

set up in Burma and elsewhere after Japanese occupation,[7] but these were difficult to monitor from Britain. Few of them appear in the daily monitors' reports in the archives, and Orwell probably left them to be refuted by the men at All India Radio in New Delhi. He rarely mentions anything likely to have come from these stations. He seems to have realised that he was best occupied countering Azad Hind and the speeches of Hitler, Goebbels and the other Axis leaders, all of which could be heard in India on world-wide link-ups and were frequently referred to in the Indian press. He also used items of news that were put out on the Axis domestic radio networks which could never have been heard in India. He was fully justified in this by the in-depth picture he gained of what life was really like in Europe under Hitler's 'New Order', the model for Japan's 'Co-Prosperity Sphere'.

The first of Orwell's scripts contains a resumé of the progress of the war up to that time, but only in broad outline to put across his own perspective. The facts would have been known to his listeners, although they had only followed the war from a distance. Like the First World War, the Second began in Europe. At that time the ordinary Indian's view must have been very much as Anand described it in his brilliant novel *Across the Dark Waters* (1940). Individual families knew that their fathers and sons were once more fighting overseas; the Indian intellectuals, no doubt, followed what was happening with some understanding beyond a simple view of victories and defeats.

At first there was little major conflict. Britain's declaration of war in September 1939, consequent on Germany's invasion of Poland, inaugurated what came to be known as the 'phoney war'. But German advances continued, absorbing most of Europe. France herself, after her sudden capitulation in June 1940, was split in two, one part occupied directly by the Germans and the other, 'Vichy France', left as a nominally independent but pro-German country under the ageing Marshall Pétain. Indian listeners, who had followed the catastrophes in Europe, ending for Britain with her ignominious withdrawal from the continent at Dunkirk, now heard of the long fight back in North Africa – a theatre much closer to India, with Indian as well as other Empire troops fighting alongside native British.[8] Germany's allies, Vichy

---

[7] There is an interesting account of Japanese radio warfare in an essay by Namikawa Ryo, 'Japanese overseas broadcasting: a personal view', included in K.R.M. Short (ed.), *Film and Radio Propaganda in World War II* (1983). About the Burma broadcasts Ryo says: 'The radio war aimed at India is said to have been particularly appalling. The chief of the station was Matsuchi Novizo a famous baseball commentator in Japan.'

[8] For the role of the Indian Army in the Second World War, see Philip Mason, *A Matter of Honour: an account of the Indian Army, its Officers and Men* (1974).

France and Italy, both had colonial possessions in North Africa and the Middle East, and it was there that Britain obtained her first sizeable victories, in all of which Indian troops played a notable part. These initial successes were followed by defeats, and the battles in the desert continued with varying fortunes throughout the period of Orwell's commentaries. The Indians were well aware of the significance of the Suez Canal for Indian links with Europe, and Orwell kept them abreast of every development in this area.

The Russian front, so important throughout the First World War, played no part in the Second until 1941. The non-aggression pact between Hitler and Stalin signed at the outbreak of war held for nearly two years, and the unholy alliance between the two alien totalitarian powers looked like becoming permanent. But German suspicion of Russia, combined with Hitler's judgment of his best opportunity for an attack, culminated on 22 June 1941 in a German invasion of Russia. The consequences were incalculable, and from now on the Russian front was followed with keen interest both by those observing the war and by others concerned for the fate of international Communism.

Indian intellectuals were only too conscious of Russia and her role in the world since the revolution of 1917. The Communist Party was active in India, and there were many who looked to it rather than to Congress for liberation from the British Raj. The sudden change of the Party's official sympathy for Germany, based on the German-Russian pact, to total and outright hostility towards Germany had its effect in India.[9] Whatever the view of Indian Congress leaders about the war in Europe, Russia's entry into the conflict had brought matters closer to home. But they were to be brought closer still, to India's very gates, with the dropping of Japanese bombs on Indian soil.

After the attack on Pearl Harbor in December 1941, which brought America into the war, the unthinkable – an attack on Singapore – seemed more and more likely as the Japanese offensive developed. The Japanese advance and the events it unfolded form the heart of Orwell's commentaries.

Besides the reporting of the war on the main fronts – the Russian front, North Africa, the Middle East, the Far East – Orwell took account of many local campaigns, such as the invasion of Madagascar and the early experimental landings on the coast of Europe itself. These must have seemed as remote to the average Indian listener as

[9] At the time that Nehru, Gandhi and other Congress leaders were being imprisoned Communist leaders were being released.

Czechoslovakia had to the British in 1938; Orwell frequently advised his listeners to consult an atlas if they were to understand the scope of the conflict. Finally there were the other campaigns, of great significance, carried on in worlds without frontiers: the war at sea, the war in the air – and the propaganda war.

At sea the activities of the great battleships unfailingly attracted headlines; there was always the hope that some cataclysmic contest between these giant ships would settle the war in a morning. But such days were over, and there were hardly any set-piece naval battles in the old tradition. For the most part the day-to-day sea war that Orwell had to report was against the submarine and the dive-bomber. Accounts of these battles were statistical, with lists of tonnage lost versus tonnage saved, which were both difficult to describe and difficult for land-locked Indian audiences to follow.

The air war, on the other hand, was known and understood in India. It had begun in earnest during the Battle of Britain in 1940 with the bombing of London and other cities in the Blitz. Anand and Orwell's other Indian colleagues at the BBC spent the entire war in London, experiencing the Blitz at close hand, sharing in the losses and sufferings of the people and describing them vividly in broadcasts to India. This bombing was seen as a logical extension of the bombing in Spain during the Civil War and came to represent for Orwell and the rest the real face of the totalitarian threat. At first British answering raids were on a small scale, but they increased enormously as the war developed, culminating in massive thousand-bomber strikes that were designed to create huge 'firestorms' which would destroy great cities in a single night with immense civilian casualties. Orwell's talks contain many references to them, usually with a note of triumph, which would not have been lost on Indian audiences, that here at least the tables were being turned.

Since the sea and air wars were wars without frontiers they made highly suitable material for the propaganda war. A convoy at one point is described by German radio as totally destroyed; Orwell counters by stating that it got through unscathed. Japanese radio refers to a sea battle in the Pacific as one of the greatest Japanese naval victories of all time; Orwell quotes American sources describing it as a defeat for Japan which has started a process leading to her ultimate collapse. Only the passage of time would enable listeners to tell which side was right.[10]

After the scripts were written they were passed to a censor, in the first instance a colleague within the BBC instructed in the arcana of

[10] See below, p.118 and p. 133, n. 217.

Government policy by the MOI. These instructions took several forms. There were frequent briefs passed to the BBC from the MOI by telegraph, but there were also more detailed guidelines, among them reports prepared by 'Special Issue' Sub-Committees of the Overseas Planning Committee of the Ministry. Over the months Orwell must have got to know the basic guidelines well and learnt to live with them, but the Special Issue reports would have been more of a challenge to his integrity.

As an example, the following is a report advising how to deal with the seriously deteriorating situation in India after the failure of the Cripps Mission in March 1942 sent to conciliate the Congress leaders. The report was urgent because actual detention of Nehru, Gandhi and the other Congress leaders was imminent, and it was felt essential for Orwell and his colleagues to be clear on the line to take.

> The decision of the Indian Congress Working Committee to appeal for British withdrawal from India means that the Government of India may be compelled at some stage to take drastic action against Mr Gandhi and other Congress leaders. This raises problems of a twofold nature in day-to-day publicity overseas:
>
> (a) What line should be taken now and in the immediate future about the situation as a whole.
> (b) What line should be taken if and when the Government of India is compelled to take drastic action.
>
> These two problems interact closely. The line taken in the immediate future must be such as to prepare opinion so as to cushion the shock if drastic action becomes necessary.

> *Comment on the attitude of Gandhi and other Congress leaders*

> A serious difficulty arises under this head. On the one hand it is most important that opinion in the US, the USSR, China and elsewhere should be adequately prepared for drastic action against Congress leaders; and that the charges levelled against them in case of such action should be fully clear and consistent with our past attitude towards them.
>
> On the other hand, while Mr Gandhi's reputation has recently suffered a sharp decline both in the US and in the USSR, and possibly even in China, and action against him therefore stands a reasonable chance of being well understood in those countries, it should be remembered that Mr Nehru's name still stands high in those countries and elsewhere.
>
> Further, Mr Gandhi's own standing in India is still such that open attacks upon him personally which could be directly attributed to official sources whether here or in India would antagonise or embarrass

many of those in India who are co-operating in the war effort, and would help to cement the unity of Mr Gandhi's following.

Therefore, unless and until Mr Gandhi forces the Government to take action against him, our *official* publicity should refrain from attacking him or his colleagues directly, and should limit itself to (a) quoting critical comment about him, whether by Indians themselves, or by Americans, Russians, etc., (b) quoting favourable references to him in Japanese and other enemy propaganda.

At the same time we should use every available channel in which we can be sure that the results cannot be attributed by Indians to us (and this entails the *utmost discretion* in their use) to explain the real facts of the case; to make clear that it was Congress, acting under Mr Gandhi's influence, which was responsible for the breakdown of the Cripps Mission; that their motive was their unwillingness to accept any solution which did not give them complete power to override the interests of all other groups in India, and notably the 100 million Moslems; that it is their responsibility as the largest party in India to work out with the Moslems and others a solution of the communal problem, and that they have made no effort to tackle that responsibility, having forced into resignation the one member of their Working Committee – Mr Rajagopalachari – who had the courage to make such an attempt.

The limelight should throughout be focussed (still bearing in mind the need for discretion) on the figure of Mr Gandhi, the inconsistencies of whose policy should be exposed, and who should be gradually built up as a backward-looking pacifist and Petainist (in this connexion his associations with prominent Indian industrialists such as Mr Birla could usefully be stressed) who has become a dangerous obstacle to the defence of India, and whose policies in fact if not in design play straight into Japanese hands. Such comment on Mr Gandhi should be positive and aggressive, and not apologetic. (WAC: MOI file)

Orwell ignored these instructions completely. He bitterly resented the attacks on Gandhi and Nehru, as did his fellow broadcasters. When the clamp-down actually came, he passed over the episode in silence. In his diary he commented frankly on broadcasts put out from the Empire section that followed the line recommended on the report.[11] Had Orwell tried to go further and put forward a pro-Congress view he would immediately have been silenced by the switch censor but, as a colleague of the time recalls, he was always trying to test the frontiers, resisting the temptation to conform and to police his own thoughts by 'self-censorship'.[12]

[11] *OWB*, p.37.
[12] Tosco Fyvel in an interview with the editor broadcast on 9 October 1984, produced by Angela Hind.

Having his integrity tested in this way directly, through censorship, must have created pressures on Orwell that helped toward the evolution of *Nineteen Eighty-Four* in which censorship is universal and a way has been found to police your thoughts for you if you can't or won't do it for yourself. Winston Smith in *Nineteen Eighty-Four* is employed in rewriting history. Every piece of 'real' news that survives from the past is consigned to the flames, and those who have gone before him have done their job so efficiently that only once has he held in his hands indisputable proof of an earlier version of 'the truth'. Orwell lived through just as dramatic changes in political and historic truth as Winston Smith. We print here a classic example of 'truth' which was current during the war but which, even a few years later, would have seemed unthinkable treason. It is another Special Issue report from the MOI dealing with the problem of German anti-Communist propaganda. Russia was Britain's ally, of course, at this time, but the report shows in detail how thoroughly steeped in Communist Party propaganda some of the officials of the Ministry were:

Arguments to counter the ideological fear of 'Bolshevism'

(1) We should show that all the horrors associated by German propaganda with the Bolshevik Bogey – destruction of culture, break-up of family life, forced labour, prison camps, seizure of property, destruction of religion, elimination of freedom, etc. – have in fact been perpetrated by the Nazis themselves in Occupied Europe. In short the so-called 'Red Terror' is merely a reflection in the Nazi propaganda mirror of the reality of the Nazi Terror.

(2) We should build up a positive picture of Russia which implicitly refutes the Nazi picture of the Bolshevik Bogey, stressing such points as:

> (a) The patriotic feelings increasingly displayed by the Russian people and encouraged by Soviet leaders during the war, with appeals to past Russian national glories, etc.
> (b) The great contributions made by Soviet Russia (in contrast to Nazi Germany) to science, learning and culture, and the continuity which they show with Russian cultural and scientific tradition from the past.
> (c) The development of small savings and personal property and individual initiative in the USSR, as showing that the 'small man' thrives in Russia. By contrast the small man has been completely betrayed by Hitler, who, having climbed to power on his shoulders, now proceeds to liquidate him.
> (d) The creditworthiness of the USSR as contrasted with the Germans in international business transactions.

(e) The increasingly tolerant attitude of the Soviet authorities towards religion. (Note: this argument must be used with great discretion and supported with evidence that is likely to command respect. It should be accompanied by reasoned explanations of the changed attitude of the Soviet Government towards religion, viz: their increasing confidence in the stability of the regime and the loyalty of the Churches in Russia; and even then it should only be used in addressing people already sympathetic to the USSR on other grounds. For the rest it is best to try to remove the question from the sphere of religious controversy altogether; or to take the line – adopted by certain Portuguese and Spanish bishops – that in respect of religion Soviet policy is certainly no worse than that of the Nazis, and that while the Soviet attitude to the Churches has been improving, that of the Nazis has steadily deteriorated. At the same time we should expose the hypocrisy of the Nazis' propaganda line on this point, and their inability to convince – e.g. their own bishops, who did not rally to the anti-Bolshevik crusade.)

(f) In building up this positive picture of the USSR, we should encourage all *specialist* interest in Russian achievements, e.g. by interesting military audiences in Russian military techniques or doctors in Russian medical services, etc.

(3) We should point to the major change of direction which has taken place in Soviet policy under Stalin. While the Trotskyist policy was to bolster up the security of a weak USSR by means of subversive movements in other countries controlled by the Comintern, Stalin's policy has been and continues to be one of maintaining a strong Russia maintaining friendly diplomatic relations with other governments – a policy which has been justified and confirmed by the events of the past two years. If Stalin maintains the Comintern in being, it is merely as a second line of defence which will be proved superfluous to the extent that he can rely on the co-operation of Britain and the USA.

We should quote evidence to show that parallel with this development in Soviet policy there has been a change in the type of personnel in power in the USSR. The ideologues and doctrinaire international revolutionary types have increasingly been replaced by people of the managerial and technical type, both military and civil, who are interested in getting practical results.

(4) Bearing in mind that in many countries fear of Bolshevism arises, particularly amongst the ruling classes, as a reflection of their fear of internal disaffection owing to inadequate social conditions, or to the atmosphere of unrest and disorder following on the cessation of hostilities, we should stress:

(a) That countries with a progressive social policy at home have nothing to fear from Bolshevism. The best antidote to internal 'Bolshevism' is an internal policy designed to provide decent standards of living and security.

(b) That Britain and the USA, with the other United Nations, intend to restore and maintain military security, law and order, and economic stability both in Europe and the world, and are preparing plans to that end.

(5) We should point out that, even supposing the USSR wanted to extend its influence throughout Europe, it will not, in the immediate post-war period, have the physical resources to exert undue influence. The food, consumer goods, etc. which Europe will so urgently need when hostilities cease can come only from the West and not from Russia, which will itself be a deficit area. (WAC: MOI file)

Orwell's views on Russia were in total opposition to the sympathies expressed in this document, which was meant to govern the tone and content of any relevant news programmes he might write. The Ministry of Information issued later editions of this report, all of which went further towards the Russian point of view. When Orwell left the BBC in November 1943 it was to write *Animal Farm*, an intensely felt satire directed at Russia. Predictably, this appears to have been banned by the MOI.[13] It was not published until after the war. At the same time he was working out the structure of *Nineteen Eighty-Four*, which was to be the ultimate attack on *all* totalitarian systems of government. Ironically the year 1984 itself, in which truth might have vanished completely, saw proof that in Britain, at least, there was some hope for its survival. The BBC's archives were seen not to have been consigned to the flames – or to their modern equivalent, the shredder – but to have survived largely intact. The propaganda war that Orwell fought is there for us to read. The distortions and suppressions, such as they were, have indeed survived, allowing us to see 'the truth' as it was sent out to those in India who looked to the BBC for truth above all else. Had Winston Smith really lived in 1984 he could have found out all he wanted about the past by merely looking.

In his last talk Orwell gave what was clearly his own assessment of the world situation and of the way things were likely to develop. There can have been few people, outside the offices of political leaders and their advisors, who were called upon to keep a clear and valid picture of the entire war on all its fronts in their mind's eye at all times, and who were asked to create immediately an authoritative picture of the war as Britain wished the world to see it. It may be remarked that

[13] See *OWB*, p.61.

it was only *radio* with its extraordinary power over people's minds that put Orwell in this position. And there is here, perhaps, a central reason why it was Orwell who successfully created that vision of the way the world was going in *Nineteen Eighty-Four*, rather than a more conventional 'literary' figure who had never sat behind a microphone, conscious that tens of millions would be listening to everything he had to say as being the truth about the greatest world struggle of the twentieth century.

The talks were weekly and cover the period from December 1941, immediately after the Japanese bombing of Pearl Harbor, which heralded the worst phase of the war for the Allies, to March 1943, when the tide had definitely turned in their favour after Germany's losses at Stalingrad. There are some weeks for which the texts have not been found. The reasons for these gaps can only be guessed at. For example, Orwell was very ill at the beginning of 1943, which may be why five scripts are missing from this period.[14] Two more gaps, for the last week of June and first week of July 1942, during which Sebastopol fell,[15] correspond with his annual leave. There is also a gap for the fall of Singapore, but for no apparent reason. Perhaps it was thought impolitic to broadcast such bad news at all; alternatively a script may once have existed which was subsequently lost. But apart from these few breaks the run of talks is complete, forty-nine in all.

The texts presented are those actually read at the microphone after censorship. In some cases, where legible beneath the censor's ink, it has been possible to restore deleted passages; such are printed in brackets. The few literal errors and inconsistencies of punctuation and orthography have been silently corrected, but otherwise the texts are printed exactly as typed.

Some maps have been included drawn and published at the time by Orwell's friend and collaborator J.F. Horrabin (see *OWB*, p.27f).

[14] Orwell took official sick leave from 20 January to 11 February 1943 and he was also away for shorter periods about this time.

[15] For a contemporary account of this neglected battle, written from a Russian standpoint, see Boris Voyetekhov, *The Last Days of Sebastopol* (1943).

THE WAR COMMENTARIES

20 December 1941

In making a survey of this week, we have a less resounding period to look back on than we had last week.[1] But one cannot say that the position is stabilized on any of the fronts. The Germans are still being beaten back in Russia and Libya, and in the Far East the Japanese are still getting further advantages from their first treacherous surprise attack. Penang has been evacuated, and the Japanese have landed on the island of Hong Kong.[2] The war is at present one of rapid changes but though the events come quickly their effects will be slow.

People easily forget what they felt about the news, and it may be worth while to look back a bit to another time when there were quick changes. Last winter the British overran Cyrenaica in a rapid campaign of two months or so; we captured Benghazi on the seventh of February. Then the Germans in answer began a drive on Greece, and we were bound in honour to send help to that brave ally. Mr Churchill and General Wavell had in view a large strategy; they were ready to maintain their obligations everywhere, and keep moving, and take risks. The troops sent to Greece had largely to be taken from Libya. On 7th April the British Expeditionary Force entered Greece, and the Axis drive back into Libya began at once. Next day the Italians were already claiming the recapture of Derna. By the 18th of April, the very rapid Axis advance had been finally held. It had recaptured the whole of Cyrenaica. The Germans succeeded in occupying Greece and Crete, and what we now hear from our brave Greek allies are tragic and horrible stories of starvation. Mr Churchill, no less than Hitler, had to consider the strategy of the war as a whole. It was on the 19th April that the British troops moved into Iraq, only just in time to prevent the Germans from taking a strong hold there. We thus stopped the

[1] News talks that reached India had been put out in the general overseas programmes.

[2] Penang was evacuated by 19 December. Hong Kong had been invited to surrender by the Japanese for the first time on 14 December and the surrender itself was reported on 25 December. Duff Cooper, previously Minister of Information, in his first broadcast as Minister for Far Eastern Affairs said: 'Let us not blind ourselves to the gravity of the situation, or the seriousness of the task that awaits us. Let us frankly admit that so far the Japanese have been extremely successful.' Broadcasts of this type were rare, and it gives the official atmosphere in which Orwell began his broadcasts.

German pincer movement, and from then on we had a comparatively stable front, behind which we could pile up in Egypt the supplies of war munitions from America. It was not till last month that we again took the offensive in Libya. By then we had the Russians as our allies, we had secured Iran against German domination and we had great supplies of munitions in Egypt. The position had changed entirely. It is in this way that we must consider the periods of rapid change in a vast war of grand strategy. We must use big maps before we can see how things are going at all; and we have been through worse times than this one.

At present the pursuit of the enemy in Libya is still going on. We have captured Derna aerodrome, on the coast, and are driving towards Mekili, on the desert road further south. In these two directions, our columns have covered a hundred miles in two days. Our main attacking force is already west of these two points. The delaying action fought by General Rommel seems now to have exhausted him, but he may make another stand. General Auchinleck, now in command of the Libyan campaign,[3] is a great believer in Indian troops. When serving in India he was anxious to create a corps from the more pacific peoples of the south. 'Start a tradition now,' he said, 'and in fifty years they will fight as well as the Sikhs.' When he was given his army corps it was suggested that its emblem should be the auk, an extinct bird because that is his nickname, but he said, 'I learned my soldiering in India; the corps shall bear the emblem of India.'

The Russians have recaptured three more towns on the Moscow front. The town of Rusa, fifty-five miles due west of Moscow, an important junction, was recaptured after desperate German resistance. It is reported that the Russian headquarters on this front has been moving its base forward twice a day. It was last Wednesday that the Germans first used the word 'retreat' about their own army, but they have thought of another word now, and say that they are 'rationalising their eastern front'.[4] They have admitted a Russian breakthrough in the south. Hitler in his last speech said that there were 162,000 German casualties in the whole Russian campaign. It is always interesting to consider how these lies are invented.[5] The campaign had then lasted

---

[3] Auchinleck was appointed Commander-in-Chief in the Middle East; a professional Indian Army soldier, he had previously been Commander-in-Chief in India and had created a favourable impression by his role in the suppression of the revolt in Iraq.

[4] The recapture of Rusa had only been announced in Moscow on the previous day, 19 December. Orwell was to have plenty of opportunity to invent his own euphemisms for 'retreat' in the months to come. He eventually acquired great skill in avoiding such traps for himself.

[5] Hitler's speech in fact gave precise details of how this figure was arrived at; here Orwell gives his own version.

just 162 days. It looks as if the Germans decided to admit a thousand men lost a day, but not more, and then a patient clerk worked out the sum exactly.

The Japanese successes are still very serious for us. At present the pressure of Japanese troops has died down in Malaya, where heavy casualties have been inflicted upon them. Large Indian reinforcements have been landed in Rangoon.[6] The Governor of Hong Kong[7] states that heavy fighting is in progress, on the island itself. The telegraphic lines to Hong Kong have been repaired, but the Japanese claim to have occupied most of the island. They are also making further attacks on the Philippines, where there is heavy fighting. Meanwhile our troops have entered the Portuguese port of Timor island, near Australia, to prevent the Japanese landing which seemed imminent. Dr Salazar has stated that Portugal will be faithful to her friends and allies.[8]

In all this we must remember that the Japanese power, though great, can only aim at a rapid outright victory. The three Axis powers together can produce 60 million tons of steel every year, whereas the USA alone can produce about 88 million. This in itself is not a striking difference. But Japan cannot send help to Germany, and Germany cannot send help to Japan. For the Japanese only produce 7 million tons of steel a year. For steel, as for many other things, they must depend on the stores they have ready.

If the Japanese seem to be making a wild attempt, we must remember that many of them think it their duty to their Emperor, who is their God, to conquer the whole world. This is not a new idea in Japan. Hideyoshi when he died in 1598 was trying to conquer the whole world known to him, and he knew about India and Persia. It was because he failed that Japan closed the country to all foreigners. In January of this year, to take a recent example, a manifesto appeared in the Japanese press signed by Japanese Admirals and Generals stating that it was Japan's mission to set Burma and India free. Japan was of course to do this by conquering them. What it would be like to be free under the heel of Japan the Chinese can tell us, and the Koreans. The Japanese will have to listen to China. In the famous Tanaka Memorial, a secret document presented to the Emperor of Japan in 1927, Baron Tanaka made one very true remark. 'In order to conquer the world,' he said, 'we must first conquer China.' Japan would have been wiser to follow the advice of this militarist leader

[6] The Governor of Rangoon, Sir Reginald Dorman-Smith, announced the arrival of strong Indian forces on 18 December.

[7] Japanese troops had landed on the night of 19 December. The Governor of Hong Kong, Sir Mark Young, was also Commander-in-Chief.

[8] Like General Franco, Salazar remained neutral throughout the war.

more exactly. She has let herself in for trying to conquer the world, and she has certainly not yet conquered China. The Chinese Government, as was stated by the Chinese Ambassador in London[9] has instructed all Chinese everywhere to assist the allied armies, and Chinese in Malaya and the Philippines, for example, are volunteering under the British and American flags. At home China has already a million men under arms and her manpower is almost inexhaustible.

Meanwhile America is in the long run an inexhaustible arsenal, and the Americans are determined not to have their help limited to the Pacific area. They have decided to use British Eritrea as the centre at which American experts will receive the great supplies of amunition which America will continue to send to the Near East.[10]

3 January 1942

During a week in which there has been fighting in almost every quarter of the globe, the two most significant events have not happened upon the battlefield. The first of these events was the signing in Washington of a pact by which no less than twenty-six nations pledge themselves to put an end to Fascist aggression.[11] The second was the entry of Chinese troops into Burma to take part in the defence of that country. In both these events we can see a demonstration of the solidarity of the free nations of the world, which is ultimately more important than guns and aeroplanes. For if four-fifths of humanity stand together, the other fifth cannot defeat them in the long run, however well armed and however cunning they may be.

We have to keep this fact in mind when we assess the news from the Far East and the Pacific. Temporarily the advantage is with the

---

[9] The Chinese Ambassador, Dr Wellington Koo, confirmed China's declaration of war on Japan, Germany and Italy on 9 December.

[10] The Italian colony of Eritrea surrendered on 5 April 1941 and was subsequently administered by the British Occupied Enemy Territories Administration. It was reported that when the capital, Asmara, was reached large machine tool and engineering shops installed by the Italians were discovered. These were taken over and run with American assistance.

[11] The joint declaration by all twenty-six nations at war with the Axis powers was signed in Washington on 1 January 1942. The nations were: the United States, the United Kingdom, the Soviet Union, China, the Netherlands, Australia, Belgium, Canada, Costa Rica, Cuba, Czechoslovakia, the Dominican Republic, El Salvador, Greece, Guatemala, Haiti, Honduras, India, Luxembourg, New Zealand, Nicaragua, Norway, Panama, Poland, South Africa and Yugoslavia.

Japanese; it may remain with them for a long time to come. The Americans have been unable to reinforce the heroic garrison of the Philippine Islands, and it is already reported that Manila, the chief town, has fallen into Japanese hands.[12] That does not mean that the fighting in the Philippines is ended, but it does mean that the Japanese are established in another advantageous spot for their attack on Singapore. Simultaneously they have occupied Sarawak in the north of Borneo. This is a strategic rather than an economic gain, for the British forces in Sarawak took care to blow up the oil wells and render them useless before they retreated.[13]

But in order to follow the events of this war, it is more than ever necessary to study the map of the world, and in addition to remember that the world is round.[14] When we hear of those early successes of the Japanese in the Pacific, we may be inclined to think that they offset the defeats which the Germans have received in Russia and Libya. But when we look at the map, we see a different picture, and we see one immense advantage which the democratic powers have over the Fascists. This is that they can communicate with one another. Between the two main Axis powers all inter-communication is impossible.[15] It is quite likely that within the next few months the Japanese will overrun so much territory in Asia and the Pacific that they will acquire enough tin, rubber, oil and food to keep their own war machine running for several years.[16] But they cannot send one single pound of these materials to the Germans, who will soon be needing them desperately. Similarly, when heavy air warfare develops in the Far East, the enormous aircraft factories of Germany will be of no value to Japan.

Meanwhile, in the other hemisphere the German retreats continue. In Libya the fighting is now at Agedabia, a hundred miles beyond

[12] On 2 January the United States announced that Manila and the Cavite Naval base had been evacuated, although troops held on at the island fortress of Corregidor in what was to develop into a classic siege.

[13] The British withdrew from Sarawak to Dutch Borneo on 3 January. On 28 December GHQ Singapore had confirmed Japanese claims that they were in control of the capital, Kuching. Despite Orwell's statement that a 'scorched earth' policy had been followed by the British before they left, Japanese radio claimed that the local population had prevented this from being carried out, as they did not wish to lose their jobs.

[14] 'The world is round' was the title of a talk Orwell commissioned from J.F. Horrabin for broadcasting to India. See *OWB*, p. 193.

[15] This had repercussions for Axis propagandists. For example, German cinema audiences were unable to see films of the Japanese victories because the film could not get to them from Japan, except by lengthy 'underground' connexions through neutral states.

[16] It was this fear that led Orwell to treat the Japanese invasion of Australia and India as real possibilities.

Benghazi. The German and Italian aeroplanes are fiercely attacking Malta, the British island which lies between Italy and Africa, and which has remained impregnable for ten months. The British and Indian troops[17] have taken thousands of prisoners, who will be sent back to join the Italians who were captured last year and who are now being employed on the making of roads in Africa and the Middle East. Simultaneously a number of American technical experts have arrived in Eritrea, the last African colony of the Italians, which we acquired last year. There they are setting up factories for the manufacture of aeroplanes and other war material, Eritrea being a convenient centre from which to supply both Russia, the Mediterranean and the Far East.

In Russia it is now hardly disguised even by the German propagandists that things are going disastrously for the Germans. Having announced nearly two months ago that Moscow was about to fall, the Germans found themselves compelled instead to retreat, and are now trying to cover up this fact by explaining that they find it convenient to shorten their lines and thus relieve some of the front line troops. But every time that the line is straightened and thus made shorter, another attack from the Russians dents it again, and the Germans are once more forced to retreat. In the centre of the front the chief damage that they are suffering is in the loss of material and also the loss of men, owing to the terrible cold of the Russian winter. In the far north and in the far south the Russians are winning a more definite strategic advantage. Leningrad, which has been almost in a state of siege for five months, is now in all probability about to be relieved.[18] It will be remembered that back in the summer the Germans described the Russian defence of Leningrad as 'criminal', declaring that the city could not possibly hold out, and that it was the duty of the Russians to surrender in order to save bloodshed. Now, five months later, the German grip on Leningrad is being forced open. This means not only a loss of prestige for the Germans. If Leningrad is fully relieved it will probably be possible for the Russians to drive Finland out of the war, and once this is done a way of communication between Britain and Russia easier than any that now exists will have been opened up.

In the Black Sea the Germans are also in great danger. When they first entered the Crimean Peninsula, and captured Odessa, it seemed as though they were going to have everything their own way. From the

---

[17] Large numbers of Indian troops were fighting in the Middle East. Orwell's broadcasts were aimed at these men and their families back in India as much as anyone else.

[18] Leningrad had been brought into the front line in August 1941. It was not finally relieved from German forces until 1943.

Crimea they were expected to cross the narrow strait to the Caucasus and at the worst, the Crimea, which is a comparatively warm climate, would be a valuable place in which to winter a great number of their troops. Nevertheless, they failed to capture the great Russian naval base of Sebastopol, and when the Russians re-captured Rostov the whole picture changed. The Russians are now advancing along the shore of the Black Sea, and at the same time, by the use of their navy, they have landed troops on the coast of the Crimea. The German Army in the Crimea is thus in danger of being cut off on the land side and simultaneously attacked from the sea. It is quite likely that it will be forced to beat a hurried retreat before the Russian armies reach the isthmus that divides the Crimea from the mainland, and in this way another valuable territory in which hundreds of thousands of Germans might have been preserved from the cold of the winter will have been lost.[19]

If we want the most revealing comment on the events in 1941, we can best get it by comparing Hitler's New Year speech with the speech he made just a year ago. At that date he had the victories of 1940 behind him and Britain stood completely alone. Now, the three greatest population blocks of the world, the USA, Soviet Russia and China are on Britain's side, and in return Germany has only gained the assistance of Japan. The German leaders are aware now that they cannot win in the long run, and every word of their speeches reveals this. They say nothing now about a speedy end to the war. At the beginning of 1941, they declared with absolute certainty that there should never be another winter of war. Now they can say only that there is a long war ahead. Admiral Tojo also bids his people prepare for a long war, and the Italian broadcasts also have strangely altered in tone. In the speeches of these men one can read their real determination. They have gambled and lost, and they are determined that since their schemes cannot be carried out, they will at least pull the world down in ruins before they perish. But even the peoples of the Fascist countries who have been so long stupefied by propaganda[20] are not incapable of thought, and it will not be long before they begin to ask themselves how many more years of war and suffering their leaders are going to offer them.

[19] Orwell, like everyone else, had overrated the effect of the Russian winter on the German forces. The Russian advances at this time were to be lost as rapidly later, and in particular the naval base of Sebastopol was to fall after a bitter siege by German and Romanian forces.

[20] Compare Orwell's ideas of super-powers whose peoples are totally dominated by propaganda, developed in *Nineteen Eighty-Four*.

10 January 1942

The greatest military event of this week has occurred on a battlefield about which we have not lately heard so much as we have heard about either Russia or Malaya, and that is the battlefield in China. The Japanese invaders have suffered a great defeat at the city of Changsha.[21] If you look at the map, you will see that Changsha is an important railway junction lying on the line between Canton and Hangkow. The Japanese are in possession of Canton, but only precariously, as they won it by means of sea invasion and the Chinese forces are all round them. If they could capture Changsha they might be able to cut off the whole south-eastern corner of China. They have now made three determined attempts in three years to capture it, and every time, after proclaiming that it was captured, they have had to fall back with heavy losses. On this occasion it is thought that they have lost twenty or thirty thousand men, and another twenty thousand are surrounded by the Chinese and likely to be destroyed.

This event is not important only for the heroic defenders of China. It cannot be too much emphasised that this is a world war, and every success or failure upon each of the various fronts has its effect upon every other front, from Norway to the Philippine Islands. The more the Japanese are compelled to tie their forces up in China, the less their chances of succeeding in an all-out attack against India and Australia; similarly, the sooner the British and Americans can bring their full power to bear against Japan, the sooner will Chinese soil be cleared of the invader.

It is good news that complete agreement has been reached between General Wavell, the Allied Commander-in-Chief in the Western Pacific, and Marshal Chiang Kai-Shek, as to the area of their commands.[22] The entry of Chinese troops into Burma, which we mentioned last week, is a sign that the alliance between Britain and

[21] After the announcement on 1 January that Japanese cavalry detachments had reached the outskirts of Changsha a stream of reports from Chungking radio ended with the claim, on 5 January, that a great victory had been achieved with 22,000 Japanese casualties and a further 30,000 trapped. Axis radio reports presented a picture of Japanese victory.

[22] In an announcement from the White House on 3 January General Sir Archibald Wavell was appointed Supreme Commander in the South West Pacific Area; Generalissimo Chiang Kai-Shek was confirmed as Supreme Commander of all Allied air and land forces in the Chinese sphere.

China is not a mere scrap of paper. No one doubts that the war in the Far East will be long and hard. The American forces in the Philippines have been compelled to abandon Manila, the principal town, and the fortress of Corregidor, which guards the entrance of Manila Bay, is under constant attack by sea and air. In Malaya the British have fallen back before Japanese forces which greatly outnumber them, and Kuala Lumpur is in danger. The Japanese are now near enough to Singapore for their fighter aeroplanes as well as bombers to fly there; this means that they may now be able to bomb Singapore by day as well as by night. The immediate situation in the Far East turns upon the arrival of British and American reinforcements, especially of aeroplanes, which have to travel enormous distances to get there. The short-term outlook in this theatre of war, therefore, is bad. But as to the long-term outlook, no one who knows how to estimate the relative forces involved is in doubt about the issue.

President Roosevelt's recent speech announcing the war budget has cleared up any doubts that might have remained as to America's willingness to prosecute the war to the very end.[23] The figures for tanks, aeroplanes and other armaments which it will be possible for American industry to produce during 1942 and 1943 are so enormous that the Axis propagandists are making every effort to prevent their peoples from even hearing about them. It indicates a great change in American public opinion that the American Government is now ready to send its forces to fight in no matter what theatre of war. Previously, there were large numbers of Americans who were willing to defend their own country against attack, but who were very hostile to the idea of being involved in war abroad, and specially in Europe. Now this objection has entirely disappeared. Preparations are being made to send American armies not only to the Pacific area, but also to Britain, to take part in the land conquest of Germany which will ultimately be necessary. This was what the Japanese achieved when they made their treacherous attack on December 7th.

On the Russian fronts the Germans are still retreating, and what is perhaps even more significant, the tone of their official pronouncements has abruptly changed. Until a week or two ago, the German military spokesmen were explaining that the attack on Moscow would have to

[23] Orwell is referring here to the President's message to Congress on the State of the Union delivered on 6 January. Roosevelt's talk described the extensive preparations being made, and the United Nations aims: 'For the first time since the Japanese and Fascists and Nazis started along their blood-stained course of conquest, they now have to face the fact that superior forces are assembling against them. The militarists in Berlin and Tokyo started this war, but the massed, angered forces of common humanity will finish it.'

be postponed until the spring, but that the German armies could quite easily remain on the line they now occupied. Already however, they are admitting that a further retreat – or, as they prefer to call it, a rectification of the line – will be necessary, and though they do not say so, it seems probable that they will have to retreat a very long way if they are to improve the situation of their troops perceptibly. [*Censored:* It has to be remembered that the Germans are fighting both against the Russian cold and against a great Russian army which is far better accustomed to the climate than themselves. Before the end of February, the Germans may well be faced with the alternative of abandoning nearly all their conquests in the northern part of the Russian front, or of seeing hundreds of thousands of soldiers freeze to death.]

Mr Anthony Eden, the British Foreign Secretary, returned only a few days ago from his visit to Moscow. In the speech which he made soon after his arrival,[24] he emphasised the complete agreement that exists between the British and Russian Governments. The Axis broadcasters are now spreading the rumour that Britain and Russia have agreed to carve up the world between them, and that Europe is to be forced at the point of the sword to accept Communism. This is simply a lie.[25] Great Britain and Soviet Russia have reached complete agreement as to their peace aims, which guarantee to every nation both access to materials necessary for life, and the right to live under the form of government which it chooses for itself.

In Libya, German and Italian forces are again in retreat. They have managed to make a stand for some days at Jedabia, south west of Benghazi, chiefly because heavy rain prevented the British tanks from attacking. General Rommel, the German commander of the Axis forces, probably also hoped that further reinforcements might reach him from Italy. If so, he has been disappointed, and the Axis forces are in flight westward, with the British and Indians in pursuit.[26]

Rommel's army will probably attempt another stand at Sirte, about halfway between Benghazi and Tripoli. The further west the battle moves, the greater the advantage for the Allied forces, because they

[24] Anthony Eden broadcast an extensive account of his visit to Russia on 4 January. He mentioned his visit to Stalin in 1935 saying: 'I believed then, as I believe now, that there is no real conflict of interest between the Soviet Union and this country. I believed then, as I believe now, that, despite the many obvious differences, our overriding purpose was the same. We both wished to maintain the peace.'

[25] This aspect of Axis propaganda must have caused Orwell some difficulty as he personally despised Stalinist Communism. It was a consistent note in Axis propaganda, although Orwell later refers to it as a fresh invention of theirs (see p.214).

[26] The position was shortly to be reversed, presenting Orwell with the classic problem of all propagandists, how to go back on his previous assertions.

have more bases from which their ships and aeroplanes can patrol the middle of the Mediterranean. The Germans are still fiercely attacking Malta in hopes of cutting out one of the most important bases from which our aeroplanes operate. But so far they have made very little impression. Meanwhile, our prisoners in Libya number more than 20,000, of whom about a quarter are Germans. [*Censored:* It is significant that though by far the greater number of Axis troops in Africa are Italians, the higher Command is entirely in the hands of the Germans. This is a sign of the relationship between the two nations, Germany and Italy, which is essentially the relationship of master and servant.]

What is perhaps the most interesting and important aspect of the North African campaign came to light recently, when it was revealed that since the autumn of 1940 forces of volunteers from the Arab tribe, the Senussi, have been fighting on the side of the British. The Senussi have been treated with peculiar atrocity by the Italians, who evicted them from the more fertile parts of Cyrenaica and penned them up in small areas with the almost openly declared intention of reducing their numbers by starvation. On more than one occasion when there were attempts at revolt, the Italians replied by taking the leading men of the Senussi up in aeroplanes and throwing them from mid-air over their native villages, so that they were dashed to pieces before the eyes of their fellow countrymen.[27] Yesterday, Mr Eden issued on behalf of the British Government a statement that at the end of the war, Britain would in no circumstances allow these ill-treated Arabs to pass once again under Italian rule.[28] Taken together with the liberation of Ethiopia, from which British troops are to be withdrawn as soon as the Italian civil population have gone, this is a better demonstration of Allied war aims than any mere pronouncement unaccompanied by concrete action.

17 January 1942

During the present week, there has not been any very great change in the strategy of the war. The Japanese advance in Malaya is

---

[27] The same story was told, years later, of British troops in Cyprus, and the problem of starvation there is still with us, war or no war.

[28] On 8 January Anthony Eden in a written reply to a question in the House of Commons said that, after approaches from Syed Idris es-Senussi, a Senussi force had been set up which had been fighting with the British. Orwell's last sentence echoes almost word for word Eden's note.

continuing, and the Japanese are also attacking Celebes and Dutch Borneo, partly with a view to seizing the oil fields, and partly in order to find a jumping-off place for fresh attacks against Java, Sumatra and possibly Australia. The little island of Tarakan, off the coast of Borneo, was overrun by the Japanese after a few days' fighting. Tarakan is very important because it produces natural oil of such purity that it can be used for aeroplanes without any refinement. The Dutch, however, had made elaborate preparations to wreck the oil wells and the machinery, and it is doubtful whether much of value fell into Japanese hands.

The biggest event of the week has been the Russian advance on Kharkov. They are now within gunshot of the city. Kharkov, besides being a great industrial town, is a road and rail junction of the greatest importance, and it may be said that whoever holds it, holds the way of entry into the Caucasus. The Germans claimed its capture some months back as a great victory, and if they now relinquish it, it will certainly not be willingly. Outside Moscow the German troops at Mojaisk are in a more and more dangerous situation, and will almost certainly have to retreat to avoid encirclement. Outside Leningrad, also, the situation has improved, and railway communications between Moscow and Leningrad have been re-established. The German withdrawal in Russia is 'proceeding according to plan', indeed, but it begins to look more and more like a Russian plan.

Meanwhile from Egypt there comes the good news that the Germans and Italians in the fortress of Halfaya have unconditionally surrendered.[29] This means not only that a large number of Axis prisoners have passed into Allied hands, but that there is now no enemy force to contend with between the Egyptian frontier and El Agheila, hundreds of miles to the west.

During a week in which not much has changed in the actual theatres of war, rumour has been busier than ever, and it becomes necessary to consider what steps the Axis powers are likely to take next and to distinguish between probable moves and stories which are put abroad with the idea of misleading public opinion in the democratic countries.

One thing that is almost certain is that the Germans must attack in a new direction within a short time. It is not very much use for Hitler and Mussolini to tell their peoples about the Japanese successes in the Pacific, for the Germans and Italians are well aware that what happens at the other end of the world does not put any food into their bellies.

In what directions could the Germans win quick victories which could be represented as offsetting the failure in Russia? The possibilities

---

[29] The garrison surrendered to General de Villairs on 16 January. Official reports put the number of prisoners at 5,500.

are: invasion of Britain; a move through Spain[30] and down the West African coast to seize Dakar and Casablanca;[31] a fresh offensive in the Central Mediterranean; or an invasion of Turkey. We can rule out the first as improbable, though not unthinkable. It is very unlikely that the Germans could succeed in a sea-borne invasion of Britain, and if attempting an airborne invasion they are more likely to aim at Ireland, which, even if it succeeded, would be embarrassing for Britain, but not fatal. The move through Spain is likely sooner or later, but it would have certain political disadvantages from the German point of view. The Germans know that they would be bound to lose heavily in attacking Gibraltar, and in crossing the sea to Africa. The move in the Central Mediterranean seems much more likely. The other possible German move, an attack on Turkey, is a likelihood sooner or later, and might form part of the fresh German offensive against Russia in the spring, but the consensus of opinion seems to be that it is not likely to be attempted this year.

Meanwhile, even when there is a lull in the actual fighting, there is one kind of war that never stops for an instant, night or day, and that is the propaganda war. To the Axis powers, propaganda is an actual weapon, like guns or bombs, and to learn how to discount it is as important as taking cover during an air raid.

The Germans, even more than the Japanese, are adepts at propaganda. They cover up every military move by spreading misleading rumours beforehand, they use threats and bribes with equal skill, and they are entirely cynical in promising everything to everybody. To the rich they promise bigger profits, and to the poor they promise higher wages. To the coloured races they promise liberty, and simultaneously they appeal to the white races to combine for the exploitation of the coloured races.[32] The object is always the same to divide and confuse their enemies, so that they can conquer them more easily. The Japanese methods are in essence the same. It is quite impossible to examine and refute every lie that they tell, and much of what they say is extremely persuasive. And yet one can remain quite untouched by Axis propaganda if one follows a simple rule which never fails.

[30] A recurring theme that Orwell returned to later (see below, p.212).

[31] Dakar and Casablanca were in the hands of Vichy France. An allied invasion attempt in September 1940 had failed in the face of fierce opposition. The effect of Orwell's suggestion here on an Indian audience would be to confuse it about the actual situation there.

[32] It is difficult to find examples of Orwell's suggestion that the Axis propagandists offered profits to the rich: their talks were filled with tirades against profit-making 'plutocrats'. However, appeals to the white races were common, most often in talks to South Africa. See for example Appendix, no. 9.

This is, to compare what the Axis powers say they will do with what they are actually doing. The Japanese propaganda line at this moment is an extremely clever one. They claim that all they are doing is to set Asia free from European domination.[33] They will drive the British out of India and the Americans out of the Pacific, and as soon as that is done, economic exploitation will be at an end. There will be no more poverty, no more taxation, no more need to be ruled ever by foreigners. And in building up the picture of a war of Asia against Europe, they try to rouse as much race hatred as possible by spreading stories of imaginary outrages – rapes, murders and so forth, committed by British and Americans.[34]

It is a very clever line of propaganda and is bound to find some sympathetic hearers. But it is a different matter if one compares these high-sounding promises of the Japanese with their actual behaviour.

For the past four and a half years they have been waging war not against any European power, but against another Asiatic nation, the Chinese. This is their third war of aggression against China in fifty years. On each occasion they have wrenched away a piece of Chinese territory and then exploited it for the benefit of the two or three wealthy families who rule Japan, with absolutely no regard for the native inhabitants. Even in the present war, they are fighting far more against Asiatics than against Europeans. In the Philippine Islands the resistance to Japanese attack is kept up mainly by Filipinos, in Malaya by Indians as much as by the British, in the Dutch East Indies by Javanese and Sumatrans. One of the opening acts of the war was the wanton bombing of Rangoon by the Japanese, in which hundreds of innocent Burmese were killed.[35] Moreover, in these Asiatic territories which the Japanese have ruled over for a long time, we can see what their behaviour actually is towards subject peoples. Not only do they show no sign of setting Korea or Manchuria free, but they do not allow any sort of political liberty to exist. Trade unions are forbidden throughout Japanese territory, including Japan itself. No one in Japan is allowed to listen in to a foreign radio station, on pain of death.[36] In the island of Formosa, where the Japanese found themselves faced with the problem of ruling over a people more primitive than

[33] The Japanese proposed an eastern equivalent of Hitler's 'New Order' in Europe, to be known as 'The Co-Prosperity Sphere'. The same themes naturally occurred in Subhas Chandra Bose's broadcasts, which Orwell is here answering (see below Appendix, no. 8).

[34] As a propagandist Orwell played the same game; see for example his requests for stories of rape and so on from Hsiao Ch'ien in *OWB*, p.177.

[35] There were 600 civilian casualties reported in the raid on 23 December 1941.

[36] Similar edicts were issued in occupied Europe by the German authorities. See also below, p.199 with n.350.

themselves, they dealt with it by simply wiping the aboriginal inhabitants out.

We can see from this what the behaviour of the Japanese, who describe themselves as the deliverers of Asia, is actually like when they have other Asiatic races in their power. Yet it is possible to forget all this if one simply listens to the Japanese promises and forgets about their actions. As the war moves closer to India, Japanese propaganda will become more insistent. At times it may need firm nerves and a clear mind to disregard it. The one safe rule is to remember that acts count for more than words, and that the Japanese must be judged not by what they promise to do to-morrow in India or Burma, but what they did yesterday[37] and are still doing in Korea, Manchuria and China.

24 January 1942

On the Far Eastern Front the Japanese advance continues, but somewhat less rapidly than before, and there are signs that Allied air power in the Pacific is gradually growing stronger. Meanwhile the Japanese have made two moves in new directions. One is towards New Guinea, which is a possible jumping-off place for an attack on Australia, and the other westwards from Thailand into Burma.

The second of these moves is much the more important. An attack on Australia might be very embarrassing for the Allied powers, but it is not likely to be decisive because Australia is much too large and too far from Japan for the Japanese to be able to overrun it in any period of time in which the war is likely to last. The other move, however, if it is not countered, may have far-reaching results, both on the war in China and on the war in the South Pacific.

The Japanese have already captured the town of Tavoy in the far south of Burma, and they are attacking at the border not far from Moulmein, which is about a hundred miles from Rangoon.[38] Rangoon is immensely important; if you look at the map you will see

[37] Orwell of course does not allude here to the fact that Japan was for many years Britain's ally in the East. 'Yesterday' means here literally that – not 'the day before yesterday'. Nor does he leave himself the loophole of blaming the Japanese rulers rather than the Japanese people.

[38] Orwell had visited Moulmein when working in Burma in the Indian Imperial Police in the twenties. All the details of the Burma campaign, such as the bombing of Rangoon which he also knew well, must have affected him deeply. For an internal BBC memorandum on Burma which he circulated at the time see *OWB*, pp.34-5.

that almost all the communications, road, rail and waterways, in Burma, run north and south – that is important, north and south – and that practically there is no route by which goods can travel to the interior of Burma without passing through the port of Rangoon. This means that the Burma Road, along which the Chinese armies draw their chief supplies of war material, depends for its usefulness on Rangoon's remaining securely in Allied hands. Fortunately, it will be very difficult for the Japanese to launch a full-scale attack in this area, for the reason already given, that natural communications all run from north to south and not east and west. It is doubtful whether tanks or heavy artillery can be brought directly from Thailand into the southern part of Burma, and the attacks the Japanese are now making seem to be carried out only by infantry and aeroplanes. It should be possible for British forces to hold them back, especially with the aid of the large number of Chinese reinforcements who are known to have arrived.

If we look further south, the situation is even more critical. It is doubtful whether a fortress as strong as Singapore can be taken by storm,[39] but we have to face the possibility that it may be at least neutralised and rendered almost useless as a base for Allied shipping during a long period. All depends upon the speed with which the Allies can bring reinforcements, especially of fighter aeroplanes, across the immense distances that have to be travelled. But if we look at the Japanese successes, not on a scale of weeks or months, but on a scale of years, then the very fact of these successes gives good ground for hope. All of these successes are due to Japanese naval and air superiority in a given area. Now the combined naval power of the Allied powers, taking the world as a whole, is very much greater than that of the Axis powers, and their combined air power is already about equally great, and is rapidly forging ahead. Germany can still produce aeroplanes and submarines in very large numbers, but a country at the industrial level of Japan cannot compete in what is essentially a war of machines, with the manufacturing capacity of great modern states such as the USA, Britain and the USSR. In the long run the factor that has been temporarily in Japan's favour, superiority in numbers of ships and aeroplanes, will be reversed, even if it should take several years to do this.

In Russia, the Germans are still retreating and during this week the Russians won a great victory by the capture of Mojaisk, from which

[39] The image of Singapore built up by such news items as this would have misled anyone who did not know the size of the island; Orwell was to describe Gibraltar in exactly the same terms. For those who thought of Singapore as a fortress, the shock of the subsequent collapse of British forces there was all the greater.

the Germans had once hoped to advance for the attack upon Moscow.[40] Seeing that any hope of capturing Moscow this year had obviously been abandoned, the loss of Mojaisk is less important strategically than for its effects on prestige and morale. It is highly significant that up till yesterday the German propagandists had not dared to inform their own people of this disaster, and no doubt they are still searching for some way of presenting the news so that it may seem unimportant.[41] This is very difficult because of the violence with which they had trumpeted the capture of Mojaisk when they took it themselves. The formula of the German military spokesmen continues to be that they are not being driven back, but are merely shortening their line with a view to settling into winter quarters, but they have twice announced what their final winter line will be, and have twice been compelled to retreat to positions further back.

The way in which the world picture is gradually changing in favour of the Allies can be seen in the swing of opinion in countries which were recently neutral or in some cases even inclined to favour the Axis. The most important symptom of this has been the outcome of the Pan-American Conference at Rio de Janeiro,[42] an outcome far more favourable to the Allies than would have been possible a year ago.

At this conference all the American republics have come to a substantial agreement and are almost unanimous in their readiness to break off relations with the Axis Powers. Some of the Central American republics have already done this. Of the larger South American states, the only two which have shown any reluctance are Argentina and Chile. The two Latin American countries which count for most, Mexico and Brazil, have already ranged themselves with the United States.

Parallel with these changes of opinion in South America, there exists almost certainly a widespread stirring of unrest in Europe. The iron censorship[43] imposed by the Nazis makes it very difficult to know for certain what is happening in the conquered countries. But we have a valuable source of information in broadcasts and other propaganda of the Nazis themselves. Both from what they say and from what they do not say it can be inferred with practical certainty that Europe

[40] Mozhaisk fell on 19 January.

[41] Such delays were frequent on both sides, partly for propaganda reasons, and partly because, in a war of movement, the final taking of an objective was not always clear-cut. There were numerous instances in the months that followed of Russia's delaying as long as a fortnight before admitting a defeat.

[42] The Pan-American Conference, attended by the Foreign Ministers of all twenty-one American republics met from 15 to 28 January.

[43] Orwell's broadcasts were themselves censored, though perhaps not to the same extent. For details see *OWB*, Appendix A.

generally is disgusted with the so-called 'New Order'. Hitler promised
the peoples of Europe work, peace and food, and of these he has only
been able to give them work in increasing quantities at lower and
lower wages. We ought not to assume that the morale of the German
people themselves will break down at any time in the near future. But
so far as the rest of Europe goes, it is clear that the picture which
German propagandists were lately building up of a united Europe all
working as one great arsenal for the war against Russia and the
Anglo-Saxon powers was simply a mirage.

In Libya the campaign has slowed down after the capture of Halfaya.
It is still uncertain whether General Rommel is about to make a fresh
attempt to recapture what he has lost – he has certainly made one
big-scale reconnaissance before which our light forces had to
withdraw[44] – or whether he is still trying to extricate his forces and
retire to Tripoli, but even when events appear to be moving slowly and
indecisively, we ought not to lose sight of the North African Front,
which ties up great quantities of trained men, shipping, and above all,
aeroplanes, which the Germans might otherwise be able to use against
our Allies in Russia.

31 January 1942

In the Far East the war situation is still serious for the Allies, but there
are certain changes in the situation which indicate that British and
American reinforcements are reaching the scene of battle. The most
important event has been the very heavy losses inflicted on a convoy of
Japanese ships in the Straits of Macassar,[45] between Borneo and
Celebes. At least ten ships full of Japanese troops have been sunk, and a
number of Japanese warships either sunk or damaged. This has been
possible because, apart from the powerful Dutch forces on the spot,
American ships and aeroplanes have already been able to reach the
Dutch East Indies. At present it is still impossible to prevent the
Japanese from making landings, but the fate of this convoy points to
the difficulties which they will experience in the future. Wherever they

[44] This was in fact the beginning of Rommel's counter-stroke. Starting in the early
morning of 21 January, the attack gave Orwell the task of dealing with defeat in his
broadcasts, for it began a campaign that brought the British army in Egypt to its
lowest ebb until the battle of El Alamein on July 19 turned the tide.

[45] The first communiqué from General Wavell's HQ of the Allied SW Pacific
Command reported attacks on a large Japanese convoy in the Macassar Straits. They
went on for at least four days from 23 to 27 January, and heavy losses were inflicted.

have made a landing they have got to supply their troops with arms and usually with food, which have to travel in ships across thousands of miles of sea, with aeroplanes and submarines waiting to attack them. Even now, with all the initial advantages on their side, the Japanese have been losing ships since the outbreak of war at the rate of one a day, and their supply of shipping is very far from inexhaustible.

Simultaneously, in their attacks on Rangoon, the Japanese have lost very heavily in aeroplanes. But further south, in Malaya, they have continued to advance, and it is probable that the British and Indian troops on the mainland of Malaya will have to fall back on the island of Singapore. [*Censored:* If they do so they will blow up the causeway that connects the island with the mainland.][46] Singapore is a powerful fortress with very heavy guns, with several airfields, and with a population of 600,000, largely composed of Chinese, from which it has been possible to raise a strong defence force to aid the regular forces. [*Censored:* It is unlikely that it can be taken by storm.] It remains to be seen whether the Japanese will risk the enormous losses that are bound to result from any direct attack.

On the Russian front the Russian armies have advanced so deeply into the German lines that they are now threatening both Kharkov, the great industrial city in Southern Russia, and Smolensk, on the road to Poland. Smolensk was, till recently, the headquarters of the German High Command, which has now had to remove itself a hundred miles further back. Perhaps the most significant thing about the Russian campaign is the fact that the Germans barely mention it in their radio announcements. They have still not told their home public about the fall of Mojaisk. To foreign audiences, realising that a piece of news of this kind could not be kept secret outside Germany, they admitted that Mojaisk had fallen, but declared that it was a town of no importance, though they had said just the contrary when they occupied it themselves.[47] People who feel confident about the future do not falsify news in this fashion. [*Censored:* The successes which the Red Army is now having ought not to give us the idea that German resistance is broken. On the contrary, they will certainly stage another

---

[46] This sentence was deleted by the censor, presumably because it was not wished to give the Japanese prior knowledge of Britain's intentions. In fact, the three-quarter mile causeway had already been blown up on the night of 30 January, but the news had not reached the BBC.

[47] The Axis broadcasters in fact pointed out that the Russians had applied the scorched-earth policy to such effect that, together with the results of having been fought over twice, it was no longer a town of any importance.

big offensive in the spring. But meanwhile they are losing heavily in men and material, and until the end of February, or much later in northern Russia, the snow and ice will be powerful allies on the side of the Russians, who are better equipped for winter warfare. Premier Stalin declared recently that he expected to have destroyed the German armies by the end of 1942, and it is worth remembering that Stalin is not a man who makes boasts lightly.][48]

In North Africa the battle is still swaying to and fro. After a campaign of two months the Germans are back in Benghazi, which has now changed hands four times. We do not know yet whether the Germans will be able to continue their advance. Probably this will depend upon the amount of material, especially heavy tanks, that they have been able to get across the sea from Italy. But even if they should be able to drive their way back to the position they occupied in November, close to the Egyptian frontier, the balance of advantage will be with the British, for the Germans and Italians have lost heavily in men and in materials of war. [*Censored:* The German army in North Africa was placed there as part of a double-flanking movement intended to converge on the oil wells of Baku and of Irak and Iran. The northern attack was to move into the Crimea and the Caucasus, and the southern was to move through Egypt and Palestine. Both moves have so far failed. The Germans have been unable to get beyond the Crimea, or even to establish their position in the Crimea itself, for the great Russian fortress of Sebastopol withstands all attacks. As to the southern flank, the Germans have failed to set foot on Egyptian soil, and indeed are a long way from it at this moment. This is not to deny that the North African campaign has been disappointing to the Allies. It would make a great deal of difference, militarily and politically, if the British could reach Tripoli and thus dominate the central Mediterranean. For as long as the two essential fronts, in the Caucasus and in Egypt, hold firm, the oil which the Germans covet and which they are in ever growing need of is out of their reach.]

Far-reaching political changes are taking place in Britain and a number of other countries as a result of the new turn that the war took when the Japanese launched their attack. One can see the main happenings in better perspective if one starts by only listing them. After this the connection between events which at first sight may not seem to have anything to do with one another, becomes clear.

---

[48] Orwell was projecting here from the sudden turn-around that had taken place in Africa. Presumably the censor did not approve of this suggestion, or of giving such hostages to fortune as Stalin's view that the war would soon be over.

In the first place, American troops have landed in the British Isles.[49] In the second place, a war council which will cover the whole Pacific area is to be set up, probably with headquarters in Washington. Thirdly, it has been arranged that Australia and New Zealand are to have direct representation in the War Cabinet in London.[50] Fourthly, all but two of the Latin-American republics have severed diplomatic relations with the Axis powers. Finally, after a debate on the conduct of the war which lasted for three days, Mr Churchill, the British Prime Minister, has asked the House of Commons for a vote of confidence and has been given it with only one dissentient vote.[51]

When taken together, these events, happening in widely separated parts of the earth, all have the same meaning. They mean that the various countries menaced by Axis aggression are coming into closer and closer agreement, both military and political. The United States, Britain and the Dominions are now pooling their troops, their resources and their naval bases, almost as though they were a single nation acting under a common ruler.[52] At the same time, the co-operation of the Anglo-Saxon powers with Soviet Russia and China becomes closer and more friendly. Chinese troops are standing side by side to the British in Burma. Just as British tanks and aeroplanes are fighting on the Russian front. In spite of the danger in the Pacific, the American Government has already declared that it looks on Hitler as the principal enemy, and the sending of American troops to Britain, to play a part in the western theatre of war, is a concrete sign of this. The resolution which eighteen American republics have signed in Rio de Janeiro is of great importance. It is of the highest importance that Brazil, the biggest and most populous country of South America, has ranged itself against the Axis. [*Censored:* Brazil is within flying range of West Africa and for at least fifty years the Germans have had designs

[49] These troops were the vanguard of the Second American Expeditionary Force in Europe under the command of Major General Russell P. Hartle. They landed in Northern Ireland on the morning of 26 January and were welcomed by the Duke of Abercorn, Governor of Northern Ireland, and other dignitaries.

[50] Mr Curtin, the Australian Prime Minister, announced on 24 January that he had asked for Australia to have a place in the Imperial War Cabinet, and for the formation of a Pacific War Council. Churchill had mentioned both matters in the speech that Orwell later refers to.

[51] The debate took place between 27 and 29 January. The dissentient vote mentioned by Orwell was that of James Maxton, leader of the Independent Labour Party. As Churchill remarked, there were only three members of the ILP, and two were required as tellers; nevertheless he was grateful to Maxton for causing the division (Winston S. Churchill, *The Second World War*, vol.4, p.62).

[52] Orwell developed this idea in *Nineteen Eighty-Four*, creating the super-power of Oceania. See also George Catlin, *One Anglo-American Nation* (1941), a much-discussed book at the time.

on it.] The Japanese have similar designs on several South American countries. Now that the whole American continent is forming itself into a common front against the aggressor, these designs – which were to have been carried out in the first place by fifth columns, aided in some cases by local Fascist parties – will be much easier to frustrate. Simultaneously the Russian radio has issued a significant warning to the Japanese. In 1938 the Japanese attempted an attack on Vladivostock, and got a lesson which they may forget under the influence of successes elsewhere. The Russians have warned them not to make the same mistake as the Germans – who also imagined that the Red Army was no good – and, in the words of the Russian proverb – 'not to sell the bearskin before you have caught the bear'.

Finally, one event has happened this week which is not strictly an act of war, but which should be mentioned. The British Government has arranged to relax the blockade and send 8,000 tons of wheat to Greece. They have done this for the quite simple reason that Greece is starving. This is the result of German and Italian rule. The German and Italian Fascists have simply plundered the country for their own benefit, with utter disregard for its Greek inhabitants. The wheat will be sent to Greece through the International Red Cross. There is no guarantee that the Germans will not seize it when it gets there, as they have seized similar supplies sent to France, but the British Government prefers to take this risk, and to send the wheat, rather than stand by and watch a whole innocent population starve. The contrast between the Fascist powers that steal food, and the anti-Fascist powers who bring it to starving people, will not go unnoticed in conquered Europe.[53]

7 February 1942

The siege of Singapore has begun.[54] As yet, no major move has been made, and it would be very rash to prophesy the outcome. Looking back over the history of this war, we notice that the siege of fortresses

[53] A propaganda point that had immediate effect. Both the Romanians and the Germans announced that they were sending food shipments to Greece and proceeded to do so.

[54] After the causeway had been blown, Lt. General A.E. Percival said in a broadcast on 31 January: 'The battle of Malaya has come to an end and the battle of Singapore has started ... Today we stand beleaguered in our island fortress. Our task is to hold this fortress until help can come, as assuredly it will come ... Our duty is clear. With firm resolve and fixed determination we shall win through.'

and fortified towns has had such varied results that it is difficult to draw any sure inference from them. Sebastopol and Tobruk held out against all attacks, but in these cases it was possible for the defenders to be supplied by sea. Hong Kong, which had only a small garrison, and no water supply of its own, was easily taken. Corregidor, in the Philippine Islands, is still holding out, although the defenders are not being supplied by sea and have hardly any aeroplanes. Leningrad successfully repulsed all attacks, although its supply route by sea was cut off, or almost cut off. From these varied experiences no definite rule can be deduced, but in forming our conclusions, it is worth keeping these considerations in mind.

The Japanese are bound to be immensely superior in numbers of trained men, and in aeroplanes.

Even if air reinforcements in large quantities arrive, the defence of Singapore will be hampered by lack of airfields,[55] unless it is possible to establish emergency airfields at Sumatra and on the various small islands which lie between Sumatra and the Malayan mainland.

Singapore has a powerful garrison, with very heavy guns, and also a large civilian population, principally Chinese, who are willing and anxious to take part in its defence.

The water supply of Singapore is adequate, and food is not likely to run seriously short, at any rate for several months, even if no supplies can be brought from the outside.

Bearing all these considerations in mind, the one thing we can say with certainty is that the capture of Singapore cannot be an easy business, and that even if it can be taken by direct assault, this would be impossible without enormous losses, which the Japanese may not be ready to face.

This week, the British Government has granted to the Chinese Republic a loan of 50 million pounds for the purchase of munitions of war.[56] The supply of arms to China is largely dependent on keeping the supply routes open, especially the Burma Road, but even if the Burma Road should be cut, or rendered inaccessible, other routes into China exist, and yet others can be contrived. The Japanese are already uttering threats to India upon the mere rumour of the building of another road from Assam. Meanwhile the loan, which will allow an

[55] Of the airfields mentioned by Orwell earlier, three were unusable, as they were within range of Japanese guns on the mainland. The British guns which he goes on to mention were, as has so often been said, sited for defence against an attack from the sea.

[56] Besides the loan, the British Government also agreed, on 2 February, to make available to China on lend-lease terms all the material it could supply. Simultaneously the American Government loaned $500,000,000.

enormous quantity of materials to be bought and if necessary stored until they can be transported, is the token of the reality of the Alliance between Free Britain and Free China.

Meanwhile, the delaying action in Burma, in the Dutch East Indies and in the Philippines, continues. The Japanese have lost very heavily in ships and men, in the Straits of Macassar, chiefly owing to the operation of Dutch aircraft, which work from airfields hidden in the jungles. It may ultimately be possible for the Japanese to bring the whole of Borneo under their control, in which case this particular danger will have been eliminated, but their heavy losses in shipping, occurring so early in the war, when all the advantages are on their side, do not augur very well for the future. In their inroads on the Dutch East Indies they are suffering from the 'scorched earth' policy as much as from the Dutch and American aircraft and submarines. It is, in fact, not much use to them to overrun territories where they will afterwards have to supply their troops by sea, if those territories have been systematically devastated beforehand. How much the Japanese fear this can be seen from their savage threat to massacre the garrison at Balik Papan, in Borneo, if the oil refineries there were destroyed. In fact, the oil refineries were destroyed,[57] and the garrison succeeded in fighting its way out, instead of being massacred. The 'scorched earth' policy has its limitations, because certain things, for instance, metallic ores, cannot be destroyed, but on the other hand, certain products, such as crude petroleum, are of little value to anyone who captures them if the necessary machinery is lacking. It is comparatively of little use for the Japanese to overrun the various oil-bearing areas, if they have got to take the oil back to Japan to be refined. At the same time, their shipping is needed for transporting foodstuffs and men, and is dwindling, owing to submarine attacks. In spite of the successes which the Japanese have won, it seems probable that their campaign is behind time, and that an Allied counter-attack has been made possible by the delaying battle which is being fought by Chinese, Dutch, British, Indians and Javanese, in the south-west Pacific.

In the Battle of Russia, there is not much to report this week. The Russians are still advancing, but they have not yet captured Kharkov or Smolensk. It now becomes clear that the campaign in Libya should probably be regarded as part of, or at any rate complementary to, the Battle of Russia, and that both this and the Japanese campaign in Asia are part of a single strategic manoeuvre. Almost certainly the plan is

[57] Batavia announced the destruction of the oil wells on 22 January and their capture two days later. The Axis propagandists claimed that they had been captured intact, citing in this case the reluctance of the owners to destroy their capital when the Japanese had announced that they would make terms.

for the Germans to break through to the Persian Gulf, capturing the Suez Canal with the southern arm of their attack, and the Caucasian oilfields with the northern arm, at the same time as the Japanese break through to the Indian Ocean, if possible capturing Rangoon and the naval bases of Ceylon on their way. The two main Axis powers would then be in communication with one another, and Germany's desperate needs for oil, rubber, tin, and other commodities, could be supplied. It can therefore be taken as almost certain that the Germans are making ready for fresh offensives against Southern Russia and against Egypt in the spring, but it is very doubtful whether these offensives can be any more successful than those which have been made during the past autumn and winter. The Russians have made good most of their industrial losses by establishing new industrial areas beyond the Ural Mountains, and the British armies in the Middle East are far stronger than they were. They are not even dependent to the same extent as before on sea-borne supplies, because by this time great armament factories have been set up in Eritrea, the province on the Red Sea which was captured from the Italians. There is, unquestionably, hard fighting and perhaps heavy losses ahead of the Allies in the spring, but on a long-term view the odds are much more heavily against the Axis than they were at the beginning of 1941.

An extremely important political event has taken place in the Treaty now signed between Abyssinia and Great Britain.[58] The Emperor Haile Selassie, driven out by the cowardly aggression of the Italians six years ago, returns to his throne, Abyssinia takes its place again among the free nations, and the attempted economic domination of the country by foreign interests is at an end. Simultaneously with this there goes a political change in Egypt, which will be to the advantage of the Allied cause. The Wafdists, the Egyptian nationalist party, who negotiated the Anglo-Egyptian treaty of 1936, have formed a new government.[59] The Wafdists are a progressive left-wing party, genuinely representative of the Egyptian people, especially the poorer peasants, and extremely anti-Nazi in sentiment.

Finally, a political event about which it is too early to make exact predictions, but which is almost certain to have good results, is the

[58] The Anglo-Ethiopian Agreement had been signed at Addis Ababa on 31 January and was announced in the House of Commons on 3 February. The agreement provided for British assistance in Ethiopia's financial and military affairs, thus filling the gap left by the departing Italians.

[59] On the resignation of the party in power, led by Sirry Pasha, the Wafdist Party under Nahas Pasha accepted King Farouk's request to form a government. They were in fact the minority party, but with the large following among the people that Orwell mentions. A Royal Decree on 7 February dissolved Parliament prior to new elections, with Nahas Pasha as Military Governor.

appointment of Lord Beaverbrook as British Minister of Production.[60]
In this position he can co-ordinate the entire output of materials of war
in Britain, and any administrative muddles or jealousies between the
different services can be eliminated. Lord Beaverbrook is a man of
enormous energy, and his efforts as Minister of Aircraft Production
probably did as much as any one thing to turn the scale and defeat the
German invaders in the summer of 1940. His wide range of personal
contacts in the USA on the one hand, and in Soviet Russia on the
other, will be of the greatest value to the Allied cause.

                                                    14 February 1942

At this moment of speaking the struggle for Singapore is still going on,
and the vital reservoirs which hold the island's water are still in the
hands of the defenders. But we must face the fact that it is unlikely
that Singapore can be kept out of Japanese hands much longer. This is
a very serious piece of news, and even more serious for Asia than for
the West. One American expert has already estimated that the loss of
Singapore will lengthen the war by about a year. It is worth, therefore,
trying to predict as fully as possible the strategic consequences which
this loss entails.[61] Once they are in possession of Singapore, the
Japanese surface ships as well as submarines can enter the Indian
Ocean. If their forthcoming attacks on the Dutch islands of Sumatra
and more particularly Java should also succeed, then they are in entire
possession of the main route across the Pacific, leading from America
to Africa. If you look at the map, you will see that communications
between the United States and India and Africa are not indeed cut off,
but that American ships have to travel by a roundabout route
southward to Australia or New Zealand, and then north again over
immense distances, which confer a great strategical advantage on the
Japanese, who are in a more central position, and will, if they can
overrun the Dutch East Indies, possess airfields and naval bases
covering the whole of this area.

Supposing that the Japanese can succeed to the extent which we

[60] His appointment was announced on 4 February. He had previously been
Minister of Supply.

[61] Japanese broadcasts were making frequent references to their plans, following
their most recent success. Orwell counters this by the drastic assumption that
Singapore would fall, and then going on to make the worst possible case from the
Allies' point of view.

have imagined, what will their next step be? In the first place, they will intensify their attack on Burma, in hopes of capturing Rangoon, the only port through which the Burma Road can be easily supplied. They will make air and naval attacks against the islands in the Indian Ocean, probably beginning with the Andaman Islands, and they will probably attempt an invasion of Ceylon, or of some area in southern India. Could they get control of Ceylon, they would command the Bay of Bengal sufficiently to prevent any Allied shipping crossing it, and though they would not have complete control of the eastern part of the Indian Ocean, they would at least be able to make damaging attacks on British shipping which has passed round the Cape and is on its way to supply the British armies in the Middle East, and our Allies in Russia.

This is not an encouraging picture, and we have deliberately put it at its worst, in order to get a realistic and unvarnished view of the situation. We may even go a step further and consider what the consequences would be if the grandiose Axis offensive, of which the Japanese naval offensive is only a part, were totally successful.

It is becoming clearer and clearer, as we have emphasised in earlier news reviews, that the general plan is for the Germans to break through by land, so as to reach the Persian Gulf, while the Japanese gain mastery of the Indian Ocean. In this way, three objects would be achieved at the same time. In the first place, Germany and Japan would be in direct communication with one another, though perhaps only rather precariously so. In the second place, the Burma Road would have ceased to be of much value as a supply route to China, and in the third place, the best supply route to Russia, that is, through the Persian Gulf and Iran, would have been cut. The Germans and Japanese have evidently staked everything on this manoeuvre, in the confidence that if they can bring it off, it will have won them the war. The conclusion evidently is that, if cut off from Western supplies, China will stop fighting, or at least China's armies will be reduced to guerilla activity, and the Russian army will have to retreat behind the Ural mountains. Simultaneously the British Empire will have been cut into two parts, and both Australia and the British dependencies in Africa can be attacked at leisure.

This is the worst that can happen and during the coming months the Axis powers will make tremendous efforts to bring it about by renewed offensives in Southern Russia, in North Africa, in Burma, and in the Indian Ocean. It should be emphasised that even should this grandiose plan succeed in its entirety, it would not give the Axis Powers victory, unless the Allied peoples of America, Soviet Russia, Britain and China lost heart. It still remains true that the balance of power both in men, materials and industrial plant, is heavily against the Axis Powers, and that the main manufacturing centres of the Allied Powers are in places where neither the Germans nor the Japanese can get at them. These main centres where aeroplanes, tanks, ships and guns are being forged are in North America, which for practical purposes is outside the sphere of war, in equally inaccessible parts of Central Russia and Siberia, and in Britain, which is much nearer the scene of danger but which the Germans have failed to invade or even to damage severely by air bombing. The Allied Powers, therefore, are able immensely to outbuild the Axis Powers, and in a year or two years bring together a force which will be all but irresistible.[62] But they undoubtedly have a difficult time ahead, and they may have a period when they are almost in conditions of siege, and when resolution, calmness and faith in final victory will be at least as important as physical weapons of war.

Meanwhile the immediate effect of events in the Western Pacific is to make the position of India more dangerous and also immensely more important. With the loss of Singapore, India becomes for the time being the centre of the war, one might say, the centre of the world. With its central position, and its wealth in manpower and raw materials, India will become a more and more important source of supply for China on the one hand and Russia and the Middle East on the other. It should be emphasised that even if Rangoon is lost, with the consequence that the Burma Road ceases to be usable, that does not mean that communication between China and her allies becomes impossible. There are several other roads into China, both actual and potential. In the first place, there exists the route through Soviet Russia and Sinkiang in Central Asia; secondly, the route already projected, through Assam; thirdly, there is the possibility of a northern route through Alaska and Manchuria; and fourthly it may be possible to establish American naval control of the Pacific at some time within the next year. But at the moment, India's position is of vital importance, and Chinese-Indian solidarity will be one of the foremost factors in the war. It is therefore most encouraging news that General Chiang Kai-Shek, the leader of Republican China, has already visited India, and had an interview both with the Viceroy and with Mr

[62] Orwell has used as the basis of his argument here a recent publication by the US Census Bureau analysing the relative strengths of the Allied and Axis powers. Presumably it had been made available in Britain through the Ministry of Information.

Nehru.[63] We do not yet know the results of these interviews, but we can at least safely prophesy that if the great peoples of China and India stand together, they cannot be overwhelmed even by the most powerful and ruthless aggressor.

In Britain there have been one or two internal events which have a bearing on the world aspect of the war. Lord Beaverbrook, now in supreme control of production, has made his first speech,[64] and given some important figures about British production during the last year. He revealed that during 1941, Great Britain sent abroad nearly 3,000 tanks, and between nine and ten thousand aeroplanes. Since the bulk of these vast supplies must have gone to Soviet Russia, we can say that the British factories have played an important part in the defeat which the Russians inflicted on the Germans when they kept them out of Moscow and Leningrad. The British factories are now producing at even greater speed than before, but these things are not achieved without sacrifices on the part of the common people, and now that war extends to the Pacific, the calls upon British shipping are even more urgent than before. Soap has just been rationed for the first time during this war. Even now the British soap ration, like nearly all the other rations, is much bigger than what is received by people living under Axis rule, but the fact that one article of daily use after another has to be rationed is a sign that British industry is moving more and more from a peace to a war economy. The ordinary people who have to put up with these restrictions do not grumble, and are even heard to say that they would welcome greater sacrifices,[65] if these would set free more shipping for the war effort, since they have a clear understanding of the issue, and set much more store by their liberty than by the comforts they have been accustomed to in peacetime.

[63] Chiang Kai-Shek arrived in New Delhi on 10 February, accompanied by Sir Archibald Clark Kerr, then Minister in Chungking. Chiang Kai-Shek saw Nehru on no fewer than four occasions. The day before leaving for China, Nehru introduced him to Gandhi, who had come especially from his home, Wardha. The Axis broadcasters immediately warned Indians against the visit as an attempt to swing Nehru and Gandhi over to the Allied cause.

[64] In the House of Lords, on 23 February.

[65] The resemblance between Orwell's writing here and the voice screeching about rationing over the telescreens in *Nineteen Eighty-Four* is striking. 'The ordinary people' who 'would welcome greater sacrifices' are very clearly the basis for Orwell's creation in that book, the 'Proles'.

21 February 1942

With the fall of Singapore, the war in the Far East enters into its second phase.

It is evident that the Japanese now have two main objectives: one is to cut the Burma Road, in hopes of thus knocking China out of the war, and the other is to widen the sphere of Japanese control in the Western Pacific, to such an extent that the Allies shall have no air or naval bases within attacking distance of Japan. In order to achieve this plan completely, the Japanese would have to control the whole of the East Indies, the whole of Burma, Northern Australia and probably New Zealand and Hawaii. Could they control all these areas, they would have eliminated the danger of British or American counter-attack for the time being, though even then their safety would depend on keeping Russia out of the war. They are not likely to attain the whole even of these objectives, but they may go some way towards it, and it is clear that their first step must be the conquest of Rangoon and of the big seaports of Java. The battle in Burma is already raging, and the attack on Java is obviously imminent.

We cannot say yet how the battle in Burma will end. The Japanese have advanced, but not very rapidly, and the British have been reinforced both with aeroplanes and with Chinese troops. The supply difficulties which decided the issue in Malaya are less acute in the Burma area. If Rangoon should fall, that is an end not actually of the Burma Road, but of the present route by which supplies can reach the Burma Road from India or from Britain. The capture of Rangoon by the Japanese would not end the campaign in Burma because in this case the direction of the Japanese advance must be northward, and there is no question of the Allied army being driven into the sea.[66] But it may be asked: if Rangoon should fall, would it be of any value to continue the campaign in Burma? Yes, because the existing Burma Road is not the only possible route from India into China. Another route is projected and can be brought into use within measurable time, so long as China's resistance can be kept going in the interval.

In this connection, the recent visit of Marshal Chiang Kai-Shek to India is of the highest importance. We know now that Marshal Chiang Kai-Shek had interviews not only with Mr Nehru, but with Mr Jinnah and with Mahatma Gandhi. What the political outcome of

[66] An echo, perhaps subconscious, of the fate of the British Expeditionary Force at Dunkirk.

these interviews was we do not precisely know,[67] but we do know that Marshal Chiang Kai-Shek has affirmed the solidarity of India and China, and has spoken of the projected new route which will enter China far to the north of the present Burma Road. It is clear, therefore, that even if Rangoon is lost, and with it the possibilities of supplying China on any large scale by sea, the retention of Upper Burma will be immensely important to the Allies. Probably the next few months will decide the issue, for during the monsoon which begins in Burma about the end of May, the passage of mechanised troops will be very difficult in Burma, except along the railways and waterways. We must not underrate the power of the Japanese, who largely possess control of the sea in the eastern part of the Bay of Bengal, and who will be heavily reinforced now that they can withdraw most of their troops from Malaya.

We must expect also the intensification of the attack on the Americans in the Philippine Islands and in the very near future an all-out offensive against Java. It is certain that Java will be a tough nut to crack. The Dutch lack aeroplanes[68] and it has been very difficult to reinforce them to any extent, but they have a large army partly Dutch and partly Javanese, which is well trained and determined to resist fiercely. It is unlikely that there will be much fifth-column activity. Even the Nationalists among the Javanese are aware that they have nothing to hope from a Japanese conquest. They realise that the independence which they wish for is not likely to be gained by passing under Fascist rule. Both the Dutch and the Asiatic inhabitants of the islands have shown themselves devoted and ruthless in applying the scorched earth policy.[69] They destroyed the oil installations at Palembang on the island of Sumatra so completely that it will be a long time before the Japanese can get any oil out of them, and they are ready to do the same wherever the invaders may advance.

[67] Churchill's summary of what occurred is succinct: 'The attitude of the Congress Party worsened with the Japanese menace. This became very clear when, in February 1942, General Chiang Kai-Shek and his wife visited India. The object of their journey was to rally Indian opinion against Japan and emphasise the importance for Asia as a whole and India and China in particular of the defeat of Japan. The Indian party leaders used the occasion to bring pressure upon the British Government through the Generalissimo to yield to the demand of Congress.' Churchill, *SWW*, vol.4, p.183. It is by no means clear whether the details of what occurred would have been known to Orwell when he wrote his broadcast.

[68] Orwell had earlier referred to their planes hidden in the jungle, but these presumably had either been destroyed or had never existed in the first place.

[69] This is a direct answer to the Axis broadcasts mentioned above which claimed that the local people, or the owners, had prevented the scorched-earth action from being carried out.

The first bombs have fallen on Australian soil. Darwin, in the northern tip of Queensland, was heavily bombed two days ago.[70] Australia has mobilised the whole of its manpower and is ready to go to extreme lengths in the conscription of property as well in order to put the country completely on a war footing. It is unlikely however that the Japanese will attempt a full-scale invasion of Australia at this stage. The country is too big to be overrun completely, and there are more pressing tasks on hand. Although geographically the Japanese are nearer to Australia, India is in acuter danger, and the solidarity of the Asiatic nations against the common enemy is the most important factor in the war.

In the Western hemisphere, the issue is still in the balance, and will probably remain so until the late spring. The German plan to knock Russia out at one blow has failed, and German prestige has suffered all over Europe, almost as much as the German army has suffered in the cold of the Russian winter. But that winter is drawing to an end, and it is clear that the Germans are making ready to launch another huge offensive towards the Caucasus, as soon as the weather makes this possible, probably about May. In the southern section of this campaign neither side has gained a decisive advantage. The German attempt to invade Egypt has hitherto failed, but so also has the British attempt to drive westwards as far as Tripoli and thus obtain control of the Central Mediterranean. At this date the result of three months' battle has been to leave the British in possession of a portion of Cyrenaica, including the powerful frontier forts of Sollum, Bardea and Halfaya previously held by the Germans. Both sides have supply difficulties to face, The Germans need only bring their supplies across the narrow waist of the Mediterranean, but the British submarines are waiting for them on the way, and have sunk an immense number of ships during the past three months. The British ships supplying the Middle East, on the other hand, have to travel from England, round the Cape of Good Hope, a journey which can only be made three times in a year. Sometimes, however, when supplies of men and materials are urgently needed, the British prefer to send their convoys straight up the Mediterranean, which they are able to do if they choose to escort them heavily enough. Recently a large convoy made the passage through the Mediterranean with the loss of only two ships, and its escorting

---

[70] The bombing raids on Darwin took place on 19 February. There were two raids and altogether fifty tons of bombs were dropped. Three people were killed, with a number of wounded and considerable damage to property.

warships sank or damaged four Italian warships on the way.[71]

The British War Cabinet has been reconstructed.[72] This was in accord with the wishes of the majority of the English people, who wished for the establishment of a smaller War Cabinet, composed of men who are free from departmental duties. The most notable change is the inclusion of Sir Stafford Cripps, recently our Ambassador in Moscow. Sir Stafford Cripps is a man of very varied talents, and is certainly the outstanding figure in the British Socialist movement. His inclusion in the Government will probably strengthen the ties between Britain and Soviet Russia, and will make negotiations with the Indian and Chinese political leaders a good deal easier. He enjoys immense prestige in this country because of the uncompromising attitude he has always taken since the German Fascism first became a menace, and because of the success of his recent mission in Moscow. The fact that such a man, without any party machine backing him, can be put into the Government in direct response to the wishes of the common people, is a testimony to the strength of British democracy.[73]

28 February 1942

During the last week not much has happened in the narrow military sense.

In Burma, the Japanese have advanced somewhat, and Rangoon is definitely in danger. On the other hand, in the air fighting, the British and American pilots defending Rangoon have had the better of it, and the Japanese have lost a large number of planes. The Japanese are now in possession of the whole of the island of Sumatra, and have got a footing on the island of Bali. From these two bases they are in a position to launch a full-scale attack on Java, which is the main stronghold of the Allies in the Far East. As yet, however, they have not been able to attack Java except by air, because the ships in which they hoped to make the invasion have been roughly handled by Dutch and American planes and warships, and a considerable number have been

[71] The convoy passed through the Mediterranean on 13 to 16 February. One of the Italian ships was sunk by a British submarine. Axis broadcasts were claiming that no ships had got through.

[72] The reconstruction was announced from Downing Street on 19 February; the number in it was reduced from nine to seven. Sir Stafford Cripps was appointed Lord Privy Seal.

[73] Stafford Cripps exercised some fascination for Orwell at this time. Orwell followed Cripps's career over the next months closely. See *OWB*, pp.33-4, etc.

sunk. Probably a Japanese landing on Java cannot be prevented, but from what has happened already it is clear that they are going to lose very heavily, probably more heavily than they can afford.

It cannot be repeated too often that this war turns principally upon the question of supplies, and though the Japanese have won great victories and inflicted great damage on their adversaries, it is doubtful whether they have yet gained much in a material sense. They have certainly gained rubber, tin ore, and territories from which, at least in the future, they may be able to obtain rice; but on the other hand, they have lost a great deal of shipping which they will have difficulty in replacing, and it is doubtful whether they have gained much of their most pressing necessity – oil. In their attack on Palembang in Sumatra, which is by far the richest oilfield in the Far East, the Japanese were so anxious to capture it intact that they tried to do so by means of a surprise attack with parachutists. This failed, however, and though Palembang was ultimately taken, we know now that the Dutch destroyed both the oil wells, and the surface plant, in a most thorough and ruthless manner. The next greatest oil fields of the Far East, those of Burma, are now similarly menaced. If, however, it becomes clear that Rangoon must fall, the oil refineries, which are at Syriam – a few miles from Rangoon – will be blown up, and probably the pipe line which brings oil from Yenangyaung, four hundred miles away, will be destroyed as well. If this scorched earth policy is carried out with sufficient thoroughness, their gains will be of no benefit to the Japanese for at least a year, for even where they are able to extract the crude oil from the earth, it is of little value if the refineries have been destroyed. In that case, they can only make use of it by transporting it to their own refineries in Japan, which puts an extra strain on their inadequate shipping, and in any case exposes them to submarine attack on the way home.

We ought not to regard the destruction of the Far Eastern oilfields as pure gain for the Allies, since it means that they, as well as the Japanese, are deprived of the much-needed oil. Both India and China rely on the oil from Burma wells, and the loss of these imposes, or will impose, serious transport difficulties on the Allies. Nevertheless, it remains true that the Allies possess enormous stocks of oil in places, chiefly the United States, which are safe from enemy attack, whereas the Fascist powers cannot solve their oil problem, except by conquest. While we watch the more dramatic events that are happening in Asia, we ought never to forget that the real issue of the war turns upon the German effort to reach the oil wells of the Caucasus. Hitherto, they have failed. If they succeed in their spring offensive the end cannot be foreseen. If they fail again, it is very doubtful whether they will have enough oil to continue the war much longer, and once Germany is defeated, Japan does not present an equally serious problem. Germany, therefore, is the main enemy, and although it may often seem that more is happening in the Far East, it is the struggle on the Russian front and in the Atlantic Ocean that will in the long run prove serious.

Although events in a military sense have not moved so rapidly this week as in the preceding weeks, there have been political developments of the highest importance. The British Government has been almost entirely refashioned,[74] and though the results of this will not be altogether clear until after the debates which are to take place in Parliament next week, we can already see in general outline the changes which are likely to follow. The chief event has been the entry into the Government of Sir Stafford Cripps, late Ambassador in Moscow. It can be taken for granted that Sir Stafford would not have accepted office without being certain that large political changes were contemplated, both in Britain's home and foreign policy. In his first speech in his new post,[75] he has already forecast a tightening up of social legislation, which will have the effect of suppressing many useless luxuries, and in general making the way of life of all classes in Great Britain more equal. It is also known that the relationship between Great Britain and India is to be debated in Parliament next week, and it can be taken for granted that that relationship is the subject of most earnest discussion and about to undergo a great change. Public opinion in this country is very anxious for a solution of the Indian political deadlock, and equally anxious to see India a willing and active ally of Britain against the Fascist powers. This popular feeling has crystallised around Sir Stafford Cripps, whose enlightened views on India are well known, and though it is too early to anticipate, it is at least certain that some far-reaching and statesman-like offer to India will be made in the near future.

Simultaneously with these political changes in Britain, there occurred on March 24th[76] the anniversary of the Red Army, which

[74] Further changes in the Cabinet were announced on 22 February. The appointment of Sir James Grigg as Secretary of State for War was of some interest to Orwell: Lady Grigg did a weekly broadcast to India, nominally under Orwell's control (but see *OWB*, p.184).

[75] The speech was in answer to a debate on 24-25 February. The comments Orwell mentions were points made in answer to questions by F. Pethick-Lawrence complaining of 'Blimpery' and privilege. The welcoming of austerity and the rationalising of the necessity for it were always, from the first outline of the book, part of the background of *Nineteen Eighty-Four* and Orwell was at first not averse to those sentiments. Later, with the experience of post-war austerity, the bitterness of the parody in *Nineteen Eighty-Four* took over.

[76] In fact 23 February, the twenty-fourth anniversary of the Red Army.

was the occasion of a speech by Premier Stalin in which he reviewed the war situation and also made what amounted to a statement on policy. Considering the atrocious manner in which the Germans have behaved in their invasion of Russia, the speech was notable for its lack of vindictiveness and for the wise and large-minded way in which it distinguished between the German people and their rulers. Stalin ridiculed the lies put about by the German propagandists, to the effect that the Russians aim at exterminating the German race, and at dominating the whole of Europe and imposing Communism upon it by force.[77] He used the memorable phrase – 'Hitlers come and Hitlers go, but the German people and the German state remain.' And he made it quite clear that the Russian state would be glad to live in amity with a democratic Germany, which was prepared to leave its neighbours in peace; but he made it equally clear that there was no chance of this happening while the Nazi party and the clique surrounding Hitler remain in power.

The Japanese have made their first attack on the Andaman Islands, in the Indian Ocean south west of Burma, two bombing raids having taken place there recently.[78] This development, which we foretold in our earlier news commentaries, is part of the Japanese attempt to extend their control step by step across the Indian Ocean and thus blockade the main ports of India. No doubt they are also contemplating attacks on Ceylon, on the various small islands in the southern part of the Indian Ocean, and on Madagascar.[79] But they would have to establish naval and air bases in Rangoon and the Andamans before they could venture so far afield as this.

14 March 1942

The most important event this week is not military but political. It is the appointment of Sir Stafford Cripps to proceed to India by air and

[77] For further insistence on this theme, see above, n.25 and Introduction p.20.

[78] These raids on 24 and 26 February were the first actual attacks on India.

[79] This is the first mention by Orwell of Madagascar, and a possible lapse of security. The fear that the Axis powers might invade Madagascar, or that the naval base there was already being used by Axis submarines, worried Churchill greatly. Steps to counter the supposed threat were already well in train when Orwell wrote this (see Churchill, *SWW*, vol.4, p.197ff.) The only part that Madagascar had actually played in Axis plans was far more sinister: the Madagascar Plan, which envisaged all the Jews in France being sent there. The plan was dropped when it was decided to move them instead to Auschwitz.

there lay before the leaders of the Indian political parties the scheme which has been worked out by the British Government.[80]

The Government has not yet announced what its plans are and it would be unwise to make a guess at them, but it is at least certain that no one now alive in Britain is more suited to conduct the negotiations. Sir Stafford Cripps has long been recognised as the ablest man in the British socialist movement, and he is respected for his absolute integrity even by those who are at the opposite pole from him politically. He has had a varied career, and possesses knowledge and experience of a kind not often shared by professional politicians. During the last war he managed an explosives factory on behalf of the Government. After that for some years he practised as a barrister, and won for himself an enormous reputation for his skill in dealing with intricate civil cases. In spite of this, he has always lived with extreme simplicity and has given away most of his earnings at the Bar to the cause of Socialism and to the support of his weekly socialist paper, the *Tribune*. He is a man of great personal austerity, a vegetarian, a teetotaller and a devout practising Christian. So simple are his manners that he is to be seen every morning having his breakfast in a cheap London eating house, among working men and office employees.[81] In the last few years he has given up practising at the Bar in order to devote himself wholly to politics.

The outstanding thing about Sir Stafford Cripps, however, has always been his utter unwillingness to compromise his political principles. He has sometimes made mistakes, but his worst enemy has never suggested that he cared anything for money, popularity or personal power. About seven years ago, he became dissatisfied with the too cautious policy of the Labour Party, and founded the Socialist League, an organisation within the Labour Party, aiming at a more radical Socialist policy, and a firmer front against the Fascist aggression. Its main objectives were to form a Popular Front Government of the same type as then existed in France and Spain, and to bring Great Britain and the other peace-loving nations into closer association with Soviet Russia. This brought him into conflict with the

[80] The decision to send Cripps to India was supposedly taken by the War Cabinet on 9 March. However, the Axis broadcasters had mentioned the visit before Cripps had even returned from Moscow, immediately dubbing him 'Stalin's Viceroy'. There is a very extensive literature on the visit. For Churchill's view, see *SWW*, vol.4, ch.12.

[81] The eating house has not been identified. This type of public-relations exercise has had something of a revival in recent years but during the war was striking and unusual. It clearly impressed Orwell, who had had his own experiences of life on the other side of the counter at such places (see *Down and Out in Paris and London*, 1933).

official heads of the Labour Party, who did not at that time grasp the full menace of Fascism. Whereas a lesser man would have given way in order to keep his pre-eminent position within the Labour Party, Cripps preferred to resign, and for several years he was in a very isolated position, only a few members in the House of Commons and a small following in the country at large realising that his policy was the correct one. However, when the Churchill Government was formed in 1940, it was recognised on all sides that no one was so suitable as Sir Stafford Cripps for the British Ambassadorship in Moscow. He discharged his office brilliantly, and undoubtedly did a great deal to make possible a firm alliance between the British and the Russian peoples. Since his return to England, he has followed this up by a series of speeches and broadcasts,[82] by which he has brought home to the ordinary people in Britain the enormous effort which their Russian allies are making, and the necessity of supporting them by every means in our power. Everyone in Britain is delighted to see such an important mission as the one which Cripps is now undertaking conferred upon a man whom even his critics admit to be gifted, trustworthy and self-sacrificing.

The Japanese are in possession of Rangoon, and probably also of the other main port of Burma, Bassein, which lies westward of Rangoon. The British have blown up the oil refineries at Syriam, near Rangoon, so thoroughly that they will be of no use to the Japanese and they are prepared, if necessary, to destroy the oil wells at Yenangyaung so thoroughly that no one will get any oil from them for the next five years.[83] Whatever else the Japanese may gain from Burma, they will gain nothing to satisfy their most pressing need, which is for oil; nor, so far as we know, have they acquired any worthwhile quantity of oil in the Dutch East Indies.

[*Censored:* It is becoming clear that the Japanese are also preparing an attack upon Australia. In the first place presumably against Darwin and the other airfields in the north. The main Japanese aim is to dominate the Indian Ocean, and join hands with the Germans in the Middle East, should the forthcoming German offensive be successful. But as part of this plan, they must also attack Australia, in order to prevent an Allied offensive being launched from there. We know already that huge American reinforcements are pouring into the Western Pacific, and their destination must be either Australia or

[82] Recordings of some of these survive in the BBC Sound Archives, including the speech addressed to the people of India from New Delhi. Cripps's voice has a strong period flavour which today would contrast strongly with a 'man of the people' image.

[83] This is a further attempt to counter persistent Axis rumours that the destruction of such wells was not being carried out.

New Zealand. The Japanese are also preparing to attack Ceylon and probably the mainland of India, and are also likely to make an attempt upon Madagascar. There are also indications that they are planning a treacherous attack upon Russia of the same kind as they made upon America, to coincide with the German offensive in the west. But the Russians, however, are not likely to be taken unawares.][84]

During this week full and well-authenticated information has been released about the behaviour of the Japanese army in Hong Kong. It has been confirmed by several eye-witnesses who escaped from Hong Kong and have now reached Chungking.[85] Among other things, it is known that the Japanese declared a whole quarter of Hong Kong to be a military brothel, which means that any woman in it can be raped at will by the Japanese soldiers. In Singapore, according to their own statement on the Tokyo radio,[86] the Japanese have taken 73,000 Chinese civilians and subjected them to what they call 'severe interrogation', in plainer language, to torture. Exactly similar things happened in Nanking in 1937. We see here the real meaning behind the Japanese slogan 'Asia for the Asiatics'. It means 'Asia for the Japanese, and slavery, impoverishment and torture for all who are unlucky enough to live under their rule'.

The Chinese have made it clear that their resistance will continue as before, no matter what happens in Burma. The temporary stoppage of the Burma Road does not vitally matter, since supplies of war material can easily be carried to China in large bombing planes from India. Meanwhile news comes from Chungking that a Free Korean Army has been formed from men who have escaped from Japanese oppression in Korea, and is already fighting side by side with the armies of the Chinese Republic.[87]

On the northern sector of the Russian front the German Sixteenth Army, which has been cut off by the Russians, has failed to escape and the Russians have announced that its end is in sight. Even the German wireless now admits that the position of the Sixteenth Army is critical. Recently the Nazi propagandists reviewed their losses during the

[84] There are obvious reasons for the censor's intervention here. The last point Orwell makes, about the Japanese attack on Russia, was, he claimed, his own invention (see *OWB*, p. 26), but he was also echoing here a broadcast from Chungking, mentioned on 10 March, entitled 'Japanese attack on Russia inevitable' (WAC: Summary of World Broadcasts 967. 9 Far East (iii.)).

[85] Broadcasts from Chungking on 11 March contained extensive accounts by Miss Phyllis Harrop, of the Hong Kong Government Services, and others.

[86] This broadcast has not been found in the monitors' reports.

[87] The 'Free Korean Movement' was described in a talk from Chungking monitored on the same day as that mentioned in n.84 above. Orwell clearly studied this particular monitors' report closely.

Russian war and admitted to having had 1,500,000 casualties in all – killed, wounded and missing. Even if we believe these figures to be truthful, this means that on average the Germans have had between five and six thousand casualties every day from the moment when the campaign began. Every single day, during the last eight months, therefore, several thousand German families have had cause to mourn the wanton attack on the Soviet Union which their Nazi rulers have forced upon them. But, since the Germans are not in the habit of overstating their losses, we can assume that the real figures are far higher.

[*Censored:* The British people are disciplining themselves yet harder for the demands of total war. The penalties against those who operate the Black Market in food have been stiffened up, so that offenders can now get as much as fourteen years imprisonment. White flour is to be withdrawn from the market shortly, and only wheatmeal flour allowed. This alone will save half a million tons of shipping space every year. It is probable also that the use of petrol for mere pleasure or convenience will shortly be prohibited. No one complains of these restrictions – on the contrary, the general public are demanding that the restrictions shall be made even stricter, so that the selfish minority who behave as though Britain were not at war can be dealt with once and for all.][88]

21 March 1942

It is now clearer than it was last week that the Japanese are preparing to attack Australia. Their main aim is what it has always been – to join hands with the Germans in the Middle East – but to do this they have got to make sure of their position in both the north and the south Pacific. There have been several indications that they are planning a sudden treacherous attack against Russia, of the same type as they previously made against America. There is no reason to think that the Russians will be taken unawares. The present aim of the Japanese is to capture the main ports in the northern part of Australia so that Australian and American and British troops will have no base nearer than New Zealand from which to make their attack.

At present the Japanese are directing their attacks chiefly against Port Moresby on the island of New Guinea opposite the northern tip of

[88] This time Orwell's comments on rationing did not pass the censor. The authentic 'Cripps' tone of the last sentence could be taken straight from *Nineteen Eighty-Four*.

Australia.[89] They are being strongly resisted but whether a landing on the Australian mainland can be prevented is not yet clear. Whether once they have landed the Japanese will find their task an easy one is a different question. Australia is an enormous country which it would take several years to overrun completely, even if there were little or no resistance. It seems probable, even though the Japanese may succeed in making their landing and in securing what at first sight appears to be a firm foothold, they will end by letting themselves in for rather the same kind of war as they have been waging for four years in China, that is to say, a war in which it is possible to conquer empty territory, but next door to impossible to destroy the enemy.

We do not know how strong are the forces which are assembled in Australia to meet the invasion; the Allies lost heavily in ships in the sea battle off Java,[90] and numerically they are not likely to be as strong in the air as the Japanese, because of the enormous distances across which air reinforcements have to be brought. We do know, however, that American reinforcements, both ground troops and aeroplanes, have reached Australia in large quantities, and have been reaching it throughout the last two months, although until now it was considered wiser not to reveal this. Meanwhile General MacArthur, who was commanding the American forces in the Philippines, has been brought to Australia to act as Commander-in-Chief of the Allied forces there.[91] General MacArthur's force has now held out in the peninsula south of Manila for three and a half months against an enormously more numerous enemy. The Japanese imagined when they first attacked the Philippines that they had an easy task before them, but they soon found that they were mistaken. This was due primarily to two causes. The first was the fact that General MacArthur, who had foreseen the Japanese invasion many years earlier, had prepared every move in advance. The second was the courage and devotion of the Philippine population, who, instead of going to the Japanese, as the latter had foolishly expected, fought bravely in defence of their country,[92] and thus allowed General

[89] The Japanese campaign in New Guinea and against Port Moresby went on throughout the period of Orwell's broadcasts, with imminent victory announced by the Japanese on many occasions. They failed to make any serious impression on the Australians.

[90] A frank admission. According to Admiralty figures the Allies lost five cruisers, seven destroyers and a sloop. Among the cruisers was HMS *Exeter*.

[91] General MacArthur's arrival in Australia as Supreme Commander of the United Nations forces in the SW Pacific was formally announced in Washington on 17 March. It was also stated that the appointment was at the request of Mr Curtin, Prime Minister of Australia, after discussion with President Roosevelt.

[92] Addressed to an Indian audience, these remarks show Orwell making the fundamental point 'Do thou likewise'.

MacArthur to possess a far larger army than would have been possible if he had been relying only on American troops. General MacArthur's arrival has been warmly welcomed in Australia, where he is generally recognised to be the best man to conduct the defence. Australia has now mobilised the whole of its manpower, which would give it, if necessary, a front line army of about half a million men, besides several millions of war workers of all kinds.

Three days ago news came from Australia of the heavy damage inflicted on the fleet with which the Japanese are attempting their invasion. American aeroplanes raided the base in New Guinea which the Japanese are occupying and either sank or damaged more than twenty Japanese ships. This included two heavy cruisers sunk, and five troop-ships either sunk or set on fire.[93] All this was accomplished with the loss of only one Allied aeroplane. On the following day news came of another successful raid. Nevertheless, the Japanese are proceeding with their attacks against Port Moresby, the chief Australian stronghold in New Guinea, and they will no doubt attempt to invade the mainland of Australia before long. But they can only do so at the cost of a heavy loss of ships, which they are already short of, and which they will find it harder and harder to replace.

News coming in from all parts of the world testified to the goodwill with which Sir Stafford Cripps's mission to India is regarded. It has been especially warmly welcomed in China. A Government spokesman at a Chungking press conference a few days ago remarked: 'It is not usual for the spokesman of one government to comment on the internal affairs of an allied country, but in the case of India, I would be failing in my duty if I refrained from expressing the great sympathy and interest with which we follow developments in that country. The appointment of Sir Stafford Cripps has been universally applauded by the Chinese press. It is generally felt here that if any man has the ability and insight to approach India's constitutional problem in the right spirit, that man is Sir Stafford Cripps. The British Cabinet has shown the highest political wisdom in making the appointment. When Sir Stafford meets the Indian leaders, they may find themselves to be really kindred spirits, working together for the defence of India and for a better world.'[94]

---

[93] Orwell is quoting here from a US Navy Department report. It described American and Australian land-based planes as 'inflicting losses as great or greater than those suffered by the United Nations forces in the Battle of Java'.

[94] The hopes Orwell expresses here must have been as real as anyone's. Surrounded at the BBC by such ardent supporters of Congress as Mulk Raj Anand, his view of the situation in India would have been transformed by a genuine resolution of the problems.

Sir Stafford Cripps is expected to arrive in India within the next day or two. How long he will stay is not yet known. He carries with him the united support and good wishes of the whole Government and people of Britain.

On the Russian front our allies are now fighting in the suburbs of Kharkov, and it does not seem likely that the Germans can hold on to this town much longer. Kharkov is an important industrial centre, the capture of which several months ago was proclaimed by the Germans as a great victory. They will perhaps give a different account of it when it once again falls into Russian hands. All the recent speeches of the Russian leaders display a confidence about the forthcoming spring campaign, which is in great contrast to the theatrical boasts of the German propagandists.[95] It is clear that apart from the actual fighting and apart from the mobilisation of fresh armies from Russia's enormous population, the losses which Russia suffered in her war industries when the Germans overran the Donetz Basin have been largely made good. Moreover, the stream of supplies of tanks, aeroplanes and other kinds of war material from Britain and the United States has never ceased all through the winter.[96] We may expect the Germans to make more than one attempt to cut the principal supply route which runs from Britain round the coast of Scandinavia and into the Arctic Sea. The Germans have now at least three powerful warships sheltering somewhere on the Norwegian coast, which have been placed there in order to make several raids on the supply route to Murmansk; only last week, the *Tirpitz*, Germany's biggest and newest battleship, attempted a raid of this type, but was driven back to port by British aeroplanes.[97]

28 March 1942

The Japanese have occupied the Andaman Islands, in the Indian Ocean to the south of Burma.[98] They were almost undefended, and

[95] Rarely did Orwell give a hostage to fortune that was so speedily lost as this. Germany's 'theatrical boasts' were put into immediate practice in the spring offensive.

[96] This statement was no doubt provoked by Axis broadcasts that claimed a marked falling-off in American shipments to Russia now that she had to fight the war against Japan.

[97] On 11 March the Admiralty announced that the *Tirpitz* had been attacked two days previously with the loss of two torpedo bombers. She was undamaged but returned to her base at Trondheim.

[98] They were occupied on 23 March. As Orwell suggests, the British force and most of the population had been evacuated, according to Government press releases.

the British command decided some time back to abandon them, evacuating a considerable proportion of the civilian population beforehand. The Andamans are eight hundred miles from Colombo and are about the same from the port of Madras, both of which are now liable to be subjected to air raids. This is the first step in the Japanese attempt to dominate the Indian Ocean from island bases, which we foretold in earlier newsletters.

[*Censored:* Apart from this, there has been no great change in the situation on the Eastern fronts during the past week. The chief activity has been in Burma where the situation is described as serious. The airfield at Toungoo in Central Burma has been lost to the Japanese. A small Chinese force has been cut off in Toungoo, but it is fighting back successfully and this morning news came that it had been reinforced. In Burma the Japanese have several possible objectives, and we do not yet know which they regard as the most important. One objective is the oilfield of Yenangyaung, another is the new road which runs via Burma from India into China. This road is still in process of construction but it could be brought into use quite shortly, and if the Japanese could succeed in cutting it, they would compel supplies from India to China to be sent by a more northerly and more difficult route. The other possible objective of the Japanese is the route leading directly overland from Burma into India by way of Assam. It is quite possible that they are contemplating a land attack upon India, especially Bengal, by this route. Owing to the wild nature of the country, however, they will probably not be able to take a highly mechanised army but will have to rely on infantry and aeroplanes. Against this kind of attack, guerilla forces can be very effective as we have seen in China, and consequently the factor of popular resistance in India will be of the highest importance.

The monsoon begins in Burma about the end of May. After that it is very difficult to move except by water or along the roads and railways. We ought not to assume, however, that this will make the country impassable for the Japanese infantry.][99] Meanwhile both British and Chinese forces in Burma are fighting back strongly. Two divisions[100] of Chinese troops are serving under the American

[99] Orwell felt the situation in Burma acutely, having worked there. His assessment of the situation did not pass the censor's scrutiny.

[100] The Chinese Expeditionary Force consisted of the Chinese Fifth and Sixth Armies, in all six divisions; however, in terms of numbers a Chinese division was about one third of a British division. General Joseph W. Stilwell was Chief of Staff to Generalissimo Chiang Kai-Shek; he had previously been military attaché at Peking for many years. Both he and the head of Chiang Kai-Shek's secret service, General Tai Li, were very anti-British, which did not help matters.

General Stilwell who is himself under the orders of Generalissimo Chiang Kai-Shek.

The Japanese moves against Australia have not made very much progress since last week. Heavy fighting is going on in the interior of the island of New Guinea, but so far the only attacks the Japanese have made against the principal Australian stronghold in the island, Port Moresby, have been air attacks. It will be recalled that last week Australian and American aeroplanes made a very successful attack against the Japanese sea forces, sinking or disabling a number of warships and troop transports, and this has probably set the Japanese plan back. General MacArthur, who made such a successful defence in the Philippines, is busy organising the forces in Australia, and has stated already that though he cannot work miracles, he regards himself as being in Australia, not merely to defend, but to attack at the first possible moment. Mr Curtin, the Premier of Australia, has described Australia as the base from which the Allies can take offensive action against Japan, and has expressed his hope of seeing a speedy settlement of Indian political problems, so that India can take her rightful place at the side of the Allies.[101]

There are signs that the war in the Mediterranean may shortly flare up again. The British navy have just brought off a brilliant feat by getting a large convoy of ships to the Island of Malta. One ship in the convoy was sunk by enemy aircraft, but the Italian naval force which attempted to attack it was driven off and one of Italy's biggest and newest battleships was hit by a torpedo.[102] The little island of Malta has now had over sixteen hundred air raids. This is a sign of its strategic importance and of the anxiety of the Axis powers to put it out of action as a base for warships and aeroplanes. As long as Malta, which lies between Italy and Africa, remains in British hands, it is both difficult and dangerous for the Axis to convey their troops to Libya. They have, indeed, lost a vast number of ships containing soldiers or materials of war during the last few months. If you look at the map, you can see that German reinforcements for Libya only have to travel a few hundred miles across the Mediterranean – whereas most of the British reinforcements have to sail thousands of miles

[101] Speaking in the House of Representatives on 25 March, Curtin said: 'The Government hope profoundly that the full moral and material resources of India may be mobilised in the common struggle through a settlement of the Constitutional problem. Australia and India must be held as the two pillars of the Allied position in Asia and the Pacific.'

[102] The battleship *Littorio*. The convoy crossed the Mediterranean during 22-24 March. Axis propaganda broadcasts claimed that Britain lost a cruiser and three destroyers, as well as the merchant ship mentioned; Orwell gives Britain's counter-claim.

round the Cape of Good Hope and up through the Indian Ocean and the Red Sea to Egypt. In spite of this disadvantage, the British and other Allied forces in Egypt have more than held their own, and besides conquering Abyssinia, have made advances into Libya which have twice taken them as far as Benghazi. It can be seen, therefore, that the sea warfare in the Mediterranean is extremely important because, if the Axis could attain control of those waters for only a few weeks, they might be able to pour into Libya an army overwhelmingly greater than the one the British have in Egypt. This army would make the southern arm of the Axis's attack against the Caucasus and the Middle East. As long as the British can hold fast in Egypt therefore, the harder is the task of the Axis forces in the North and the more our Russian allies are benefited.

The Germans are making great efforts to add to their depleted armies by recruiting fresh troops from Rumania and by bringing Bulgaria more actively into the war. King Boris of Bulgaria, who has always been an Axis sympathiser, is probably in favour of a closer alliance with Germany;[103] but it is doubtful whether the mass of the Bulgarian people, who are very pro-Russian in their sympathies and indeed almost regard themselves as Russians, can be persuaded into a war against the Soviet Union. There are also signs that Hitler is making renewed efforts to get hold of the remnants of the French fleet for use against Britain. It remains to be seen whether Marshal Pétain, who is at any rate the nominal ruler of unoccupied France, will violate his pledged word by handing the French warships over. Even if he does so, it remains to be seen whether the French sailors will be ready to fire their guns against people who, as they are well aware, are fighting for the liberty of France.[104]

The *Daily Mirror*, one of the most widely read of English newspapers, has been threatened with suppression because of its violent and sometimes irresponsible criticisms of the Government. The question was debated in both Houses of Parliament with the greatest

---

[103] The Germans were very successful in Romania, as Russia was to find to her cost at Sebastopol. For an Axis propagandist's view of the German-Romanian Alliance and of the other Axis allies, see Appendix, no.1. For a quite different view of King Boris and the likelihood that his assassination was by German agents, see now Hannah Arendt, *Eichmann in Jerusalem* (1963, Penguin 1977), p. 187.

[104] When dealing with France at this stage of the war, Orwell, like other Allied broadcasters, frequently resorted to half-truths of the sort used here; they may well have been following a censor's policy line. The feelings of French troops were soon to be tested at Madagascar.

vigour.[105] This may seem a waste of time in the middle of a world war, but in fact it is evidence of the extreme regard for freedom of the press which exists in this country. It is very unlikely that the *Daily Mirror* will actually be suppressed. Even those who are out of sympathy with it politically are against taking so drastic a step, because they know that a free press is one of the strongest supports of national unity and morale, even when it occasionally leads to the publication of undesirable matter. When we look at the newspapers of Germany or Japan, which are simply the mouthpieces of the Government, and then at the British newspapers, which are free to criticise or attack the government in any way that does not actually assist the enemy, we see how profound is the difference between totalitarianism and democracy.[106]

Manuel Quezon, President of the Philippine Islands, has arrived in Australia to join General MacArthur and to carry on the business of the Free Filipino Government. It is amusing to record that the Fascist radio has put out no less than three reports that President Quezon had been assassinated by the Americans.[107] They reported this on March 22nd, and later on the same day, they added that Quezon had been assassinated 'on the orders of MacArthur because he refused to travel with him to Australia'. On March 24th the Rome radio announced yet again that Quezon had been assassinated by British and American agents. And now Quezon has travelled to Australia of his own accord and there affirmed his unconditional loyalty to the Allied cause, and the resolve of the Filipino people to continue the fight against the

[105] The debate took place on 26 March after a written reply on 19 March by Herbert Morrison to a question raised in the Commons about a cartoon by Philip Zec published in the paper which showed a merchant seaman clinging to a life raft with the caption: 'The price of petrol has been raised by a penny. (Official.)' Morrison said: 'The cartoon in question is only one example, but a particularly evil example, of the policy and method of a newspaper which, intent on exploiting an appetite for sensation and with a reckless indifference to the National interest and the prejudicial effect on the war effort has repeatedly published scurrilous misrepresentations, distorted and exaggerated statements and irresponsible generalisations.' In the heated debate which Orwell refers to here Aneurin Bevan stated: 'I agree that there must be such restrictions on personal liberty as are necessary to win the war, but I do not consider Mr Morrison, the witch-finder of the Labour Party, the man to be entrusted with arbitrary powers.' For an account defending the *Daily Mirror*, see Hugh Cudlipp, *Publish and Be Damned* (1953), pp.172-87. Cudlipp claims that Zec's cartoon was misinterpreted: it was intended as an attack, not on Government cynicism, but on the black marketeers in petrol who were hampering the war effort 'while gallant lives were being lost'.

[106] Orwell is to some extent justifying his own position here.

[107] There were broadcasts on Rome radio on 22 and 24 March, repeating a Tokyo news item of the 22 March. The text of this is reprinted in full below (Appendix, no.5).

Japanese invaders. To get to Australia, he had to travel something over a thousand miles, which was a remarkable journey for a man who has been assassinated three times. So much for the truthfulness of Fascist propaganda.

4 April 1942

There is still heavy fighting in Central Burma, but the Allies will probably be forced to retreat a good deal further in the direction of Mandalay.

The day before yesterday, news came that the Japanese had landed at Akyab, the port on the Bay of Bengal not very far from Calcutta.[108] This is a serious threat to the British forces at Prome, who might be cut off if they do not retreat and if the Japanese force which has landed is strong enough to cut their communications. The Japanese have several different objectives in their invasion of Burma, and their aims are simultaneously strategic, economic and political. Strategically, they are trying to encircle China so that no further war supplies can be sent there from India, and they are also trying to prepare the way for the invasion of India by sea and land. Overland, they might manage to enter India by the difficult route through Manipur and Assam and simultaneously they might move in the direction of Bengal by successive landing operations along the coast. We cannot be sure that either of these manoeuvres will fail, nor can we assume that the monsoon, which begins in Burma about the end of next month, will slow up the Japanese movement very seriously. We can, however, be fairly sure that either by land or sea, they will not be able to bring a very highly mechanised force, with tanks and heavy guns, to India. They will have to rely chiefly on infantry and aeroplanes, against which numerous though ill-armed forces can often put up a successful resistance. A very great deal, therefore, depends on the will of the Indian people to defend themselves and upon their feeling that they have something which is really worth fighting for.

Economically the Japanese aim at plundering Burma of its oil, of its rice, and, insofar as they need it, of its timber. The oil is not of much immediate use to them, even if they get possession of the oil wells, because the refineries near Rangoon have already been destroyed. On

---

[108] This report on Tokyo radio, which Orwell must have seen in the monitors' reports, was denied by New Delhi on 3 April. The denial cannot have reached London by the time Orwell's talk went out.

the other hand, they have the greatest need of the rice, for their armies and, if they have enough shipping to transport it, for their home population.

Politically the Japanese aim at using Burma as a base for propaganda against India. They are now near enough to India to be able to broadcast on medium wave, and we must expect their propaganda to be enormously intensified during coming weeks.[109] At the moment they are keeping rather quiet, because until the negotiations which Sir Stafford Cripps is conducting have been settled one way or the other, they are not quite certain what attitude to take towards Pandit Nehru, Mahatma Gandhi and the other Indian political leaders. Should the negotiations end in a satisfactory settlement the Japanese, through their paid Indian mouthpieces[110] will open up a campaign of libel against Pandit Nehru and the others, whom they will accuse of being the paid agents of British imperialism. Should the negotiations fail, they will praise Pandit Nehru to the skies as the man who was not deceived by British promises and who is struggling for the independence of the Indian peoples. Which line they take will depend on the outcome of the negotiations, but one way or another the barrage of propaganda will begin within a week, and it is important for Indian listeners to be prepared for it, and not deceived by it.

Simultaneously with this propaganda campaign, the Japanese will point to Burma and Siam as examples of the success of the Japanese New Order, or, as they call it, 'The Co-Prosperity Sphere'. It is clear from the reports coming in that in Lower Burma, especially in the district of Tharrawaddy, the Japanese have managed to induce large numbers of excitable and adventurous Burmese to fight on their side in the vain hopes of winning independence for Burma.[111] They will certainly try to

[109] For Cripps's response to the radio propaganda he heard in India and the need for more talks to counter it, conveyed through the Minister of Information Brendan Bracken, see *OWB*, p.33.

[110] One of Orwell's very rare references to his main opponent, Subhas Chandra Bose and his supporters. Orwell and his Indian colleagues at the BBC were, of course, paid.

[111] As Orwell knew there had been considerable opposition to the British presence before the Japanese invasion. The Burmese Premier U Saw had been arrested on 18 January and the official Government announcement said: 'From reports received about the movements of U Saw after his good-will mission to this country [he had arrived on 10 October 1941 to discuss Dominion Status for Burma] it has come to the knowledge of HM Government that he has been in contact with the Japanese authorities since the outbreak of war with Japan. This fact has been confirmed by his own admission. HM Government have accordingly been compelled to detain him, and it will not be possible for him to return to Burma.' Despite Axis references to the incident, Orwell appears to have been banned from making any allusion to it by the censor.

repeat this manoeuvre in India. It is important, therefore, to see just how the Japanese Co-Prosperity Sphere works, how it fits in with Japanese and Nazi propaganda, and how both of these compare with the true facts. We can foretell with some certainty what will happen both because of the existing situation and because of the example of what the Germans and Japanese have done in the past.

Let us imagine that the Japanese can gain undisputed possession of the whole of Burma. Let us also suppose that the conquered Burmese are more or less on their side, having believed in the Japanese promise to make Burma independent after the war and having also believed that Japan is going to enrich Burma by gifts of manufactured goods and by stimulating Burmese industries. Now in these circumstances, what will actually happen? The first thing is that the Japanese will take away from the Burmese most of their rice, not only the surplus which they usually export to India, but also a good deal of what they usually eat themselves. The Japanese are bound to do this, because they must have rice for their armies and for their home population. But, it may be said, this does not matter if they pay the Burmese for their rice. The only difficulty is, what are they to pay with? In the first place, they will pay in money which they will print off in exactly such quantities as they think necessary. The Burmese peasant whose rice has been taken from him will get paper notes in return, and it will be two or three months before he will fully grasp that these notes are worthless, because they cannot buy anything. Necessarily they cannot buy anything because, with a great war on their hands, the Japanese cannot manufacture goods for export, even if they had any wish to do so, for the benefit of the people they have conquered. The money which they print will therefore be a painless way of plundering the peoples of Burma, Siam, Malaya and the other territories they have overrun. The Germans have done exactly the same in Europe, using what are called 'occupation Marks', that is to say, money specially printed for the use of the army of occupation. This money has to be accepted by the conquered peoples in return for goods, but in practice it will not buy anything. We may assume, therefore, that should the Japanese get possession of the whole of Burma, it will be only a few months before the Burmese discover that, so far from being liberated and enriched by their Japanese friends, they are being systematically robbed. Probably even the most ignorant Burmese will have grasped this fact by the middle of this winter, when the 1942 rice crop is out.

If the swindle of the Japanese Co-Prosperity Sphere is so simple as this, why is it that Japanese propaganda should have any success? To answer this question, one should look at Europe, where the same story has been enacted a year or two earlier. There you had the same essential situation. The Germans made promises very similar to the Japanese. They divided and weakened their victims with very similar propaganda. Then they invaded and conquered them, and then they proceeded systematically to plunder them by means of worthless money, holding them down with a military occupation and a ruthless police force. When it was too late, the conquered peoples learned the truth about Hitler's New Order. Something very similar has happened in Siam and is happening or may be happening in Burma. We see, therefore, the immense importance of political consciousness and of a sceptical attitude towards tempting propaganda. Just as in Europe, so in Asia, certain peoples have fallen into the clutch of the Fascists because they listened to what the Fascists said, instead of observing what they had actually done. The words which the Japanese are now pouring out towards Burma and will soon be pouring out towards India, are extremely inviting, but their deeds in Korea, in China, in Manchukuo,[112] in Formosa, are less inviting. In all these countries they have held the peoples down with the club and the machine-gun, they have robbed them of their crops and of their raw materials, they have crushed their national movements, interfered with the education of their children, and have failed entirely to develop their resources except in the interests of Japan itself. They have been doing that to Formosa for fifty years, to Korea for forty years, to Manchukuo for ten years, and to the occupied parts of China for five years. Tomorrow they hope to do the same to India, to Australia and possibly even to parts of Africa. Very much, therefore, depends on the steadfastness and common sense of the people to whom the Fascist propaganda is addressed, for it is better to fight back and be free even though one suffers like the Chinese, than to submit and discover too late that one has been deceived like the people of Siam. To those who say that Japan will set Burma or India free, the best answer is: Why then have they not set free Korea and Formosa, which they have had in their power for so long? To those who say that the Japanese are fighting for the liberation of India, the best answer is: Why then are they fighting against the liberation of China? To those who say that the cause of Japan is the cause of Asia as against the European races, the best answer is: Why then do the Japanese constantly make war against other races who are Asiatics no less than themselves?

---

[112] Manchukuo was considered by the Allies to be purely a Japanese puppet state and it is unusual to see its existence recognised as Orwell recognises it here.

18 April 1942

During this week the principal events have been political rather than military. The news from the battle fronts is well known and may well be left out.[113] Now let's take the political situation, which is full of possibilities, both hopeful and threatening.

[*Censored:* In Burma the Japanese have received large reinforcements and have made a further advance. As we foretold in earlier letters, the British have had to abandon the Burmese oilfields. These had been systematically wrecked beforehand and will be of no direct use to the Japanese. The great oil refinery near Rangoon was in any case destroyed some time ago. Apart from the fortress of Corregidor, fighting is still going on in various parts of the Philippine Islands, and American long-range bombers, operating from bases more than a thousand miles away, have made a heavy raid on the Japanese forces. The Japanese plans to invade Australia do not seem to have made any further progress. From the Western theatre of war there is not much to report. The snow in Russia is thawing and for the time being the mud slows down operations, but the heroic Red Army continues to make small advances and the British bombing planes continue their raids on Western Germany.]

Sir Stafford Cripps is expected to reach Britain shortly. Now that a week has gone by since the breakdown of negotiations between Sir Stafford Cripps and the Indian political leaders, it is possible to see his mission in clearer perspective and to say something about the reactions to it in various parts of the world.

It is clear from the reports that have come in from many countries that only the supporters of Fascism are pleased by the failure of Sir Stafford Cripps's mission. On the other hand, there is a general feeling that the failure was not complete, in so much that the negotiations have clarified the issue and did not end in such a way as to make further advances impossible. However deep the disagreement, there was no ill-feeling on either side and no suggestion that either Sir Stafford Cripps or the Indian political leaders were acting other than in

---

[113] This sentence was inserted by the censor after he had deleted Orwell's original sentence which ran: 'We can summarise the news from the battle fronts in a few words before proceeding to discuss the political situation which is full of possibilities both hopeful and threatening.' The censor then deleted the whole of the following paragraph.

good faith.[114] In Britain and the United States Sir Stafford has actually enhanced his already high reputation. He undertook a difficult job in which he risked being personally discredited, and his obvious sincerity has impressed the whole world. The Axis propagandists are attempting to represent the breakdown as a refusal on the part of India to defend herself, and an actual Indian desire to pass under Japanese rule. This is a direct lie, and the Axis broadcasters are only able to support it by deliberately not quoting from the speeches of Mr Nehru and the other political leaders. Even Mr Gandhi, though remaining faithful to his programme of non-violence, has not suggested that he wishes to see the Japanese in India, merely that he believes that they should be resisted by spiritual rather than material weapons. Mr Nehru has not ceased to be anti-British, but he is even more emphatically anti-Japanese. He has asserted in the most vigorous terms possible that Indian resistance will continue and that the Congress Party will do nothing to hamper the British war effort, although the failure to alter the political status quo will prevent their taking a very direct part in it. He has said, as on many other occasions, that however deep his own objections to the British Government may be, the fact remains that the cause of Britain, of Soviet Russia and China, represents progress, while the cause of Germany and Japan represents reaction, barbarism and oppression. In spite of the difficulty, therefore, of collaborating directly with the British forces, he will do all in his power to raise popular Indian feeling against the aggressor and to make Indians realise that their liberty is inextricably bound up with an Allied victory. For even at the worst, India may get its independence from Britain, whereas the idea of India or any other subject nation winning its liberty in a Fascist-ruled world is laughable.

These are not empty words, and the attitude of the mass of the Indian people, and also of the leading political parties such as the Congress movement, can undoubtedly make a very great difference to the outcome of the war. Even the fact that it would be difficult for

[114] As always when Orwell alludes to reports coming in from many countries, he is referring to the monitored broadcasts of the non-Axis powers. Orwell's plain statement of 'good faith on both sides' presaged a storm culminating in the arrest and detention of the Congress leaders. Orwell goes on to mention that Nehru did not support the Japanese, and had the assurance of his colleague Mulk Raj Anand, a close friend of Nehru's, on this. Nevertheless the Government of India was later to release documents seized at raids on Congress Party offices purporting to show that, as in the case of U Saw, suggestions had been made that the Japanese be approached directly in the event of an invasion, which was likely. The BBC was given special instructions on how to deal with the situation in India shortly before Nehru's arrest (see above, p.18f.).

India to equip every Indian with modern weapons does not alter this.[115] Back in 1935 or 1936 when it became clear that a Japanese invasion of China was imminent, many outside observers considered that nothing could be done to stop the Japanese, because the Chinese peasants had little sense of nationality and modern armaments hardly existed on the Chinese side. As it turned out, these predictions were quite false. Ever since 1937 the Japanese have been engaged in an exhausting war in which they have gained very little material benefit, lost great numbers of men, reduced the standard of living of their own working class[116] and alienated millions of Orientals who might otherwise have been on their side. The reason was that there existed in China a strong popular political movement which could fire the peasants and the town working class and make them ready to struggle against the invader, pitting their numbers and their courage against superior armaments. Against very heavily mechanised armies, such as the German army, mere popular resistance with rifles and hand grenades may perhaps be ineffective, though the success of the Russian guerillas makes even this doubtful. But against the sort of army that the Japanese have employed in China, or the sort of army that they are likely to be able to use for the invasion of India – that is an army mainly of infantry – guerilla methods can be highly successful and the 'scorched earth' policy can immensely hamper the invader. Very much, therefore, turns upon Indian popular enthusiasm and the efforts of Mr Nehru may turn out to be a thorn in the Japanese side. There is no doubt that the Axis propagandists are well aware that Mr Nehru, Mr Azad and the other leading Congress personalities are heart and soul against them, and it will not be very long before they once again begin libelling them as the agents of British imperialism.

[*Censored:* The British Budget was announced three days ago, and on the whole has caused satisfaction. Summarising it briefly, its provisions are as follows. It does not add to direct taxation and it actually remits income tax on the lower levels. Roughly speaking the poorer grades of manual workers will be paying less in direct taxation during the current year. On the other hand, the Budget adds heavily to indirect taxation, almost all of it on luxuries. Tobacco and alcohol

[115] There was a strong romantic attachment to guerrilla warfare at the time; the early Local Defence Volunteers, which Orwell joined, had some of that spirit. But the arming of all Indian civilians, as some Congress members had naively suggested, would have been impossible logistically, as well as a certain recipe for civil war.

[116] Axis propaganda made much of the fact that, before Pearl Harbor, the accepted opinion of world military experts was that Japan was exhausted by her wars with China and the standard of living of her workers had been reduced to critically low levels. Orwell is here repeating exactly the same propaganda line even after the greatest Japanese victories of the war.

are both very heavily taxed, so also are all kinds of luxuries such as fur coats, silk dresses and the like. Certain kinds of very cheap clothes intended to be worn at work will be exempted from taxation. The tax on tobacco will not apply to the armed forces, who will be able to buy each day a certain number of cigarettes at the old price. In general, it is felt to be a democratic Budget, which will hasten the equalisation in the standard of living and the wiping out of class distinctions which is happening in Britain as a result of the war.]

There is very bad news in the fact that Laval has returned to the French Cabinet.[117] Laval is a French millionaire who has been known for many years to be a direct agent of the Nazi Government. He played a leading part in the intrigues which led to the downfall of France and since the Armistice has steadily worked for what is called 'collaboration' between France and Germany, meaning that France should throw in its lot with the Axis, send an army to take part in the war against Russia, and use the French Fleet against Britain. For over a year he has been kept out of office, thanks to American pressure, and his return probably means that diplomatic relations between France and the USA will now come to an end.[118] The American Government is already recalling its ambassador and has advised its nationals to leave France. This is perhaps no bad thing in itself, for there is very little doubt that German submarines operating in the Atlantic have habitually made use of French ports, both in Africa and in the West Indies, and the fact that France and America were theoretically on friendly terms has made these manoeuvres harder to deal with. If relations are broken off, the Americans will at any rate not feel that their hands are tied by the so-called neutrality of France. Nevertheless, there is very great danger that at some critical moment Laval may succeed in throwing the French Fleet into battle against the British Navy, which is already struggling against the combined

[117] On 14 April Admiral Darlan was dropped from the Vichy cabinet and the post he held of Vice-Premier was abolished; he remained head of the armed forces. Laval took his place in the newly created post of Chief of Government.

[118] In a speech delivered on 13 April by the politician Marcel Deat the new administration's view of America is clearly foreshadowed: 'There are two choices for France: either she comes out openly for collaboration in the New Europe, or Germany will have recourse to force and take such measures as she may judge necessary. We can participate in a European victory or a British defeat. For 18 months France has been governed by the American Ambassador, Admiral Leahy. We must make our choice – the Anglo-Saxons or Europe. Britain bombs our cities, murders our workmen in the Paris suburbs, steals our colonies, sinks our ships and tries to starve us by blockade. America has occupied St Pierre et Miquelon and New Caledonia and would attack Morocco tomorrow if she could!' On 17 April Admiral Leahy was recalled by President Roosevelt. American citizens in Vichy France had been advised to leave the previous day.

navies of three nations. That undoubtedly is what he aims at doing, but he may be frustrated by the fact that the common people of France are whole-heartedly anti-Nazi. There is some reason to think that the French sailors would refuse to use their guns against the British, whom they well understand to be fighting for the liberty of France. Disturbances, riots and sabotage continue in Occupied France, and almost every day the German newspapers announce the shooting of fresh batches of hostages. The Germans themselves appear to believe that if a British and American invading force landed in France it would be eagerly helped by the French population. Meanwhile, however, the situation is full of danger, and we can be sure that the Quisling element in France has been assigned some fairly important part in the great spring campaign which the Germans are now preparing.

25 April 1942

During this week the military situation in Asia has not greatly changed. It is known that the Japanese in Burma have been heavily reinforced. The Allies have made a further withdrawal since last week. The Japanese efforts to encircle the British forces at Yenangyaung and the Chinese forces at Loikaw have failed. General Wavell's speech of April 21st[119] made it clear that India's air defences have been greatly strengthened, both in planes and in personnel, and this improvement will probably make itself felt on the Burma front, though the lack of airfields in Upper Burma adds to the difficulties of the Allies. The return to Madras of the Provincial Government, which had been temporarily evacuated,[120] is no doubt a result of the improved situation in the air. In their raids on Ceylon and Madras the Japanese are believed to have lost about a hundred planes, and as these planes must have come from aircraft carriers, they cannot be replaced without some delay. In their Burma campaign the Japanese are racing against time and the weather. They hope to cut not only the Burma Road which runs from Lashio, but also the new roads now under

[119] In a broadcast to the Indian people from New Delhi calculated to boost morale Wavell made general references to hoped-for improvements, which Orwell here puts the best face on that he can.

[120] The first air-raid alert had sounded in Madras on 7 April. Systematic evacuation of all non-essential citizens had continued from then on, with the Provincial Government, seemingly also in this category, going as well. By the time the alarm was over more than 100,000 had left the city.

construction between India and China, before the onset of the monsoon, which begins about the middle of May. By the middle of June all low-lying ground in Burma is waterlogged. We ought not to make the mistake of assuming that the coming of the monsoon will completely immobilise the Japanese forces. Even in the most rainy months it is possible to move large bodies of infantry by means of rafts and shallow boats. But the transport of tanks and heavy guns is very difficult and suitable landing grounds for aeroplanes are much fewer.[121] On the whole, therefore, the beginning of the monsoon will be advantageous to the Allies and will offset to some extent the advantage in numbers and armaments by which the Japanese have won their successes hitherto.

The Americans and Filipinos continue their resistance in the fortress of Corregidor and in various other parts of the Philippine Islands.[122] On April 18th Tokyo was bombed by American aeroplanes, in all probability operating from aeroplane carriers. The Japanese profess great indignation and make the claim, which is usual with Axis propagandists, that only non-military objectives were hit. Indeed, to judge from the Axis broadcasts, any bombs that drop from Allied aeroplanes fall so invariably on schools and hospitals that one must assume that Tokyo, Berlin, and the other chief cities of the Axis countries contain no other buildings than these. But when we remember that for five years past the Japanese have been bombing totally undefended towns in China, their indignation seems a little ridiculous.

In the Western struggle there are three all-important questions which cannot yet be answered with certainty but which we must do our best to answer in order to get a clear picture of the future. These questions are, first, in what direction will the Germans make their main offensive? Secondly, will the British and Americans attempt an invasion of the continent of Europe? Thirdly, what part will France, now under the control of the pro-Nazi millionaire Laval, play in the forthcoming operations?

We have pointed out in earlier newsletters that the Germans are bound to make their greatest effort in the direction of the Caucasus and the Middle East. Their chief needs are to obtain fresh supplies of oil and to join hands with their Japanese allies, and therefore the general direction in which they must move can hardly be questioned.

[121] Here again Orwell draws on his experience in Burma.

[122] Axis propaganda was still making great play of Japanese victories. On 7 April the US War Department admitted that 65,000 US and Filipino troops and civilians on Bataan were now prisoners. Orwell, understandably, makes mention only of the resistance at Corregidor.

The only doubt hitherto has been as to whether they will make an all-out effort to defeat the Red Army and reach the Caspian Sea, or whether they will attempt to move eastward by a more southerly route. The fact that France is now more closely under German control than before may decide the Germans to make a direct attack on the island of Cyprus and then on Syria. For if they can get control of the French fleet, they may have enough warships at their disposal to challenge the British control of the Eastern Mediterranean. To capture Cyprus and Syria by air attack alone would be very difficult. It is also quite possible that simultaneously with their main offensive the Germans will make some kind of attack in the west, either against Spain, Gibraltar and West Africa, or against the British Isles. A full-scale invasion of Britain is not likely to succeed, but even an unsuccessful invasion might cause great disorganisation of industry, and for this purpose Hitler, who does not care how much blood he sheds, might be ready to risk quite a large force at a critical moment. Britain, however, is well prepared for any such attempt, both on land, on sea and in the air.

We prefer not to make any definite prediction as to whether the Allies will invade Europe this year. [*Four lines illegible.*] It seems clear that the Germans expect one such invasion to be made, and believe that either Norway or France will be the scene of it. They are feverishly at work strengthening their defences in the west, and have probably already withdrawn troops and aeroplanes from the Russian front for this purpose. The British have made another successful commando raid, this time at Boulogne.[123] These commando raids not only do damage to important military objectives but force the Germans to divert a disproportionately large number of men for the defence of their long coast line. Beneath their habitual boasting, the speeches of the German leaders betray great anxiety. They are aware that in the war of 1914-1918 it was the necessity of fighting on two fronts, in Russia and in France, that wore out the German army, and they are afraid of the same thing happening again if the British and the Americans can secure a footing in Europe. In his speech broadcast on April 22nd Hitler once more attempted to frighten the German people into greater efforts by telling them that defeat would mean the utter destruction of Germany. Needless to say this is a lie: a German defeat would mean merely the destruction of the Nazis. But it is a significant change to find the German dictator even discussing the possibility of defeat. It is strange to look back and remember that in the summer of

---

[123] On 22 April. The raid, led by Major Lord Lovat, was described as a small-scale reconnaissance raid.

1940 the Germans were told that the war would be ended in a few weeks, and that at the beginning of 1941 Hitler solemnly promised his people that they would never have to endure another winter of war.

As to developments in France, it seems clear, as we predicted last week, that Laval is bent on co-operating closely with the Germans. Indirectly he may be of great use to them but he will have to go very carefully, for he is hated in France, and popular feeling runs high. Probably he will endeavour to secure his aims little by little: indeed his past record shows that he prefers to work quickly underground and afford his critics little opportunity to find out what he is doing. But his accession to power has shown how weak is the Vichy regime and how little it can be relied upon to stand against German demands – whether these include the cession of French possessions overseas or the use of French shipping. South Africa has now severed relations with the Vichy government, and prior to this General Smuts had already announced that any attempt to seize Madagascar on behalf of the Axis would be resisted.[124] There is no further news as yet as to whether Laval will endeavour to place the French fleet at the disposal of the Axis. It is probably safe to assume that the French sailors, or most of them, would not fight against their former allies at the bidding of the Germans. But there remains the danger that during the past year and a half the Germans may have been training crews of their own for this purpose; for though they agreed under the Armistice terms not to make use of the French navy, it is not usual with them to abide by agreements which have become inconvenient. It is clear that anti-Nazi feeling in France is stronger than ever since Laval's accession to power. An attempt has been made on the life of Doriot, the French Fascist and pro-Nazi politician.[125] Statements that fresh batches of French or Belgian hostages have been shot are now almost daily items in the German press.

[*Censored:* Fresh rationing arrangements have been announced in Britain. From June 1st fuel for domestic use is to be rationed which is expected to save about 10 million tons of coal annually.][126]

Sir Stafford Cripps arrived in England on April 21st. A survey of the world's press shows that even though his mission has failed for the

[124] In the context of the Allied plans to invade Madagascar which were at an advanced stage, this remark of Smuts and the earlier reference to cession of Vichy territory to the Axis powers seem to be a deliberate propaganda smoke-screen.

[125] On 20 April a bomb was thrown at Doriot while he was speaking at Rennes. It failed to explode but the offices of his anti-Bolshevist organisation were successfully attacked a few days later.

[126] A further attempt by Orwell to give the tiniest glimpse of the reality of war-time life in London that caught the censor's eye.

time being, the world at large, especially in China and the United States, admires him for his integrity and hopes that the negotiations may be reopened at some time in the future. During this week the Cripps mission will no doubt be debated in the Houses of Parliament, and in our next newsletter we hope to be able to comment more fully upon the reactions in this country.

2 May 1942

The Japanese have captured Lashio, which is on the main branch of the Burma Road, running eastwards from Mandalay. There is another road further to the north, which runs south-eastward from Bhamo and enters China a good deal to the east of Lashio. This, of course, is still in Allied hands, but it is not a first-class road, and Bhamo is only connected with Mandalay by river. If Mandalay should fall, China is for the time being cut off from the outside world and the Chinese armies will be dependent on airborne supplies until the new roads from India into China are completed. As much as possible of the war materials which had been piled up at Lashio had been removed into China and it is known that the rest were destroyed before the Japanese got there.

At such moments as this it is more than ever necessary to see the whole war, as well as the Burma campaign, in perspective, and to pay no attention either to enemy propaganda or to the rumours brought by refugees from Burma, which may often be exaggerated and misleading. The loss of the greater part of Burma is a setback for the Allied cause, but not an overwhelming one, and cannot be decisive in the major strategy of the war.

There is little to report from either the Philippine Islands or from Australia. The Australian and American aeroplanes continue heavily bombing the Japanese forces in the island of New Guinea and have destroyed much war material and a number of enemy planes. Nevertheless, observers on the spot believe that the Japanese intend launching their attack on Australia at some time in the near future.

Comparison of Stalin's Order of the Day[127] with the hysterical speeches which came from Hitler and Mussolini earlier in the week leaves no doubt that the Axis tyrants feel the chill of their twilight while the Russian leader is more confident, and has stronger reasons

[127] The major speeches of all wartime leaders were broadcast worldwide and Orwell here assumes that his audiences in India and the Middle East would be free to listen to them.

for confidence, than ever. The meeting of Fuehrer and Duce by the wayside in the mountains of the Salzkammergut was doubtless intended to make the world's flesh creep; but even their own peoples cannot now be completely deceived by the pretence that these conferences produce miracles of victory. Though the two friends met on the eve of Hitler's invasion of Norway and of the ignominy with which Mussolini covered himself and the Fascist army by the invasion of Greece, it will not be forgotten in their two countries that they put their heads together before Hitler plunged into the Russian adventure, and their last meeting was the prologue to the smashing repulse of what the Nazi commander intended for the final assault on the Russian people.

When the couple meet now, Mussolini must be haunted by bitter memories of the days when he could approach Hitler as an equal. As the most helpless of quislings he went to Salzburg, and the result of the conference, according to his own mouthpiece, Gayda, must be to rivet the chains more closely on himself and the Italian people.[128] Larger numbers of Italian troops are to be flung into the fire of the Russian front, still stronger forces of the Nazi army admitted to Italy, to pillage at their will. On this occasion at least we may be sure Gayda has told the truth. Hitler had with him Marshal Keitel, the Chief of the Nazi High Command, who has been running round the other slave states of Eastern Europe to collect troops for slaughter and would not let Italy off lightly. The official report of the conference, jejune as usual, nevertheless betrays the nervous confusion of Fuehrer and Duce: they have won, they say – an 'overwhelming victory', but they renew in their own words 'stern determination to ensure final victory by all means in their power'.

If words were among the means which overwhelm, Russia would have been annihilated several times last summer and last autumn. There is no doubt of the justice of Stalin's estimate that the German army is weaker now than it was ten months ago. The best officers, the best troops and masses of material of the Wehrmacht have been destroyed. Russian resources of manpower are incomparably greater than Hitler can scourge to the front from the Reich and all his slave States.[129] Heavy handicaps have been inflicted on Russia's productive power by the loss of the Ukraine, which is not only a rich granary but

[128] Verginio Gayda was editor of the *Giornale d'Italia*. The meeting of Hitler and Mussolini had taken place at Salzburg on 29-30 April.

[129] This and the previous paragraph show Orwell striking his most populist propaganda note. It is difficult to surmise his own view of the two million Indian troops, all volunteers, fighting with the Allies, but the Axis broadcasters used almost the same words about them as Orwell uses about Germany and her allies.

furnishes over half the normal coal and iron supply of Russian industry. On the other hand, remarkable success in the movement of factory equipment eastward, in holding the Moscow area and in the expansion of Ural and Siberian production has ensured that the decline of armament manufacture through the overrunning of the Ukraine is far less serious than was feared. More and more munitions and aircraft, Stalin is able to say, are now reaching the front from Russian workshops, while Great Britain and the United States give 'ever-greater war assistance'.

It is no doubt in Stalin's calculations that grandiose attacks will be delivered. The weight of machinery and men which Nazism can put into such blows is still formidable. Points of the first importance to Russia, such as the Moscow area and the oilfields of the Caucasus, to say nothing of Leningrad, are much nearer the German lines now than they were last summer. It must, however, be far more difficult to concentrate powerful striking forces on the tortuous front than it was in Poland. Stalin tells his people that the German reserves of men, of oil and of raw materials are at an end. With Hitler in command we must expect that any such approach to exhaustion will produce the fiercest efforts which brutality can extort from a nation trained in a barbarous discipline. The Russian people are assured by their leader that they can make 1942 the year of final defeat for Germany. We may depend on them to do their utmost, convinced that there can be no peace upon earth, no security of freedom or of life worth living, till Nazism is extirpated. Whatever the course of the struggle, they may count on the maximum strength that we and the other allied nations can exert for swift and complete victory.

In their 'all-out' war effort, Russian workers have sacrificed the more popular one of their two annual festivals. May Day this year was a working day for the first time since 1918. The occasion was, none the less, observed by the holding of meetings and the display of red streamer banners bearing slogans.

Since the Soviet power was established, the prime significance of May Day for the Russian people has been a patriotic one, and since Stalin told the Stakhanovite workers seven years ago that 'life is growing better, life is growing happier', the day has been the occasion of a temporary relaxation from the strain and effort demanded of Soviet workers, and has had something of the quality of the Fourteenth of July in France.[130]

In the celebrations held in past years in the Red Square in Moscow, the Uritsky Square in Leningrad, the Kretchadik in Kiev, and in

---

[130] Contrast Orwell's view of the Russians' sacrifice of their Labour Day holiday with the Frenchmen's sacrifice of their Fourteenth of July celebrations (below, p.118).

thousands of towns and villages, there has been more thought for Socialist achievement in the Soviet Union than for the international implications of a day which, as a demonstration of working-class solidarity, had its origin in the Chicago strike of forty-six years ago.

This year, more than ever, the patriotic note was dominant, and it was to the events that have happened since last May Day that thoughts were directed – the sudden impinging of German might on the Russian frontiers; the long and bitterly fought withdrawal to the outskirts of the two greatest Russian cities and to the banks of the Volga and Don; the crashing counter-offensive which developed, as winter deepened, into a persistent, dogged advance; and to the allies of Russia, active or potential, the proletariat of all lands, European patriots, oppressed brother Slavs, and the workers of Germany.

It is the firm belief among Russian workers that it is because their land is a socialist one that it has withstood Hitler's attempts to disrupt it politically, on the battlefield, and economically. For many years the factory wheels ceased to turn on May 1st as a protest against a system the workers believed exploited them. For twenty-four years they stopped while the Russian workers celebrated their change of system. This year, on the Volga, in the Urals, in Siberia and Central Asia, and in the workshops near the battle-zone, in besieged Leningrad as in liberated Kalinin, the wheels continued to turn in order to defend that system.

9 May 1942

On May 5th British forces landed on the island of Madagascar. The Vichy government ordered the garrison to resist, and there was indeed fierce resistance for a short time, but Diego Suarez, the naval base, had surrendered by the evening of May 7th, and almost all the Vichy forces in the island laid down their arms. A certain amount of mopping up may now be necessary, but it can be taken that Madagascar is now under British control.[131] This is an extremely important move in the

[131] The surprise of the attack was such that a French naval captain in charge of a squadron was under the impression that he was being attacked by the Japanese. Despite Orwell's repeated statements of the sympathetic views of French sailors, the battle for the naval base of Diego Suarez was bitter. Of the sailors 114 were reported dead in the first twenty-four hours as well as 180 from the air force. The claim that Madagascar was under British control was premature; Vichy ordered a continued resistance, and Orwell did not report the final capitulation of their forces until 5 November.

general strategy of the war against Germany and Japan.

If you look at the map, you can see that this large island dominates the route by which ships coming round the Cape of Good Hope travel either towards Ceylon and India, or towards the Red Sea and the Middle East. In enemy hands, therefore, Madagascar would constitute a most deadly threat to the Allies' war effort; for since it is difficult for British merchant ships to pass through the Mediterranean, the armies in the Middle East and India have to be supplied largely round the Cape. In addition, the supplies that are sent to our Russian allies, and which are put ashore in the Persian Gulf, go by the same route.

In spite of this danger, the British Government would probably have preferred to take the risk of not occupying Madagascar if a reliable government had been in power in France. However, during the last few weeks effective power in the Vichy Government has passed into the hands of Laval, who hardly pretends to be anything more than a tool of the Germans. More than a year ago, while Pétain was still in power, the French handed over Indo-China to the Japanese, to be used as a base for attacks on Siam and Malaya. If even Pétain was willing to do this, it was much more certain that Laval would do the same with Madagascar. Apart from this general probability, it had been known that for months past more and more Japanese in the guise of traders, military attachés, tourists and whatnot, had been pouring into Madagascar in order to prepare the way for a coup d'état.[132] In the circumstances, the British Government had no choice but to forestall the Japanese by entering Madagascar first. It has been made clear that Britain has no intention of annexing Madagascar or of interfering more than is necessary in its internal administration. The British will probably not occupy the whole of the island, but merely the ports, airfields and other places of military importance. Their first task will be to round up the Japanese fifth columnists. Apart from these, the bulk of the inhaitants are probably pro-Ally. The Malagasy population of the island is about four million, and the French population about 25,000. It is known that these are divided in sympathies. Earlier in the war, the then Governor of Madagascar was in favour of continuing resistance against the Germans, and in consequence Pétain replaced him by a more pro-Nazi official. Recently a secret radio, supporting General de Gaulle, has been heard broadcasting from Madag-

---

[132] Presumably Orwell is here repeating an MOI propaganda briefing. In fact no Japanese were found on the island, with the exception of two domestic servants, and the use of 20,000 troops in the invasion to fight against a 1500 Vichy garrison, white and coloured, proved excessive.

ascar.[133] We know, therefore, that at least some of the French population are on our side, and the indigenous population, with the threat of German or Japanese tyranny before them, are almost certain to be so. It is regretted that both French and British blood had to be shed in carrying out this operation, but by arriving in overwhelming force the British managed to reduce the bloodshed to a minimum.

Once Madagascar is occupied, it becomes necessary to defend it, and the other islands in the Indian Ocean assume an increased importance. In particular, there are the islands of Mauritius and Reunion, lying somewhat to the east of Madagascar. The Japanese are almost certain at some time to make an attempt upon these islands in order to use them as stepping stones for further attacks. Mauritius is a British possession, but Reunion is under the control of Vichy France and there exists the danger that its rulers may make an attempt to hand it over to the Japanese. However, the British occupation of Madagascar may make a political difference in Reunion, where, as elsewhere throughout the French Empire, the Vichy elements are only very insecurely in control.

In Burma, the Japanese have entered Mandalay, and the eastern wing of their army, driving from Lashio, has crossed the China border. On the western flank, British and Chinese forces previously defending Mandalay are retreating northward. By these operations the Japanese have succeeded in temporarily isolating China, which for the time being can only be supplied by air. On the other hand, their other objective of encircling the British and Chinese armies in Upper Burma is not likely to succeed. Some material may have to be abandoned, but the main British and Chinese forces in the eastern part of Upper Burma will probably get away. They may move up the railway to Myitkyina and thence into China, but more likely will have to retreat over the mountains of Manipur into Assam. It is a difficult route, but not impossible, and it is made easier by the fact that great numbers of Indian refugees have passed that way already.[134] Meanwhile the Chinese Republican armies have made a series of daring raids on Shanghai, Nanking, Hanyihow and several other cities in the heart of Japanese-occupied China, and two days ago they made another similar raid on Canton. The fact that Chinese armies can thus operate right inside their territory shows how precarious is the Japanese hold even on the parts of China that are marked 'Japanese' on

---

[133] Again, this information seems to have come from the MOI or Gaullist sources, as no broadcasts of this type have been found in the BBC monitors' reports available to Orwell. The Vichy Governor was M. Annet.

[134] It was against believing these and their stories that Orwell elsewhere had warned his listeners (above, p. 84).

the map. On May 5th the Japanese succeeded in landing on the island of Corregidor, and on May 6th the fortress was forced to surrender, after a resistance of four months. This long delaying action in the Philippines has held up the Japanese attack on Australia, just as the delaying action in Burma has held up the attack on India. Yesterday came news of an air and naval action near the Solomon Islands between the American navy and a Japanese fleet evidently making for Australia. At the moment of speaking the battle is probably still continuing. It is too early to give a detailed account, but it is certain that the Japanese have had very heavy losses, including two aircraft carriers, two or more cruisers, two destroyers and a number of smaller ships, besides transports.[135] The Allies have not yet published figures of their own losses. Until further reports come in a final verdict is not possible, but it can be taken that in all probability this battle has resulted in a serious setback for the Japanese.

With the coming of spring, operations on the Russian front are beginning again. Everything points to the fact that the Caucasus will be the scene of the main German offensive. The Russians are not ceasing from their attacks both there and in the Crimea, their main object being to weaken the Germans beforehand and hamper their concentration. British supplies of war material continue to pour into Russia, through the Arctic Sea, but not without difficulty, for the nights are now very short in the far north, and the Germans have strong fleets of submarines on the Norwegian coast. A few days ago, a sea battle took place in which the British lost a cruiser[136] and the Germans a destroyer, but of 30 merchant ships making up the convoy, 27 got through and delivered their cargoes to our Russian allies. In another broadcast speech, Stalin has again stated confidently that he expects final victory over the Germans during 1942.

The Royal Air Force continues to make heavy bombing raids on the German ports and armament factories. The Germans cannot at present reply by similar raids and in continuing to bomb residential areas hope that the suffering which this causes will induce the British

---

[135] This is an early report of the Battle of the Coral Sea described in the MOI releases as the largest naval battle since Jutland; it took place during 4-8 May. In fact it was a naval battle of a new type, where attacks were made with planes from the carriers on each side and none of the great surface ships ever exchanged fire. Axis propaganda reported major US losses which US propaganda duly denied, keeping secret the loss of the USS *Lexington* until the outcome of the Battle of Midway Island, which followed, was clear.

[136] HMS *Edinburgh*.

Government to stop bombing Germany.[137] In the occupied countries it is clear that the German rule is becoming more and more irksome. On May 4th, the Germans themselves announced that they had just shot seventy-two Dutchmen in one batch for pro-Allied activities,[138] and almost every day their newspapers and radio contain similar announcements, that ten, twenty, thirty, Poles, Frenchmen, Belgians, Norwegians or other citizens of the occupied countries have been shot for the same reason. When some piece of sabotage or other pro-Allied activity takes place, the German practice is to shoot at once a number of hostages who are usually described as Jews and Communists, and to threaten that if the culprits are not delivered up, further hostages will be shot on a certain date. To an extraordinary extent this method has been a failure, and the people of the occupied countries have refused to collaborate with the invader, even when not to do so means risking their own lives. [*Censored:* Some very interesting eye-witness evidence has just come to light about the British Commando raid on Saint Nazaire, which took place some weeks ago. It appears now that the local French joined in on the side of the British and that fighting actually continued for three days after the main body of the Commandos had done what it came to do and withdrawn. The Germans took reprisals of the most barbarous kind afterwards and posted notices all along the French coast, saying that hostages would be shot as a matter of routine at any place where British landing-parties appeared.][139]

In the near future what is known as luxury feeding is going to be prohibited in England. Full details of the law have not been fixed, but it is known that the amount of money anyone can spend on a meal at a hotel or restaurant is to be fixed at a small sum. Taken together with clothes rationing, petrol rationing, universal military service, and the changes which are occurring in the British educational system, this

[137] Orwell refers here to the raids on Exeter and elsewhere which the Germans mounted in answer to the British bombing of the historic centre of Lübeck. As is well known, a specific purpose of these British raids was to terrify the population of Germany, and industrial targets were not their object. Had Orwell known of this he would no doubt have spoken differently here and elsewhere when describing the progress of the RAF.

[138] This is a good instance of Orwell's close reading of the monitors' reports. The incident referred to here was broadcast on one channel only, Hilversum, for the Dutch Home Service.

[139] In future raids there were broadcasts by the BBC to the local population warning them to stay out of the fighting which was not part of an invasion attempt. See p.139 with n.229.

new law is one more step along the path by which Britain, as a result of the war, is becoming more truly a democracy.[140]

16 May 1942

India is now within measurable distance of invasion.[141] At the same time the military situation has not changed greatly during the past week, and for once, instead of my usual commentary, [*censored:* in which I try to sum up the current news from the battle events,] I want to try to give you a more general picture of the war as a whole, which may help to bring the events of the immediate future into better proportion.

War is not an event like a football match, which takes place within a measurable time and between two fixed teams. [*Four lines illegible.*] When we look at the history of this war, which has now gone on for two and a half years, we see that something which started as a localised struggle has become definitely worldwide, and that a meaning and purpose which were not apparent at the beginning have gradually become clear. More than that, we see that this war is not an isolated event, but part of a worldwide process which began more than ten years ago. It started, properly speaking, in 1931, when the Japanese invaded Manchuria, and the League of Nations failed to take action. From then onwards, we have seen a long series of aggressions, first of all unresisted, then resisted unsuccessfully, then resisted more successfully, until finally the whole picture becomes clear as the struggle of free peoples who see before them the chance of a fuller and happier existence, against comparatively small cliques who are not interested in the general development of humanity but only in advancing their individual power. One country after another is sucked into the struggle, and they are sucked in not purely for reasons of geography, and not purely from economic motives, but primarily for what are called ideological reasons – that is to say, they are practically compelled to take one side or the other, according as their national philosophy is a democratic one or the contrary. Thus it was inevitable that Soviet Russia, however anxious to remain at peace, should, sooner or later, be drawn into the war on the side of the democracies. It was inevitable that Britain and China should ultimately find themselves

---

[140] A further example of the experience which led to *Nineteen Eighty-Four*.

[141] In this talk Orwell gives his fullest account of the Allies' position and Britain's view of India.

fighting on the same side, whatever causes of difference there may have been between them in the past. It was inevitable that a progressive state like Mexico should line up with the democracies, in spite of the outstanding disputes between Mexico and the United States. Equally, it was inevitable that Japan should join hands with Germany, even though, if they should be victorious, these two will be fighting one another almost immediately.[142] The Fascist states have a common interest in suppressing liberty everywhere, because if it exists anywhere, it will ultimately spread to their own dominions. In this vast struggle, India finds itself inescapably on the democratic side, and this fact is not really altered by the ancient grievances which India may feel against Britain, nor by the very real desire of Germany and Japan to win India to their side. India is compelled to be with Britain, because a victory of the Germans or the Japanese would postpone Indian independence far longer than the most reactionary British Government would either wish or be able to do. And in fact, in spite of Japanese promises and protestations of friendship, the attack on India has already begun. Bombs have dropped on Indian soil, Japanese troops are advancing dangerously close along the eastern shore of the Bay of Bengal.[143] Willy-nilly, India is already in the struggles and the outcome of the war – and therefore India's independence – may be determined to a very great extent by the efforts that Indians themselves now make.

In these circumstances, it is useful to look back and consider what has been achieved during the past ten years by those peoples who knew what they wanted and rated liberty above safety. When the Japanese invaded Manchuria in 1931, China was in a state of chaos, and the young Chinese Republic was in no condition to resist. Six years later, however, when the invasion of China proper began, order had been restored under the leadership of Marshal Chiang Kai-Shek, and a powerful national spirit had grown up. The Japanese, therefore, were surprised to find that what they regarded as a mere military parade – the 'China incident' was their phrase for it – stretched out indefinitely, causing them endless losses in men and materials and never seeming to come within sight of its end, however many victories they might report in the newspapers. [*Censored:* That war has now been going on

---

[142] Another clear link with *Nineteen Eighty-Four*, when the alliances between superpowers change so rapidly that a public meeting called to condemn one changes in mid-course to an attack on the other. The origin of Orwell's remark here and of the idea in his book is, of course, the Russo-German pact.

[143] There were a number of false reports of Japanese landings which were later denied, but it is clear that, as far as Orwell could see, the Japanese invasion of India was already a reality.

for just over five years; all along the Japanese have seemed to have everything in their hands, modern weapons, war materials of every kind, and command of the sea. They have been able to drop bombs by the tens of thousands on Chinese towns where the inhabitants had not even an anti-aircraft gun with which to reply, much less an aeroplane. They have been able to overrun great areas and to seize the important industrial districts of the coastal towns and to kill no one knows how many thousands of Chinese men, women and children and yet somehow, China never seems any nearer to being conquered.] Scores of times the Japanese Government has announced that the 'China incident' is now nearing its end, and yet somehow the 'China incident'[144] never seems to end. What is it that enables the Chinese to fight on, in spite of their enormous physical difficulties? [Censored: The reason is partly in their vast manpower and in the industriousness and ingenuity of the Chinese people.] But the main reason is simply that they are fighting for their liberty, and the will to surrender does not exist in them. To such a people, defeats in the field are of little importance. [Censored: There are always more of them, and they are always willing to fight.] The campaign in Burma probably had as one of its main objectives the invasion of China from the west, the idea being that if the Chinese were hemmed in on all sides and finally cut off from the outer world, they would be too deeply disheartened to continue fighting. Without doubt, in these circumstances the Chinese would be defeated according to the military text-books. But so they have been many times before, yet their resistance has never slackened. We cannot doubt that it will be so again, and will continue to be so – so long as the Chinese people put the goal of liberty before their eyes.

This is not the only heroic fight against Fascist aggression which has happened during the last ten years. The Spanish people fought for two and a half years against their own quislings and against the German and Italian invaders, actually fought against odds which, relatively speaking, were greater than those facing China. Their resistance was the resistance of almost unarmed peasants and working men against hoards of trained soldiers with the resources of the German war machine behind them. [Censored: At the beginning of the Spanish Civil War, the Republic had practically no army at all, for it was precisely the regular army, under Fascist officers, which had staged the revolt and this army was even reinforced by great numbers of Italian mercenaries sent by Mussolini, and by German tanks and bombing planes. The ordinary working men of the factories, led by

[144] Japan and China had not formally declared war, and the conflict was always referred to in their communiqués as 'The China Incident'.

their trade union officials, began to organise themselves into companies and battalions to make such weapons as they could manage with the rather backward industrial equipment of Spain, and to learn the art of war virtually by practice. Men, who in private life were factory workers, or lawyers or orange growers, found themselves within a few weeks officers, commanding large bodies of men and in many cases commanded them with great competence. Apart from the inequalities of equipment, the Spanish people had great hardships to face. The food situation was none too good even from the first, and the Nazi airmen serving with General Franco carried out wherever they went the most atrocious raids on open towns, deliberately aiming their bombs on residential working-class districts, with the idea of terrorising the people into surrender. Yet in the face of all these difficulties, they fought for two and a half years, and though at the end, Franco managed to win a kind of victory, his position is now so insecure that it is thought that about a million people – that is about four per cent of the population, are in concentration camps.][145]

Britain has now been fighting for two and a half years, and she started almost unarmed against an enemy who had been preparing for six years for just this occasion. In the middle of 1940 France went out of the war, and for exactly a year Britain had to fight alone, with no very sure prospect of help, either from Russia or from America. During that time, the people of London and other towns had to endure the heaviest air raids that the world has yet known. [*Censored:* For about six months, London barely knew a night without a raid and in all, quite 50,000 non-combatants, many of them women and children, were killed.] Yet [during that time] the idea of surrender didn't occur to the British people, and the efforts of the German radio to persuade them that they were beaten and had better stop fighting simply made them laugh. Soviet Russia again has been fighting for nearly a year against the same enemy, and has had to endure great losses of territory, cruel bombing of open towns, and an appalling series of outrages by occupying troops against helpless peasants. Yet not only is the Russian army further than ever from being beaten, but behind the lines, the Russian people are resisting more and more stubbornly, so that the Germans get no benefit from the territories they have occupied. The thing which animates the Russians is the same that

[145] Spain was neutral throughout the war, and her staying that way was of great importance to the Allies. Orwell refers here to the Nazi airmen who served with Franco, without mentioning the equal numbers of Russian or Russian-trained airmen on the other side, hoping no doubt by this omission to get the piece past the censor. The censor, clearly, did not wish any reference to Spain, especially in controversial terms.

animates the Chinese and that animated the people of London under the bombs: the feeling that they are free and that if only they can hold on to their freedom and drive out this foreign invader who is trying to take it away from them, a fuller and happier life lies ahead.

I have said all this because it is quite likely that India has great and unprecedented hardship ahead of her. India has not seen warfare on her own soil for eighty-five years. She may see it, and it may be the cruel modern kind of war which makes no distinction between combatants and non-combatants. There may be hunger and other hardships ahead as well, but India's fate depends ultimately upon the attitude of Indians themselves. India is not only a great country; it is a very big country – as big for instance as Europe without Russia. It cannot be physically overrun, and the Japanese, even if they have the opportunity, will not attempt to occupy the whole of the country. Their efforts will be to paralyse Indian resistance, by terrorism, by lies and by sowing dissention among the Indians themselves.[146] They know that if India has the will to resist, India cannot be conquered, whereas if that will fails, the conquest might be comparatively easy. They will approach you therefore by telling you that they have no designs against your liberty or your territory, and simultaneously they will tell you that they are so strong that it is hopeless to resist. They will also libel those among you who are organising national resistance in the hopes of setting one faction against another. Those are the tactics of the Fascists everywhere. The thing that will defeat them is the same thing that has defeated the Japanese assault on China and the German assault on Russia – the resolution and obstinacy of the common people. The German invasion of Russia has been defeated less by weapons than by an act of will, depending on the knowledge of the Russian people that they are fighting for their liberty. If we choose, we can see today that this history is repeated in the Japanese invasion of India.

23 May 1942

The principal events this week have happened on the Russian front. We recorded last week that fighting had broken out again in the Crimean

---

[146] It is remarkable that even here Orwell makes no mention of Subhas Chandra Bose and the Axis Indian radio station. For Bose's model plans for creating civil unrest, see below, Appendix, no.13.

Peninsula.[147] Since then, the Germans have overrun most of the Kerch Peninsula, which is separated from the Caucasus only by a very narrow neck of the Sea of Azov. It is known, however, that fighting is still going on on the westward side of the Strait,[148] and the German claims to have destroyed the Russian army in that sector and to have taken an enormous number of prisoners are just as untrue as their similar reports have been in the past.[149] Meanwhile, further north the Russians have launched an offensive of their own upon a much larger scale. This is directed against the great industrial city of Kharkov, which the Germans took last autumn. As I speak, the decision is still uncertain. The Russians have advanced on a wide front, destroying great numbers of German tanks, and the communications by which the German forces in Kharkov are supplied are in great danger. The Germans, however, have launched a counter-attack in the south, which may prevent Kharkov from being encircled.

It would be unwise to expect too much from the Russian offensive, which may have been undertaken merely in order to anticipate the Germans and upset their timetable. Meanwhile, the Russians have begun another attack in the far north, against the German armies in Finland, and have already made a considerable advance.

The outlines of the spring campaign on the Eastern front are still not clear. Some observers think that the Germans, instead of making another large-scale frontal attack against the Russian armies, will strike their main blow against Turkey. If Turkey were overrun they could then make for the oil wells of Iraq and Iran, and at the same time attack Baku by the easier route from the south. It is at any rate certain that for months past the Germans have been doing all in their power to sow distrust between Turkey and Britain, and more especially between Turkey and Soviet Russia, which may be intended to prevent the Turkish Government from taking concerted defence measures beforehand in consultation with the Allies. However, there is no sign that the Turks have been deceived by the German manoeuvres. Turkey is not very well supplied with modern weapons, but imports from Britain and the USA have to some extent made this good during recent months. The people are resolute and brave

[147] Presumably in one of the brief news summaries put out during the week; there is no reference in Orwell's previous talk.

[148] The news on radio Moscow mentioned fighting on the eastward side of the Strait.

[149] The information coming from Russia was more than usually vague and misleading at this time. With little to go on, Orwell and the other BBC reporters dared not believe what was being said on the Axis radio about Hitler's spring offensive. For the difficulties of Allied reporters on the Russian fronts who never once in the war saw a shot fired in anger, see Paul Winterton, *Report on Russia* (1945), p.30f.

fighters,[150] and it is certain that should the Germans make their offensive in this direction they will have to fight hard every inch of the way.

Simultaneously with their attempts to sow distrust between Turkey and Russia, the Germans appear to be making another effort to egg on the Japanese to attack the Russians in Manchuria. They are broadcasting threatening statements about Russia, alleged to have been made by leading Japanese statesmen. These may or may not be authentic.[151] We have frequently pointed out in these newsletters that the likelihood exists of the Japanese attacking Russia sooner or later, and if they do so, we may be sure that they will do it with the maximum of treachery at a moment when they believe the Russians to be in serious difficulties. The Germans will try to provoke the clash between Russia and Japan as early as possible in hopes that this may prevent further men and materials being brought from Siberia to the Western Front.

In Burma, the greater part of the British forces have reached the Indian frontier in safety.[152] On the eastern sector of this front the Japanese attacks against Yunnan continue. The Japanese are still in possession of Tengueh, but to the south of this the Chinese have recaptured Kanlanchai. It is possible that the Japanese now intend an all-out attack against China, one column moving eastward from Burma, another northwards from Siam and another westwards, probably from Fuchow, where they have recently made a fresh landing. China's position at this moment is certainly difficult, and she needs all the help that can possibly be given to her, especially in aeroplanes. It is therefore good news that a large unit of the Royal Air Force has just reached central China.[153] We need not imagine, however, that Chinese resistance is at all likely to be crushed. Marshal Chiang Kai-Shek has repeatedly declared that he will go on fighting just as long as is necessary to drive out the invader, and that if need be, he would be ready to withdraw for years into Central Asia and reorganise his armies there. The Japanese are aware that so long as

[150] This favourable opinion of the Turks contrasts with the view to be seen in the writings of T.E. Lawrence and others about the First World War. Perhaps Orwell was harking back to earlier times and battles such as the Siege of Kars.

[151] Probably an Orwell fiction of the kind he refers to in his wartime diary (see *OWB*, p.26). No such broadcasts have been found in the monitors' reports that Orwell used.

[152] Thereby retaining the initiative. See below, p. 190.

[153] I have not been able to identify the unit that Orwell refers to. A number of American pilots with the American Volunteer Group were fighting in China at this time, but in a broadcast on 19 May the Chungking Government urgently appealed for more. Orwell may have been indicating Allied intentions, as counter-propaganda.

Chinese resistance continues, their gains elsewhere are very precarious. They may have decided that this is the moment to finish with China once and for all, or they may have the intention of capturing all the airfields which are within striking range of Japan itself. Whether they can carry out a full-scale attack against China while also proceeding with their campaigns against Australia and India, and possibly a little while hence with Russia, at the same time, is uncertain.

Bombs have already been dropped on Assam,[154] and the Japanese forces on the eastern coast of the Bay of Bengal are not very far from Chittagong, but this is not the route that they are likely to take in their main attack upon India. The Battle in the Coral Sea, in which the Japanese lost heavily, has no doubt set back their plans for attacking Australia, but those plans still exist, and there are signs of fresh activity in the Japanese-controlled islands surrounding New Guinea. Australia is now far more strongly defended than was the case three months ago, and each day that the Japanese attack is delayed gives more time for American reinforcements to arrive.

The disarmament of the French warships lying at Martinique, off the coast of the United States, is proceeding. Before long the United States Government will probably have to take similar action against the island of Guadeloupe, also under Vichy control, which has almost certainly been used as a port of call by Axis submarines, and whose wireless station is used for pro-Axis propaganda in South America.[155] The accession to power of Laval, who has hardly pretended to be more than a puppet of the Germans, has opened the eyes of the Americans to the danger presented by Vichy France, and we may expect them to take a firmer attitude from now on.[156] Laval's dealings with the Germans have also certainly caused trouble between Germany and the other Axis partner, Italy. The Italians came into the war in the summer of 1940, when they imagined that the fighting was almost over and that they would be able to grab large quantities of loot without having to shed any Italian blood.

Instead of this, they have lost most of their empire and have not received any of the bribes they were promised. In his efforts to get hold of the French fleet, Hitler has evidently made certain concessions to Laval, one of which is the dropping of Italian claims to the island of Corsica and other portions of French territory. It is clear that this

[154] In a raid reported on 8 May.

[155] Presumably Orwell obtained this information from an American source; there are no broadcasts corresponding to this description in the monitors' reports at the BBC.

[156] See above, p. 79, n.118.

causes great resentment among the Italian Fascists, but they are at present quite powerless against their German masters.

The Royal Air Force continue their heavy raids on Germany. On Wednesday they made one of the biggest raids of the war on Mannheim, the centre of the German chemical industry. Two days earlier, they had performed a brilliant feat in torpedoing the German cruiser the *Prinz Eugen*, which had been in a Norwegian port after being damaged by a British submarine and was making its way back to Germany for repairs. The *Prinz Eugen* was not sunk, but it is likely to be out of action for the rest of the summer.[157]

Another large draft of American troops, complete with tanks and all other weapons of war, have reached British soil. They crossed the Atlantic without being attacked by the Germans in any way. Public opinion in Britain is more and more anxious for the opening of a second front in Europe, so as to take the pressure off our Russian allies and to make the Germans fight simultaneously on two fronts. We prefer not to express an opinion as to whether this will be done in the near future. In all probability it is mainly a question of shipping, because not only the transporting but still more the supplying of an overseas force uses up an enormous number of ships. The Government has made no definite pronouncement upon the subject, quite naturally, for if they intend to launch an offensive, they cannot be expected to reveal their plans beforehand. In his recent speech,[158] however, Mr Churchill made the point that after two and a half years of war, so far from being war-weary, the British people are actually demanding offensive action and chiding the government for being too slow. This, as Mr Churchill pointed out, is certainly a remarkable advance, when we remember that two years ago Britain stood alone, and was only doubtfully able to defend herself, let alone to contemplate launching attacks on a foreign shore.

6 June 1942

The fighting on the Kharkov front has almost come to a standstill. This does not mean that the German offensive has been abandoned, but it does almost certainly mean that the attack staged by Marshal

---

[157] The *Prinz Eugen* had been attacked on her way to Kiel from Trondheim on 17 May. She reached Kiel on 22 May.

[158] Churchill's broadcast on 10 May, the second anniversary of his becoming Prime Minister.

Timoshenko has disrupted the German timetable and put back their plans by several weeks. Many observers now think that the main German attack will begin about the same time as it began last year, that is to say about the middle of June. The Russian summer lasts only four or five months, so that every day by which the Russians can hold up the German timetable is a great gain. The main German effort must be in the direction of the Caucasus and the Middle East, but the day before yesterday Hitler made a visit to Finland, which may possibly mean that there will also be important developments on the northern front.[159]

The heavy fighting in Libya, which had just started at the time of our last newsletter, is still going on and the issue is still uncertain. The battle has had two phases, the first of which ended favourably for the British. The German armoured forces, moving eastward, circled right round the British minefields with the evident object of destroying the British forces in that area and of attacking the seaport of Tobruk, which has been in British hands for eighteen months and lies on the flank of any possible German advance into Egypt. The brunt of the first German attack had to be taken by Indian motorised troops, who behaved with great gallantry.[160] The Germans failed in both of their objects and were driven back, losing about 250 tanks, but instead of retreating the way they had come, they managed to break their way westward through the British minefields, creating a wide gap through which they could bring up further reinforcements. They are now renewing the attack. The British are using a new type of tank which had previously been kept secret,[161] and also two types of planes which had not beforehand been used on the Libyan front and whose presence came as a surprise to the Germans. General Kruewell, second in command of the German forces in Libya, has been taken prisoner.[162] The battle will no doubt have been decided one way or another within a few days. It may end with a tactical victory for the Germans, but

[159] Hitler visited Marshall Mannerheim, Commander-in-Chief of the Finnish armed forces, on 4 June. Axis broadcasters described the visit as a good-will gesture on the occasion of the Marshall's seventy-fifth birthday.

[160] The first attack was in fact by the Italian Ariete Division which came across the Third Indian Motor Brigade by chance and wiped it out. Axis radio in Germany had accused the British of deliberately placing the Indian troops in the front line to absorb the first shock of the attack, while the Indian Axis stations warned Indians that they were being used as cannon fodder. Orwell's only possible reply to these and similar taunts was to point to the gallantry of the men fighting, and for the rest to rely on broadcasts home by Indian soldiers on other programmes.

[161] The M3 medium tank, the General Grant.

[162] On 1 June; his reconnaissance plane had been forced down.

after the failure of their first surprise attack, it is very unlikely that they will succeed in reaching Egyptian soil.

On two days of this week, two air raids, far greater in scale than anything yet seen in the history of the world, have been made on Germany. On the night of the 30th May over a thousand planes raided Cologne,[163] and on the night of the 1st June, over a thousand planes raided Essen, in the Ruhr district. These have since been followed up by two further raids, also on a big scale, though not quite so big as the first two. To realise the significance of these figures, one has got to remember the scale of the air raids made hitherto. During the autumn and winter of 1940, Britain suffered a long series of raids which at that time were quite unprecedented. Tremendous havoc was worked on London, Coventry, Bristol and various other English cities. Nevertheless, there is no reason to think that in even the biggest of these raids more than 500 planes took part. In addition, the big bombers now being used by the RAF carry a far heavier load of bombs than anything that could be managed two years ago. In sum, the amount of bombs dropped on either Cologne or Essen would be quite three times as much as the Germans ever dropped in any one of their heaviest raids on Britain. [*Censored:* We in this country know what destruction those raids accomplished and have therefore some picture of what has happened in Germany.] Two days after the Cologne raid, the British reconnaissance planes were sent over as usual to take photographs of the damage which the bombers had done, but even after that period, were unable to get any photographs because of the pall of smoke which still hung over the city. It should be noticed that these 1000-plane raids were carried out solely by the RAF with planes manufactured in Britain. Later in the year, when the American airforce begins to take a hand, it is believed that it will be possible to carry out raids with as many as 2,000 planes at a time. One German city after another will be attacked in this manner. These attacks, however, are not wanton and are not delivered against the civilian population, although non-combatants are inevitably killed in them.

[163] The city was described in the MOI press releases as being 'just one stretch of fire' far bigger than at Lübeck. Air Marshal ('Bomber') Harris had said before the raid: 'You have an opportunity to strike a blow at the enemy which will resound not only throughout Germany but throughout the world.' Whatever their military effect, very large numbers of civilians were burnt alive in these 'fire-storm' raids, culminating in the raid on Dresden. At this time the war reached new heights of inhumanity: two days after the bombing of Lübeck the first train full of Jews from Paris arrived at Auschwitz. The gassing of Jews began in May and from then on the deranged German leaders pursued their aim of the extermination of the Jewish race in Europe. See also below, p. 214 with n.381.

Cologne was attacked because it is a great railway junction in which the main German railroads cross each other and also an important manufacturing centre. Essen was attacked because it is the centre of the German armaments industry and contains the huge factories of Krupp, supposed to be the largest armaments works in the world. In 1940, when the Germans were bombing Britain, they did not expect retaliation on a very heavy scale, and therefore were not afraid to boast in their propaganda about the slaughter of civilians which they were bringing about and the terror which their raids aroused. Now, when the tables are turned, they are beginning to cry out against the whole business of aerial bombing, which they declare to be both cruel and useless. The people of this country are not revengeful, but they remember what happened to themselves two years ago, and they remember how the Germans talked when they thought themselves safe from retaliation. That they did think themselves safe there can be little doubt. Here, for example, are some extracts from the speeches of Marshal Goering, the Chief of the German Air Force. 'I have personally looked into the air-raid defences of the Ruhr. No bombing planes could get there. Not as much as a single bomb could be dropped from an enemy plane', August 9th, 1939. 'No hostile aircraft can penetrate the defences of the German air force', September 7th, 1939. Many similar statements by the German leaders could be quoted.

These prophecies have been terribly falsified and that fact is no doubt making its impression upon the Germans themselves as well as upon public opinion throughout the world.

During this week there has not been any very great development in the war in the Eastern Hemisphere. The Japanese are now making their main effort against China, and may put off the attempt to invade India for the time being, though they must make it sooner or later. We pointed out last week that the battle of the Coral Sea had not ended, though it had checked, the Japanese advance against Australia, and this has been borne out this week by an attack on Sydney Harbour made by Japanese submarines.[164] The submarines did no damage worth considering, and it is believed that three of them were sunk. But the fact that they could get there is significant, for Sydney is a very long way to the south of any island in Japanese possession and the submarines must in fact have been launched from surface ships. This suggests the possibility that a Japanese naval force is somewhere off the

[164] Orwell is clearly vague about this raid, which took place on 31 May. The submarines were in fact miniature submarines with two-man crews, and their appearance caused considerable confusion at the time. There was no official report as there had been over the bombing of Darwin. A Japanese broadcast revealed some of the background of the raid (see below, Appendix, no.15).

eastern coast of Australia, and apart from attacks on American convoys, an attempt against the mainland of Australia is always possible. In addition, Japanese aeroplanes have made several small raids on the Aleutian Islands,[165] the chain of islands which run westward from Alaska and almost connect America with Asia. It is too early to determine the object of these raids, which might either be the prelude to a naval attack or be a feint to cover operations elsewhere, but they certainly have some strategic purpose. An attack on Midway Island, in which a Japanese battleship and a plane-carrier were damaged, has just been reported.[166] It is too early to be sure about the meaning of this action, but it may be the prelude to another Japanese attack on Hawaii.

The underground struggle in the occupied countries continues. Two days ago there came the news that the editor of the best-known quisling paper in occupied France – this paper is the organ of Doriot, the French fascist leader who is one of the most ardent 'collaborators' – has been assassinated.[167] Just over a week ago there occurred a much more important event of the same kind, when an attempt was made on the life of Heydrich, the chief of the Gestapo in Czechoslovakia. Heydrich was hit by three bullets, and died two days ago, in spite of the efforts of Hitler's own physicians to save him.[168] The Germans are following their usual practice of shooting hostages with the threat that more will be shot unless the real assassins are handed over. According to the special bulletins of their own radio they have already shot over two hundred people for the assassination of Heydrich. This process of intimidation is going on all the time all over Europe. To give just one example, three days ago an official bulletin on the German wireless announced that a French girl, aged only ten, had been sentenced to twenty-five months' hard labour for assisting

---

[165] At 6 a.m. on 3 June four bombers and fifteen fighters were reported as having bombed the American naval base there.

[166] On 4 June. In official communiqués at the time this theatre of conflict was referred to as 'Oceania', the name Orwell adopted in *Nineteen Eighty-Four* for the super power formed by the amalgamation of the United States and the British Empire.

[167] At 7.30 p.m. on 2 June M. Albert Clement, editor of the 'Cri Du Peuple', was shot down in the street while taking an evening stroll with his wife.

[168] Heydrich was in fact killed by fragments from an exploding grenade thrown by a Czech soldier, one of a group trained in Britain and flown in for the specific purpose of killing Heydrich. It has been suggested that the bombs contained a lethal germ filling (see Jeremy Paxman and Robert Harris, *A Higher Form of Killing: the secret story of gas and germ warfare* (1982)).

escaped prisoners of war.[169] But the very fact that these brutal sentences and shooting of hostages go on and on as they have done now for two years, and seem if anything rather to increase in number, show how ineffective these methods are to crush the spirit of the common people of Europe.

[*Censored:* The annual conference of the British Labour Party has been held during the past week.[170] The Labour Party, as far as present political power goes is the second party in Britain, but numerically it is by far the largest, being as it is the organ of the Trade Unions and the working class generally. Some of the resolutions voiced at the conference are therefore of interest for the light they throw on British public opinion. The conference registered its complete confidence in the present Prime Minister, and decided, though only by a very small majority, to continue with the inter-party truce. This is an agreement by which the main political parties have agreed for the duration of the war not to vote or campaign against one another at by-elections. The conference urged that another effort should be made to resolve the Indian political problem and again by a small majority it voted for the raising of the ban on the *Daily Worker*. The *Daily Worker*, which was the Communist daily paper, was suppressed two years ago for what were undoubtedly defeatist activities. Since then the USSR has entered the war and the attitude of the British Communist Party has naturally become very different. This, however, is not the issue at stake, as was pointed out by one delegate after another at the Labour Party Conference. The real issue was freedom of the press. There is a profound respect for freedom of the press in this country and even people who detest the politics of the *Daily Worker* were uneasy at seeing the paper suppressed. While passing the resolution that the ban on the *Daily Worker* should be raised, the Conference also rejected by an overwhelming vote the proposal to cooperate politically with the Communist Party. The fact that this major political party should be as anxious for the freedom of expression of another party whose policy it is utterly opposed to, is a sign of the strength of British democracy, even after three and a half years of war. Besides rationing domestic fuel, the Government has just announced that it is going to take full control of

---

[169] This particular report has not been found in the monitors' reports, but Orwell may well have been using it as a counter to extensive reports of children helping to raise funds for those fighting on the Russian front and others, such as: 'Mme. Pétain visited this morning "L'enfance et la jeunesse" centres, a crèche and a youth centre' (Radio Paris, 5 June).

[170] The conference lasted from 25 to 28 May, under the chairmanship of Walter Green MP.

the British coalmines for the duration of the war.[171] We hope to comment more fully upon this next week.]

13 June 1942

By far the most important event during this week is the Anglo-Russian Treaty, the terms of which were published last night.

It would be almost impossible to overestimate the significance of this event, which may well have a beneficial effect on world history for decades to come. Before the declaration of the new treaty Britain and Russia were of course in alliance, but it was the rather loose and unsatisfactory alliance of people who are forced to fight on the same side because they are attacked by the same enemy, but who are liable to develop new disagreements as soon as the danger is over. The relationship between Soviet Russia and the United States was even more indefinite. Now, however, there is a close formal agreement between Britain and Russia for clearly stated ends, and the United States, though not as yet a signatory of the agreement, is in complete sympathy.

In this short news review we cannot give the terms of the Treaty in complete detail, but we can summarise them sufficiently. In the first place, the British and Russian Governments undertake not only to give each other all military assistance against Germany and the other European Fascist states, but undertake not to make any separate peace either with Hitlerite Germany or with any German Government which still retains aggressive intentions.

This qualification is extremely important. There is no doubt that the Germans have long hoped to buy either Russia or Britain out of the war, so as to follow their usual practice of dealing with their enemies one at a time. And one way they might possibly have done this was by a pretended change of policy, which would make it appear that the clique responsible for German aggressions had now been got rid of, and Germany had no further warlike aims. It has always been a possibility that there might be some kind of coup d'état, either by the German Army Commanders, or the so-called moderates of the Nazi Party, who would get rid of Hitler and then declare that the cause of the trouble had been removed, and there was no sense in continuing

[171] The Government's White Paper on Coal was published on 3 June. It outlined state control of the industry, the setting up of the National Coal Board and other measures constituting in real terms the nationalisation of the industry.

the war. This pretence would have been aimed at either Russia, Britain or the United States, whichever power seemed most war-weary at a given moment. The new Anglo-Russian Treaty practically removes this possibility. It means that the war is being fought not merely for the destruction of Hitler and the figure-heads of the Nazi Party, but of all those forces in Germany who are interested in aggressive foreign wars. Reduced to simple words, this part of the Anglo-Russian Treaty means that Russia and Britain will not stop fighting while Germany has an army. Secondly, Russia and Britain pledge themselves to post-war collaboration. In the first place, each promises to go to the help of the other, should either be attacked after the present war is over. Even more important than this, the two countries pledge themselves to collaborate in reestablishing the prosperity of Europe. They agree to give one another economic assistance after the war and to pool their efforts in order to restore peace, order, and a decent standard of living to the war-scarred countries of Europe. They agree also to do this without attempting any territorial acquisitions for themselves, and without attempting any interference in the internal affairs of other states. This implies, incidentally, that Russia and Britain will not interfere in the internal affairs of one another, which means that the two regimes are now in far greater political and economic agreement than would have been possible or even thinkable five years ago. It means, in fact, that the ancient ghost of Bolshevism and 'bloody revolution' has been laid for ever. The treaty will be ratified at once, and it is to operate for a period of twenty years, before coming up for renewal.

Two very significant remarks were made by Mr Eden, the British Foreign Secretary, when he announced the terms of the Treaty in the House of Commons. In the first place, he announced that it has no secret clauses.[172] In the second place, he announced that Russia, Britain and the United States had reached full agreement about the momentous task of the opening of a second front in Europe during 1942. Just what they have agreed is, needless to say, a secret.

After visiting London first, Mr Molotov also visited Washington. The terms of the treaty between Russia and the United States will no

[172] Eden gave his assurances in answer to a question from Anthony Greenwood. A Swedish newspaper in London had got wind of the existence of such clauses, and the Axis radio immediately developed the story to include an agreement between Russia and Britain to divide Europe between them after the war, to 'Bolshevise' the whole of Europe and so on. Fears of Russian intentions were widespread despite her wartime popularity; Orwell himself shared them. But the MOI had issued specific instructions on how to quell 'the menace of Bolshevism' stories (see above, p.20f.) and Orwell obeys those injunctions to the letter. We can only guess what his feelings were at having to write such things.

doubt be published shortly. The treaty was actually signed in London on May 26th. Mr Molotov's arrival and departure were very well guarded secrets; although known to a certain number of people in London, they got no further. In particular the Germans were completely in the dark about the whole visit. Although their wireless now claims to have known all about the impending treaty,[173] it in fact made absolutely no reference to it or to Molotov's visit until the news was made public in Britain.

As we have had to devote some minutes to the Anglo-Russian Treaty, we must comment on the rest of the news more briefly than usual this week. The situation in Libya is less favourable than it was a week ago. After holding out for sixteen days, the Free French and Indian garrison at Bir Hakeim has had to be evacuated,[174] which has allowed the Germans to clear their right flank and thus attack our main positions in greater force. The battle will probably continue with intensity for some time. The Germans may make further advances, and it is possible that they are planning to synchronise their tank attack with an attack by air-borne troops from Crete. But on the whole, the chances are against their capturing the stronghold of Tobruk, and still more heavily against their succeeding in breaking into Egypt.

A great naval battle has taken place in the Pacific, the full outcome of which is not yet clear.[175] A week ago we reported that the Japanese fleet had made an unsuccessful attack on Midway Island, and since then fuller figures of their losses have come in. It is now known that they lost four plane-carriers and a number of their ships. Full figures for the Battle of the Coral Sea have now been released and it appears from these that in the two battles the Japanese lost 37 ships of various classes, sunk or damaged, including a battleship and five cruisers sunk, damage to a number of other ships, including three battleships. Almost simultaneously with this the Japanese made some kind of attack upon the Aleutian Islands, the chain of islands which almost connect America with Asia in the far north. It is not certain yet what has happened, but it does not appear from American reports that the

[173] This claim is only made in one broadcast, and then by implication: a spoof interview with Molotov the day before on the 'Workers Challenge' station which, it was claimed, could not have been released earlier for security reasons.

[174] General Ritchie ordered the garrison to withdraw on 10 June.

[175] The battle of 4 June was indeed a decisive battle in the Pacific, with all four of Admiral Nagumo's aircraft carriers being lost. Orwell's reference to the figures for the Coral Sea battle in the next sentence refer to those released by the US Navy Department on 12 June. They had been held back until the Midway Island battle had been concluded; Orwell mentions this specifically because the usual Axis reason for withholding figures was to conceal a defeat.

Japanese have landed on any island which is inhabited.[176] They may be planning an attack with the object of attacking on the main American base, Dutch Harbour, or they may merely be making a demonstration in the Aleutian Islands in order to cover up their defeat on Midway Island. We shall be able to report on this more fully next week.

Heavy fighting is going on in Eastern China, in the neighbourhood of Nanchang. The Japanese also claim to have made inroads into Inner Mongolia, through which one of the routes between China and Soviet Russia runs. Although they now say that they are about to bring the so-called China incident to an end once and for all, they no doubt remember that they have been saying this for five years, and the China incident is still continuing. Probably, therefore, what the Japanese are aiming at at the moment is not so much the final conquest of China, as to capture the airfields not far from the Eastern coast, from which Japan itself might be bombed. Meanwhile, the Chinese Government has announced that fresh British and American air force units have arrived in China.

Mr Oliver Lyttelton, British Minister of Production, has just announced the truly staggering figures of Britain's current war production.[177] He announces among other things, that Britain is now producing vehicles for war purposes – this of course includes tanks – at the rate of 250,000 a year; big guns at 40,000 a year, and ammunition for those guns at the rate of 25 million rounds. He announces also that Britain's aircraft production has made a hundred per cent increase, that is to say, the rate has doubled since the last quarter of 1940, while the production of merchant shipping has increased by 57 per cent. Some of the effects of this large-scale war production can be seen in the continued air raids on Germany, which at the moment are not quite as terrible as the thousand-plane raids we reported last week, but are still very big raids by any normal standard.

We will end our review with a comparatively small item of news, which is nevertheless worth reporting, because it shows more clearly than whole books could do, what Fascism means. Following on the assassination of Heydrich, the Gestapo chief in Czechoslovakia, the Germans, up till three days ago, had already shot over two hundred

[176] This landing was at Attu, described as 'a desolate spot of little value'. The attack was originally intended as a diversion for the attacking force at Midway.

[177] Lyttelton was in America from 3 to 21 June. The facts and figures here given were in a broadcast he made from New York on 10 June. The purpose of the trip was the greater co-ordination of war production between the UK, the USA and Canada; hence, no doubt, Orwell's not mentioning the circumstances of Lyttelton's announcement.

hostages. These figures are from their own official wireless statements. Then, two days ago, they followed up these announcements of shooting by announcing over the air the action they had taken against a Czech village whose inhabitants were accused of having assisted Heydrich's assassins.

'Since the inhabitants of this village,' states the German wireless, 'have frequently violated the laws which have been issued, by their activity and by the support given to the murderers of Heydrich, the male adults have been shot, the women have been sent to a concentration camp, and the children have been handed over to appropriate educational authorities. The buildings of the locality have been levelled to the ground, and the name of the community has been obliterated.'

Notice that these are the words of the Germans themselves, broadcast to the whole world in at least two languages. The Czech village, named Lidice, was a village of about 1200 inhabitants.[178] We may assume, therefore, that the Germans have killed about 300 men, sent about 300 women to the concentration camp, and about 600 children to what they call 'appropriate educational authorities', which in practice means to labour camps, and all this upon the mere suspicion of having helped the assassins of a man who is himself known all over Europe as a bloodstained murderer. But more significant than the act, is the impudence with which it is broadcast to the world, almost as though it was something to be proud of. And most significant of all is the fact that more than three years after their seizure of Czechoslovakia, the Germans are compelled to commit these barbarities in order to hold down a people whom they pretend to be benefiting by their wise and disinterested rule.

11 July 1942

During this week the two great German offensives in Russia and Africa have continued. As you know, the long-term strategical aim of

[178] Orwell's initial description of this as 'a small item of news' adds to the horrific effect of the facts. Orwell had often commented favourably on the policy of scorched earth but, in common with most people who used the phrase glibly, he was deeply shocked when the policy was enacted before his eyes. The obliteration of a village, a commonplace event on the Eastern front in actions by both sides, seemed to add a new dimension to the war when carried out in 'civilised' Europe. Numerous books were written and published about the atrocity at the time, and new towns and villages elsewhere were named after it. For the full text of the German announcement, see below, Appendix, no.7. In line 2 Orwell has misread 'flagrantly' as 'frequently'.

the Germans is to drive through, by a vast pincer movement, to the oil of Iraq and the Caucasus, and from there to join forces with the Japanese. The essential thing for us is that this drive should be held, and if we do that we need not grudge temporary losses of territory, and may look with confidence to the future.

For the last four days, there has been a lull in the fighting in Egypt. It is now over. The battle has flared up again at the northern end of our defence line, about seventy miles west of Alexandria. The new flare-up follows an intensified day and night offensive by the Royal Air Force. Only two nights ago, our heavy bombers started an assault on great masses of Axis transport on the road to the front. The attacks went on all day, and British frontline soldiers said that the ground in front of them was sometimes obscured by bomb explosions.

After the first rush of the German tank columns had been halted, there was ground for hope that we might launch a powerful counter-offensive immediately. The German forces were extremely exhausted and their lengthened supply lines were not working smoothly. However, our own losses had also been great, and the four days had to elapse; it may be that the Germans have had time for recuperation and reinforcement. Meanwhile, though we have great stores of arms in Egypt and the Middle East, the reinforcements of those stores is necessarily a slow process. In that sense the German supply lines there in Egypt are shorter than ours.

One very encouraging feature of the war in Egypt has been the firm behaviour of the Egyptian people and their leaders. There has been no panic; the country is united under its natural leader[179] and the people are said to be treating the German propaganda, especially the leaflets which are scattered from aeroplanes, with contempt, and meanwhile strong measures have been taken against war profiteers. The struggle for Egypt will be carried on with determination by the Egyptian people as well as by the Allied armies.[180]

In Russia the Germans have launched two new offensives, well to the north of the tremendous battle still raging along the middle reaches of the Don. One is about 140 miles south-east of Kharkov, where the Germans have advanced 60 miles to the east since they captured Izyum last month. The other is 45 miles south of Rossosh, on the main Moscow-Caucasus railway, from which the Russians

[179] This would appear to be a favourable reference by Orwell to the institution of monarchy, in the person of King Farouk.

[180] On 24 June the Egyptian Premier Nahas Pasha had issued a statement denying rumours that Egyptians were being mobilised or that Egypt was being forced to declare war on the Axis powers; the Axis propagandists had made much of this and Orwell is here making a fresh statement of the position.

have already had to withdraw. Meanwhile, the heavy German offensive against Voronezh, over a 100 miles to the north, is still going on.[181] Moscow radio says the fighting there is becoming even more intense, and that on Friday morning an important position held by the Germans was recaptured. London papers emphasise the threat of this heavy German offensive and the need to send further supplies to Russia; the British as a whole feel the greatest admiration for the courageous resistance of the Russians. The most serious strategical effect of the drive is the Russian loss of their main railway from the Caucasus to Moscow.

The attack on the Don can no longer be viewed in isolation from the rest of the Soviet front. The immediate objective is undoubtedly the cutting-off of the Southern Army. Already the situation in which Timoshenko finds himself in relation to the rest of the front is serious. The Germans are trying to rupture his direct communication with the north, and they seem determined to leave him no alternative route.

The Soviet announcement of the evacuation of Rossosh is significant. This town lies one hundred miles to the south of Voronezh. A week ago the German forces were still at Volchansk, a hundred miles to the west. The rapidity of the Nazi advance indicates a general Soviet withdrawal along this stretch of the Don. The strategic sacrifice of this territory is serious because from Rossosh ran a lateral railway line to the east and connected with the Moscow railway.[182]

This was one of the many strategic lines built in recent years and is not marked on most maps. But now it, too, has passed under German control. The fact that the mass of the German armies is still on the western bank of the Don is not an insuperable difficulty for von Bock; the river in these regions is not very wide and at this time of the year is shallow and easily crossed.

The real problem for the Soviet Supreme Command is to anticipate the direction of the German attack. The general opinion, of course, is the Caucasus, oil and the Middle East. But there are equally strong indications that what Hitler needs as much as oil is a quick political as well as military victory over the Soviet Union.

It would be dangerous to overlook the sudden switching northward of von Bock's armies in a great enveloping movement to the rear of

[181] 'Flash No.60' from the Führer's Headquarters in Berlin had announced the fall of Voronezh at noon on 7 July. As the Russians did not admit this until 13 July, Orwell, like the other Allied broadcasters, had to say that the fighting was continuing.

[182] Orwell in his turn now finds suitable euphemisms for 'retreat'. 'The rapidity of Nazi advances indicating a withdrawal' and 'strategic sacrifice of territory' are masterly creations.

Moscow, while the frontal attack which is already under way is pressed from the Kalinin-rzev district.

Midway between Voronezh and Rossosh the railway from Kharkov and Kupyansk crosses the Don and runs first east, and then north-east. Just over a hundred miles from the Don it cuts the first important Moscow line and about seventy miles further, the second running south-east.

These are not the immediate possibilities but undoubted possible developments of the war. Timoshenko's forces are fighting back here and maintaining their positions there. But this is modern fluid war and once a point of the Soviet defence is penetrated, we must be prepared to see the Nazis using every possible means to widen the gap.

Further information has been coming in about the behaviour of the Japanese in territories they have overrun. The Japanese in Java are trying to blame the Dutch for the famine which they are expecting because of Japanese robbery and maladministration. In fact the Dutch never destroyed any stocks of food destined for internal consumption in the islands. The island of Amboyna, for example, is not self-supporting and had large stocks of rice; these were confiscated by the Japanese. Tokyo radio has made an urgent appeal for 30,000 Japanese to go to the Dutch East Indies for administration, the Dutch had only about half as many Europeans in their Civil Service. All small businesses in Japan, the Berlin radio said, are to be liquidated, and their owners employed in industries in the newly acquired territories. These < ?moves > are clearly < ?designed > to put the Javanese traders out of business. Furthermore, Japanese peasants and fishermen are being shipped over in large numbers. All Javanese fishing boats have been requisitioned by the Japanese, who have restarted fishing under strict government control. The population of Java is nearly 800 to the square mile. It is obvious that the Javanese must expect fearful hardships if the Japanese occupation continues. Meanwhile all Indonesian political organisations in Java have been abolished by Japanese decree; all must collaborate with the military authorities.

In New Guinea, a Japanese proclamation demands that 'all and everyone must bow their head whenever they see Japanese soldiers'. They must learn Japanese. All property has been 'frozen'. They must not write letters or listen to the wireless.

The Japanese are behaving fairly well in Burma, because they expect soon to have to fight for Burma and are anxious not to be much hated there. They are chiefly concerned to make the Burmese hate and suspect the Indians and the Chinese, the Shan tribes in the north hate and suspect the Chinese and the Burmese, the Thailanders hate and suspect the Burmese and the Chinese. Such is the Japanese plan for speedy peace and freedom in Asia.

You can now get news of the campaign as it develops direct from Russia, as the Russians are broadcasting to India themselves.[183]

Let us turn to the fighting in China.

Chungking reports that in Kiangsi the Japanese thrusts from the capital have been thrown back. The Chinese claim to have encircled 30,000 Japanese troops.[184] Further east, in Chekiang, reinforced Japanese troops are advancing towards the port of Wenehow. Far to the north-west of this fighting, in the mountains between Shanshi and Honan provinces, the Japanese are said to be withdrawing towards the bases from which they launched their offensive last month. The Chinese say that the battle is in its closing stages, and has been a defeat for the Japanese.

Thus heavy fighting is still going on in China, mainly in the Eastern provinces where the Japanese are afraid that airfields might be used to bomb Japan. The Japanese may also still hope to exhaust the Chinese by keeping up a considerable strain; it is known that most of the Japanese armies are still in China.

In this week, as you know, occurred the anniversary of the start of the Sino-Japanese war. China has now entered her sixth year of determined and successful resistance to aggression, and she calls the anniversary Reconstruction Day. There were great celebrations in England; not only the official meetings for speeches by the Chinese Ambassador and other distinguished speakers: all over the country the mayors of urban and district councils have called meetings to honour the Chinese resistance and collect gifts for the China Fund. The determination of China has excited great admiration in England.[185]

Today all the 42-year-old women of Britain are registering for National Service. Many of them are married women with children and many will only be asked to undertake part-time war work near their homes. Over 8 million women have now been registered for service in England and from 15,000 to 20,000 a week are being transferred to

[183] No examples of these broadcasts have been found in the monitors' reports, or of the various statements about Japan and Java that Orwell refers to earlier. No doubt the information came from MOI releases. Orwell's references to Burma show his detailed knowledge of the country and his best guess at the likely tactics of the Japanese.

[184] A Chungking broadcast on 10 July claimed to have trapped these men on the east bank of the river. The scale and complexity of the China campaigns, greater even than those in Russia, can be gauged by Chungking's announcement a short while later, on 14 July, that a further 6 million men aged between 18 and 40 had been called up for service in the Chinese army.

[185] The anniversary was on 7 July. Among the ceremonies which Orwell alludes to here was Lady Cripps's formal inauguration of the Aid to China Fund.

Women's Services or to war work. Britain is determined to resist the aggression to the end.

18 July 1942

The German offensive against our Russian allies is now at its height, and it would be stupid to disguise the fact that the situation is very serious. The main German drive, as we foretold in earlier newsletters, is south-east towards the region of the Caucasus. The Germans have now crossed the upper reaches of the River Don, and fighting is now going on around and inside the important town of Voronezh. They are also making fierce attacks further south in the direction of Rostov, the important city near the south of the Don and the Donets which the Russians recaptured from the Germans last year, and in the direction of Stalingrad on the Volga. Both Rostov and Stalingrad are in danger.

In these attacks the Germans' aim is evidently twofold. The final aim is, of course, to capture the oilfields of the Caucasus and the Middle East, but the more immediate aim is to cut communications between this area and the more northerly parts of Russia. By crossing the Don near Voronezh, they have already cut one important route northward, since this move has put them across the railway between Voronezh and Rostov. A further advance might leave only one railway line from this area open to the Russians, while if the Germans could get as far as Stalingrad all direct railway communication between the Caucasus region and the northern fronts of Moscow and Leningrad would be cut. This does not, of course, mean that the Russian oil would not any longer be transported, but it would mean that it would have to be transported by roundabout routes and largely by river, putting an enormous extra strain on the Russian transport system.

This phase of the war is essentially a struggle for oil. The Germans are trying to win for themselves the fresh supplies of oil that would allow them to continue their campaign of aggression, and at the same time trying to strangle the Russian people by cutting their supplies of oil and thus starving both their war industries and their agriculture. Taking the long view, we may say that either the Germans must reach the Caspian Sea this year or they have lost the war,[186] though they might be able to go on fighting for a considerable time. If they do

---

[186] In the midst of the very worst days of the war for the Allies Orwell makes a prediction of the end of the war which, ultimately, proved correct.

reach the Caspian Sea and get possession of the oil areas, that does not mean that they have won the war, but it does mean that their capacity to fight is greatly prolonged, and the task of the Allies becomes very much heavier. The Germans are throwing all they can into this battle in a desperate effort to finish with Russia before the growing strength of Britain and America can be brought against them in the west. The objective with which they actually started the Russian campaign a year ago, that of destroying the Russian armies, has not been achieved, and as they now probably realise, never will be achieved. The Russian losses have been enormous, but so have those of the Germans who are less able to bear them. The Soviet Government has just issued a casuality list giving the German losses in the last two months as 900,000 and their own at 350,000. On the whole, in spite of the gravity of the crisis at this moment, we may look forward with some confidence, remembering that last year the Germans started their offensive a month or more earlier than they started it this year, and still failed to reach a decision before winter overcame them.

In Egypt, the German attack which looked so threatening ten days ago appears to have been halted. The two armies are still almost where they were a week ago, near El Alamein on the Egyptian coast. The Germans have made and at this moment are still making strong attacks, but so far without succeeding in dislodging the British from their position. On the other hand the British have succeeded in making small advances and taking between two and three thousand prisoners. We ought not to imagine that the danger to Egypt has been removed, but at any rate the German plan of reaching Alexandria and perhaps Cairo in one swift rush has vanished. It is more easy for the German armies in Africa to receive fresh supplies than it is for the British, because their supplies are only making the short trip from Italy while ours are travelling round the Cape of Good Hope. But in the present battle the supply situation favours the British, who are nearer to their bases, and during the last ten days have been bringing up reinforcements from Egypt and probably from the Middle East. It seems likely that while the Germans have numerical superiority in tanks and possibly in men, the command of the air lies more with the British. We must expect the Germans to make further attacks because it would not only be valuable to them to capture our naval base at Alexandria, but also because this is the southern prong of the offensive against the oil regions in which the Russian attack is the northern prong. On the other hand, if the Germans do not succeed in advancing further into Egypt in the near future, they have not much to gain by staying where they are. Probably, therefore, they will make one more all-out effort to break through and if that fails, will fall back into Italian Libya.[187]

Political developments in the Middle East following on the German success in Libya have probably been very disappointing to the Axis. The German and Italian promises to liberate Egypt have not made any impression. It is indeed difficult to see how they could do so, when on one side of Egypt lies Libya, which is under the very oppressive rule of the Italians, and on the other side lies Abyssinia, which was wantonly attacked and oppressed by the Italians until the British and Abyssinian armies set it free last year. The Egyptian answer to German and Italian promises is, not unnaturally, 'If you are so anxious to set others free, why don't you start by setting free the Arabs of Libya?' We reported last week that the Turkish Premier, Dr Refik Saydam, had died,[188] and the Germans probably hoped that he would be succeeded by some statesman less friendly to the Allies. He has been succeeded, however, by Mr Sarajoglu, who is also known as a firm friend of Britain, and was one of those who drew up the Turkish-British Alliance. The American Government has notified the Vichy Government that in the case of the Germans advancing further into Egypt, they will support any move the British may make to deal with the Vichy warships now interned at Alexandria.[189] One object of the German offensive was probably to get hold of these ships, which include a battleship and some cruisers; now this design is foiled, for if Alexandria should prove to be in danger, the British will either sink these ships or remove them via the Suez Canal.

The German battleship the *Tirpitz* has been torpedoed and damaged, by a Russian submarine.[190] This is the only heavy warship left to the Germans, and though it is a new ship of enormous power it has not yet been employed very successfully. Last time it emerged in an attempt to harry the convoys going to Murmansk, it was driven back into harbour by British torpedo-carrying planes and this time it

[187] Here again Orwell was correct, and the German advances had indeed reached their limit. Fears that the Germans would reach the Suez Canal, or that they would get to Palestine and carry Nazi hatred of the Jews to the Jewish heartland were never realised. After great changes on the Allied side and a fierce campaign, the Axis armies did indeed fall back.

[188] This is not referred to in Orwell's text and, again, was probably mentioned in one of the daily news summaries. Saydam died on 8 July. Sarajoglu, a personal friend of Kemal Ataturk, had previously been Foreign Minister.

[189] It is perhaps worth observing here that America did not break off diplomatic relations with Vichy France until they were sundered, de facto, by her invasion of French North Africa.

[190] The Russian High Command had announced this ten days before, on 8 July; the report was erroneous.

has received damage which will probably keep it out of action for several months. The struggle to keep supplies flowing into Russia through the port of Murmansk continues ceaselessly, and is not achieved without losses to the Allies. Another big convoy has got there within the last week. The Germans have made fantastic claims about the number of ships sunk by their aeroplanes and submarines. Those can be disregarded, but it is known that some of the ships in the convoy were lost, a thing which cannot be avoided at this time of year when in the far north there is no night, and the sun shines continuously for about six weeks.[191]

The island of La Mayotte, near Madagascar has been taken over by the British from Vichy France.[192] This was achieved without bloodshed. Though a small operation, this was an important one, since German submarines were probably operating from the island and now that it is in British hands, the journey round Africa will be safer for our ships.

Four days ago, July 14th, was one of the great national anniversaries of France, the anniversary of the fall of the Bastille more than a hundred and fifty years ago. The Bastille was the prison in which the French kings locked up their political opponents and its capture by the people of Paris was the first step in the French Revolution and the downfall of the French monarchy. This day has been celebrated in France every year until now. This year Marshal Pétain, the puppet ruler of the Germans, forbade the usual celebrations and ordered July 14th to be observed as a day of mourning.[193] It was extensively celebrated, however, in Britain and in all the other territories where the Free French Forces are serving, and British aeroplanes marked the day by scattering over France 5 million leaflets promising that before very long July 14th should again be celebrated as the birthday of the Republic and the day of France's liberation from tyranny.

[191] This was the ill-fated convoy PQ 17. The *Tirpitz* had not in fact been damaged as the Russians claimed. She was sighted with the *Scheer* and the *Hipper* near the convoy which was ordered to disperse; 23 of the 34 ships in the convoy were sunk. The information provided here by Orwell must have originated in the MOI. It is clearly direct counter-propaganda in the face of an embarrassing truth.

[192] The landing on 8 July by British commandos assisted by Royal Marines and East African troops was unopposed. As in Madagascar, fears of an Axis presence proved groundless, though this of course did not detract from the strategic importance of the move.

[193] This departure from precedent was in answer to Stalin's cancellation of Labour Day mentioned earlier (p. 86, n.130). The mourning was for those killed in Allied bombing raids on France.

25 July 1942

This week, although very important events are happening, the situation has not altered radically since our last newsletter. We are going, therefore, to summarise the events of the week more shortly than usual, and then, as we do from time to time,to discuss the current trends of Axis propaganda addressed to India. We do this because this propaganda has no other purpose than to deceive, and by viewing it objectively, it is often possible to infer the real intentions which it conceals.

Here is a short summary of the week's events. On the southern part of the Russian front, the situation has deteriorated and Rostov is at the least in very great danger. The Germans are already claiming that Rostov has fallen.[194] This claim should be treated with scepticism until confirmed from Russian sources, but it is unquestionable that the rapid advance of the Germans into the bend of the Don river puts this important town in great danger. The vital strategic point is not so much Rostov itself as Stalingrad on the Volga, and beyond that Astrakhan on the Caspian Sea. Those are undoubtedly the German objectives, and if they have not reached Astrakhan before winter, it may be said with fair certainty that they have lost the war.[195] Further north, at Voronezh, the Russian counter-attacks have been successful. The Red Army has recrossed the Don and Germans appear to have lost heavily in men and materials.

In Egypt, the situation has greatly improved. The British have made successful counter-attacks, pushing the Germans back some miles and capturing 6,000 prisoners in the last ten days. The Indian troops have greatly distinguished themselves in these actions, several Baluchistan regiments being specially picked out for honourable mention. At the moment the Germans are probably short of aircraft, owing to the demands of the Russian front, but they are well provided with tanks,

[194] The fall of Rostov was announced by Hitler's HQ on 24 July. The Russians confirmed this after a briefer than usual delay on 27 July.

[195] Orwell repeats a statement he made earlier, but in this case it is being used in the standard propagandist's ploy of diminishing an enemy's victory by saying that he has yet to do more or he will lose.

and in particular with anti-tank artillery.[196] We must expect them to make one more large-scale attempt to break into Egypt, but their chances of doing so have grown less in the last fortnight. Should they fail in this final attempt, they will probably retreat at least to the frontiers of Libya.

There is heavy fighting in Eastern China, and the town of Wenchow has twice changed hands. It is in Japanese hands at present. The Mexican Government has taken over the oil wells in that country previously owned and operated by Japan.[197] Reports which came from usually reliable sources suggest that the Japanese are contemplating an unannounced attack on Russia about the end of this month. Naturally, they will choose the best moment and will probably wait till they believe that the Russians are in serious difficulties in the West. But we may be sure that the Soviet Government is well acquainted with their plans and has made suitable preparations.

We will now add a few notes on the nature of current Axis propaganda. We said current, because it is important to notice that this propaganda changes completely according to circumstances, not being concerned with revealing the truth in any way, but simply with influencing public opinion in a direction favourable to the Axis. The biggest example of such a change was when the Germans invaded Russia. Up to this moment, they exploited their pretended friendship with Russia for all it was worth, and described themselves as the allies of a socialist country fighting against plutocracy. They had no sooner invaded Russia than they began to describe themselves as the defenders of European civilisation against Bolshevism, appealing to the propertied classes in their second line of propaganda, just as they had appealed to the property-less classes in the first. This sudden reversal in Axis propaganda – and we choose it merely as the most outstanding example from many similar ones – should be enough to save anyone who happens to listen to it from taking Axis propaganda at its face value.

If we look at the Axis propaganda especially directed towards India at this moment,[198] we find that it all boils down to the pretence to be

[196] One of Orwell's rare mentions of actual weapons. He is referring here to the 88mm flak 18 anti-aircraft gun that the Germans also used very effectively as an anti-tank weapon. The battle referred to was the first battle of El Alamein whose final result did not match up to Orwell's optimistic description.

[197] This is a puzzling news item. All foreign oil assets had been seized years before. It is possible that Orwell was countering Axis mentions of Mexico's seizure of *American* oil wells on the occasion of Mexico's paying a first instalment of $8 million to America in agreed compensation.

[198] This broadcast was unquestionably intended as a direct answer to that given by Subhas Chandra Bose on 20 July (below, Appendix, no.8).

fighting against imperialism. The Japanese slogan is 'Asia for the Asiatics' and very similar phrases are a daily occurrence in German and Italian propaganda. The world picture presented by Axis propagandists is something like this: Britain and America are in possession of nearly the whole world, and are using their power in order to exploit the greater part of humanity and make hundreds of millions of human beings live lives of toil and misery in order to pour money into the pockets of the few hundred millionaires in London and New York. Germany, Italy and Japan are fighting against this unjust oppression, not in any way for their own interests, but simply in order to set the enslaved peoples free. When they have achieved their object, they will retire from any countries they may have had to occupy, freely granting the previously subject peoples full independence. Thus the Japanese assure the Indians that if they invade India, it would be with no intention of settling there, but merely in order to drive the British out after which they will retire again. Simultaneously, the Germans and Italians are assuring the Egyptians that they have no desire whatever upon Egyptian territory, but are merely invading Egypt in order to expel the British, after which they too will retire to their own territories. Similar promises are made all over the world, to any inhabitants of Allied countries who may be supposed to be discontented with their present lot.

Needless to say, those promises are, on the face of it, absurd. It is clear that if the Germans, Italians and Japanese were really the enemies of imperialism, they would start by liberating their own subject peoples. The Japanese would liberate Korea, Manchuria and Formosa, and would retire from the parts of China which they have overrun since 1937. The Italians, instead of making promises to the Egyptians, would set free the Arabs of Libya, and in any case would never have committed the aggression against the Abyssinians, which was justly avenged last year. As for the Germans, in order to make good their promises, they would have to liberate the whole of Europe.

These facts are self-evident. For Germany to call Britain imperialistic is at best the pot calling the kettle black. Nevertheless, the Axis propagandists are not so silly as this may seem to imply. They go upon two principles, both of them sound in the short run, though probably not in the long run. The first principle is that if you promise people what they want, they will always believe you. The second is that very few people either know or are interested in knowing what is being done or said in other parts of the world than their own. The Axis propagandists know, therefore, that in their propaganda to various countries they can contradict themselves grossly without much danger of being detected. Here, for example, is one instance of such self-contradiction. At the same moment that the Axis broadcasts are assuring India that they are the friends of the coloured peoples, as against the British, they are assuring the Dutch of South Africa that they are the friends of the white race as against the black.[199] Indeed, this conviction is inherent in the whole of Axis propaganda, since the central thesis of Nazi theory is the superiority of the white races over the Asiatic and African races and the Jews. The Germans go even further than their Italian colleagues by claiming that all that is worth while in human history has been achieved by people with blue eyes. Naturally this doctrine is left out when Berlin is broadcasting to India or Africa.[200] The Japanese might seem to be debarred from holding any such theory, but in fact they have, and for centuries have had, a racial theory even more extreme than that of the Germans. They believe the Japanese race to be divine; all other races being hereditarily inferior; and they have incidentally a contemptuous nickname ('Korumba') for the negroes and other darker-skinned races. Both of these peoples, the Germans and the Japanese, and perhaps also the Italians, commit their aggressions upon the theory firmly believed in by many of them that since they are superior races, they have a divine right to govern the earth. These ideas are mentioned quite freely in their home press and broadcasts, and even for outside consumption when they consider it suitable. A good many German broadcasts addressed to Britain, for example, have suggested fairly openly that the German and Anglo-Saxon peoples, as the principal members of the white race, have a common interest and ought to get together for the combined exploitation of the world.[201] Needless to say, neither India nor Africa are supposed to hear anything of this, and since, in fact, those people have not access to the press or radio outside their own countries, these flagrant contradictions do generally go unnoticed.

We have made this the subject of our talk this week, because we are well aware of the nature of the Axis propaganda now being addressed to India, and we think it wise to answer it from time to time, not for

[199] An Axis broadcast to Africa in Afrikaans, 'The coffee-coloured nation' (below, Appendix, no.9), had made these points on the previous day. It appeared verbatim in the monitors' reports where Orwell must have seen it, deciding to use it as a theme.

[200] As the Germans' main ally was Japan, their position was obviously a little more sophisticated than this. It was summed up in an Axis broadcast on 10 March by Fuerst Urach, 'The formation of Greater East Asia'. This concept has strong echoes in *Nineteen Eighty-Four*.

[201] It seems, from their content, that Orwell is here referring to the broadcasts of William Joyce ('Lord Haw-Haw').

the sake of exposing individual falsehoods,[202] which would take too long, and is not worth while, but merely to issue a general warning which may help our listeners to see the world situation in perspective. Next time, therefore, that you come across a piece of plausible Axis propaganda, it is worth asking yourself this question: 'If they say this to me, what are they likely to be saying to Europe, to America, to Africa, to Britain, or to China?'

A little thought along these lines will often help to counteract that other tendency which Axis broadcasters play upon, the tendency to believe any story which tells us what we want to hear.

1 August 1942

On the Russian front the news continues to be extremely grave. The Germans have now crossed the Don river, and are moving south into the Caucasus area. The important city of Rostov fell several days back, and it is south of Rostov that the German advance has been most rapid. It is uncertain how far they have yet got. They have at any rate entered Bataisk, about fifty miles south of Rostov, where there are a few oil wells. We can assume that the Russians blocked these or otherwise put them out of action when it became clear that they might fall into German hands. Simultaneously with this southward movement another body of German troops has been moving eastward into the angle of the Don, in the direction of the important town of Stalingrad. Here, however, they have been stopped, and all their efforts to cross the Don, as also further north near Voronezh, have failed. In general the position is such that the entire body of Russian troops in the Caucasus area is in danger of being cut off from the more northern parts of Russia. Even should the Germans reach Stalingrad communications between Moscow and Leningrad on the one hand, and the Caucasus region on the other, do indeed exist, but by roundabout routes which put strain on transport. Of course, even if the Germans should succeed in separating the northern and southern Russian armies, that does not mean that they have reached the oil,

[202] Monitors were always in two minds about telling the opposition that their broadcasts were being listened to. This is as far as Orwell goes towards letting Subhas Chandra Bose and the others know just how closely he was following their programmes. It is unusual for Orwell to use a word such as 'falsehood' when the more direct 'lie' was to hand; the word was frequently used at the time as being more formal and convincing, and there was also a wide circulation of the book *Falsehoods in Wartime* by Lord Ponsonby which gave an account of First World War propaganda.

which is their chief objective. They have still got to meet the Russian armies in the Caucasus, and the British Ninth Army in the Middle East. But they might, by severing the communication between this all-important oil area and the rest of Russia, starve the northern Russian armies of oil for their vehicles, and at the same time strike a very severe blow at the economic life of the whole of the Soviet Union. Russian agriculture is done mainly with tractor ploughs,[203] which need constant supplies of oil. There are natural sources of oil in Russia in several areas apart from the Caucasus, including considerable supplies beyond the Ural mountains, in places where it is impossible for the Germans to get at them. It is also probable that the Soviet Government has placed large dumps of oil all over the country, in preparation for just such an emergency as this. Meanwhile, however, the productive capacity of the Russian armaments factories must be adversely affected, both by the loss of territory and by the extra strain on communications. The war is not at its climax, but it is no use denying that the situation is very bad – as bad as, or perhaps worse than it was in the autumn of last year. Nevertheless, the campaign has not gone according to German plan. The destruction of the Red Army, which was the primary aim of the Germans, has not been accomplished, and the German commentators are beginning to admit that it cannot be accomplished. Politically, the German attempt to subjugate Soviet Russia has been an utter failure. There has been no kind of quisling activity whatever in the occupied areas and the Germans do not even pretend that the inhabitants are anything but hostile to them.[204] It is significant that recently they have enormously increased the number of their armed police force – a silent confession that the so-called New Order can only be maintained by naked force. Although the Germans have now overrun large and very rich territories, these are not of much direct use to them, since they have not the labour to exploit them, they cannot successfully force the inhabitants to work and they have to contend everywhere with the results of a scorched earth policy carried out with extreme thoroughness. In a positive sense, therefore, the Germans have not gained much by their conquests, and probably will not gain much. In

[203] A propaganda point. German radio was unashamedly broadcasting advice to her farmers on the best use of horses on the land, and even introduced legislation to ensure that none were used for other than essential war purposes.

[204] A further propaganda point. There was, of course, extensive co-operation with the German armies, culminating in the appearance of large numbers of Russian troops fighting for Germany under General Vlasov. There is now an extensive literature about the Vlasov movement, but it is unlikely that Orwell would have known of its existence. The Russian propaganda emanating from the MOI reached its peak in August/September 1942.

a negative sense however, they have gained by reducing the offensive power of our Russian allies, and this will remain so until the territories at least so far west as Kharkov have been won back.

In Egypt, there is little to report since last week. The British have made several successful attacks, but all the activities have been on a comparatively small scale. It is evident that the hope of swiftly reaching the Suez Canal, about which the Axis broadcasters were talking so unguardedly a fortnight ago, has now faded. The present stage of the Egyptian campaign is being fought largely by Indian troops,[205] who have won themselves very high praise from the Commander in Chief.

On Sunday, July 26th, a huge meeting was held in London, to demand the opening of a second front in Western Europe. It was attended by people of all kinds, and the crowd numbered not less than 50,000 people.[206] We do not care to express any opinion as to whether the British and American Governments will or will not open a second front this year. It is obvious that whatever the Government's intentions may be, it cannot disclose them prematurely, but it is important to realise that the mere idea of the opening of a second front deeply affects the strategy of the war. On their own statement, the Germans are feverishly at work fortifying the whole Western coast of Europe against a possible attack, and the danger on their flank probably prevents them from using their full air strength on the Russian front. The British air attacks on Germany continue relentlessly and the Germans are only able to retaliate against Britain on a very small scale. There have been several small air-raids on London and other British cities during the last week, but the anti-aircraft defences are now so good that in each case the raiding force lost ten per cent of its strength. On July 27th, there was another large scale British raid on Hamburg, carried out by about 500 bombing planes, which even on the German admission caused extensive damage. It was followed two days later by another raid on about the same scale. There is little doubt that these raids are going to become greater and greater both in numbers and volume. The American as well as the British airforce is now beginning to take part in them, and American planes are arriving in Britain in ever greater

[205] A reference to the Fifth Indian Division's part in the attacks of 21 and 26 July; 'largely' was a pardonable exaggeration.

[206] The meeting was held in Trafalgar Square; the meetings in 'Victory Square' described by Orwell in *Nineteen Eighty-Four* are obviously based on such events. The demonstration was followed by a mass lobby at the House of Commons by 1500 people and an address to the members of the House in secret session by Maisky, the Russian Ambassador. The Axis propaganda made a great deal of these happenings.

numbers. The Chief of Bomber Command broadcast some nights ago to the German people, warning them of the heavier and heavier raids that are to come. The Germans cry out against these raids,[207] declaring the whole policy of bombing to be wicked and inhumane, having apparently forgotten that only a year or two ago, they themselves were bombing London and other residential cities and openly boasting of the slaughter they were achieving among the civilian population. At that time Britain was not able to retaliate on a big scale, and the Germans probably imagined that this state of affairs would continue. Now that the tables are turned, they talk in a different vein. This, however, will make no difference, and the raids will increase in volume, so that before long a raid carried out by a thousand bombers will seem almost commonplace. We do not express any opinion as to whether this air activity is or is not a prelude to an Allied invasion of Europe, but we can at least say that should such an invasion be made, the raids will have weakened the German power to resist, and helped to secure air superiority over the coast, which is indispensable if any landing is to be attempted. The British people, though recognising that the decision must rest with the Government, which alone possesses the necessary information, are extremely eager for the invasion to be made, and would be willing even to risk a great disaster if this helped our Russian allies by drawing off the German armies from the Eastern front.

Fighting has flared up again in New Guinea, where the Japanese have made a fresh landing on the northern coast. [*Two lines illegible.*] The Japanese forces made another attempt to advance on Port Moresby, the possession of which is indispensable to them if they are to invade Australia, but they have been successfully beaten back.

British subjects living abroad are to be made liable for National Service.

The harvest in the British Isles is estimated to be by far the largest that has ever been known. This applies both to wheat and other cereals and even more to potatoes.[208] Since the outbreak of war an extra six million acres have been brought under cultivation in the British Isles, and Britain is now producing about two thirds of its own food. This is

---

[207] Their immediate reply was in the form of a broadcast, 'Two can play at bombing cities'. Orwell had himself experienced the London raids and had been bombed out on more than one occasion. His only piece of fiction written during these days, the first episode of 'Story by Five Authors', is set in an air raid (*OWB*, p.95ff.).

[208] Orwell is here perhaps making a private joke against himself. At the beginning of the war he had become convinced that there would be a shortage of potatoes and he had spent considerable time and energy planting a large crop on his small-holding in Hertfordshire. In the event there was a glut.

a marked change from the conditions of peace time when almost all food was imported from abroad. At the same time, so far as can be discovered from reports and observations, the German harvest this year is a very poor one.

8 August 1942

On the Russian front the general movement continues to be the same as we reported last week. The Germans are still advancing southward, though somewhat less rapidly than before, and it may be taken that they have definitely cut the railway connecting Stalingrad with the Black Sea and the Caucasus area. They claim to have reached the Kuban river, which runs into the Black Sea near Novorossiysk; but it is doubtful whether they have actually done it as yet. Further north, they have failed to make any progress towards Stalingrad. Probably they have not, in the present campaign, captured anything that is of much direct use to them, but they have succeeded in almost separating the northern and southern parts of the Russian front, and thus making it much harder for the northern Russian armies to get their supplies of oil. Much depends on the quantity of oil and other war materials which the Soviet Government had stored beforehand at strategic points. In spite of the striking German successes of the last month, the Soviet Government's pronouncements are as firm and confident as ever and we may assume that from their knowledge of the situation they know that though the campaign has reached its climax, it is far from desperate. The aim of the Germans is first to destroy the Russian armies as a fighting force, and secondly to win themselves an unlimited supply of oil. The aim of the Allied nations is to gather strength as quickly as possible and see to it that the German armies are forced to spend another winter in the Russian snow. The Germans' aims do not now look as though they can be fully achieved this year, and in spite of all the confident predictions of victory of the Nazi wireless, the prospect of another winter like the last one, with Anglo-American strength mounting up, and the German soldiers dying of cold by tens of thousands, is probably a nightmare to the leaders who have brought Germany to its present pass.[209]

[209] A provoking stance by Orwell, as the Germans' 'present pass' was that of victory on all fronts. Many German soldiers did die of cold, no doubt, but a large number were taken back to Germany to attend engineering and technical courses during the winter months at the colleges and universities, a point made by the Axis propagandists frequently at this time.

It is important, however, to see each campaign in perspective and to realise that however little they may like one another, the two major powers of the Axis are for the time being acting in concert. During recent weeks, we have not said very much in our newsletters about the Far Eastern end of the war. Except for some rather indecisive actions in China, the Japanese were not attacking, but were building up their strength for two, or possibly three, offensives which they will probably undertake in the near future. We reported last week that there has been fresh activity in New Guinea and during the last week it has become clearer that the Japanese are going to launch another attack against Port Moresby, perhaps on a bigger scale than hitherto. Air reconnaissance also shows that they have occupied some small uninhabited islands about two hundred miles north of Australia. These moves cannot have any meaning except as a prelude to an attack against the mainland of Australia and we must write this down as one of the campaigns which the Japanese are likely to undertake shortly. They will probably attack Australia, not merely because they have always coveted the possession of it, but because it is there that British and American strength is most rapidly increasing, and it is from there that a counter-attack against the Southern Asian Archipelago can be undertaken. Simultaneously, however, the Japanese seem to be also preparing attacks on both Russia and India. It is known that they have greatly increased their forces on the borders of Manchuria and also that they have been bringing reinforcements into Burma. The RAF has been bombing the port of Akyab, which probably indicates the presence there of Japanese transports. It is not certain that the Japanese will attack India but, as in the case of Australia, they must do so if they wish to prevent a counter-attack against themselves being prepared. It may be asked why they have not attacked India already, since they probably had a good opportunity to do so three or four months ago, when the British were being driven out of Burma and British naval strength in the Indian Ocean had been much weakened by the loss of the two battleships at Singapore. The reason for the Japanese not attacking India are two, or possibly three: the first is the monsoon, which makes landing operations difficult, and slows down the movement of troops in low-lying country. The second reason developed a little later in the heavy Japanese naval losses in their two unsuccessful battles against the Americans. So far as we know, the Japanese lost at least five aircraft carriers – which would also mean the loss of several hundred aeroplanes and several thousand trained men – in these two encounters; and without a sufficient force of aircraft carriers they probably do not feel equal to attacking the coast of India against land-based aircraft. The lost aircraft carriers can be replaced, but this would mean several months' work. The third possible reason was that the Japanese were hoping for political strife in India to reach such a pitch that if they made the invasion they would be greeted as friends by at least a large section of the population. In thus holding back they showed caution, but they also allowed the Allied forces in India to be immensely strengthened. It is not our place to comment on India's internal politics,[210] but we may say that the recent pronouncements of the Working Committee of the Congress Party at least do not favour the theory that the Japanese would be welcomed as friends if they came.

[*Censored:* As to the attack on Russia, it is simply a matter of choosing an opportune moment. Whereas the Japanese might possibly hold on to their conquests while leaving India and Australia alone, their aims and those of Soviet Russia are absolutely incompatible. The conquest of Siberia has, in fact, been a Japanese objective for the last forty or fifty years.] We reported in earlier newsletters that the Japanese had established themselves in the Aleutian Islands. They are only in two uninhabited islands at the top of the Archipelago, but from air-reconnaissance it is estimated that there are about 10,000 of them there. It may not be easy to get them out again, since the whole of this area is constantly enveloped in storms and mist, which makes movements by ships and aeroplanes difficult. The Japanese seizure of these two islands cannot have any purpose but to establish themselves across the route between Russia and America and thus to cut off the supplies of war materials which would flow across the northern Pacific if war should break out in Manchuria.

We may take it that an attack against Vladivostok – no doubt a treacherous[211] and unannounced attack – comes high on the Japanese programme. If it does not take place, that will only be because the Japanese fear the strength of the Red Army. We do not

[210] As far as purely Indian politics went, this period provided Orwell with the most serious test of his integrity. As he well knew, the failure of the Cripps mission, for whatever reason, had been followed by greatly increased unrest. At a meeting in Bombay on 4-5 August the Congress Party Working Committee had drawn up demands for immediate withdrawal of Britain from India and urging a mass civil disobedience campaign. Finally, the Government of India ordered the arrest of Nehru, Gandhi and other Congress leaders on the day after this broadcast. Orwell says merely that it is not his place to comment on India's internal politics, which is about all that the official directive to the censor would allow him to say. For his private opinion, see *OWB*, pp.36-7. His allusion in the rest of the sentence to the Congress Party's *not* being sympathetic to the Japanese cause is in direct contradiction to the Government of India's line, based on documents seized, that they were.

[211] Treacherous, because Japan and Russia were not at war. Finally it was Russia who declared war on Japan, on 8 August 1945.

profess to say which of these three possible moves, an offensive against India, against Australia, or against Russia, will come first, but we do say with certainty that all three are highly probable, and that so far as India is concerned, the situation depends quite largely on the courage, foresight and hard work of the peoples of India themselves.

There is little to report from Egypt. We merely mention this front in order to remind our listeners that the lack of activity there does not mean that the campaign is at an end. The fact that the Germans did not retreat again after being stopped at El Alamein must mean that they intend another attack. Otherwise, they would have had no reason for staying in so inconvenient a position. Both the Axis and the Allied forces are building up their strength in tanks and aeroplanes as quickly as possible. It must not be forgotten, as we have pointed out in earlier newsletters, that the supply problem in this area is easier for the Germans than for ourselves. Probably, therefore, another major battle is to be expected in Egypt within the next week or two.

The British have made two more heavy air raids, on Düsseldorf and on Duisburg.[212] These recent raids have not been carried out by a thousand planes, like the earlier ones, but in most cases by five or six hundred. The actual weight of bombs dropped, however, is hardly less than in the thousand-bomber raids. Exact figures cannot be given, but it appears that in the recent raids on Düsseldorf and on Hamburg the RAF each time dropped three or four hundred tons of bombs on its objectives. This is a greater weight of bombs than has ever been dropped on Britain, even including the terrible raid which almost wiped out the city of Coventry.[213] From our experience in this country, we can get some impression of what is now happening to various German industrial towns. The Germans have continued to make raids on London and other cities, but only on a very small scale, and in several of these raids, the attacking force has lost about ten per cent of its strength. It is probable, however, that these raids are made largely for reconnaissance, and to test the new anti-aircraft defences which have been developed in Britain during the past year. Large-scale raids on Britain may be resumed this autumn, at any rate, if the Germans are able to disengage a sufficient part of their air force from Russia.

From Palestine comes the very good news that a Palestinian regiment is being raised, in which both Jews and Arabs are

---

[212] On 2 and 6 August.
[213] An example often cited in the popular press when anxiety was expressed.

serving.[214] Thus the obvious, unmistakable menace of Fascist aggression is helping to solve one of the most difficult political problems the world contains, and people who only yesterday were political enemies find that they have a common interest in defending their country against the invader.

15 August 1942

The Russian front still continues to be the most important one, but during the past week there have also been new and significant developments in the South Pacific. We will deal with the Russian front first.

During the past week, until a few days ago, the main German drive was still southward in the direction of the Caucasus. During the last two days, however, the Germans have made fresh attacks eastward, in the direction of Stalingrad – an important industrial base, situated on the river Volga which is still a very important line of supply between the Caucasus and the rest of Russia. So far these eastward attacks have not had much success. The Germans have gained little if any ground, [*censored:* and the Russians are counter-attacking and in places have forced the enemy on to the defensive.] Stalingrad however, may be menaced from a new direction if the Germans gain much more ground to the south, as this might enable them to attack this very important objective from two sides. In the south, the German advance during the past week, though not very rapid, has been almost continuous. In places they are now actually in the foot-hills of the Caucasus mountains. It is uncertain whether the oil town of Maikop is actually in German hands.[215] All that is certain is that fierce

---

[214] In a debate in the House of Commons on 6 October Sir James Grigg, Secretary for War, had announced that a Palestine Regiment of the British Army, with separate Jewish and Arab infantry battalions, was being established. There was also to be a Palestine Volunteer Force that all sections of the community could join. Axis propagandists referred only to attempts to set up a Jewish army which had failed. There is some reference to this failure in Churchill's papers: 'It may be necessary to make an example of these anti-semite officers and others in high places. If three or four of them were recalled and dismissed and the reason given it would have a salutary effect' (quoted by Martin Gilbert, *Auschwitz and the Allies* (1981), p.49.)

[215] The fall of Maikop was announced by the Axis broadcasters in their usual style: 'From the Führer's Headquarters 9 August, Maikop captured: special announcement (fanfares). The High Command announces: Maikop centre of the important oil region on the northern border of the Caucasus was taken by assault by mobile units at 18.20 today.'

fighting is taking place in that area, and Maikop itself has been heavily bombed and largely destroyed. Besides their advance southward and south-westward, the Germans have also advanced westward along the foot of the Caucasus mountains and claim to be only about two hundred miles west of the Caspian Sea. The whole of this movement is full of the greatest danger for our Russian allies. By advancing so swiftly to the south, the Germans have endangered the position of the Russian armies on the shores of the Sea of Azov, and also endangered Novorossiysk as a naval base. If it should be lost, the only harbour on the Black Sea left to the Russians would be Batumi, near the Turkish border. This may not be sufficient for their purposes, since a fleet needs not only harbours, but stores and workshops of every kind. The whole situation, therefore, is full of the greatest danger, and indeed, is as menacing as it was in the autumn of last year.

However, that is not to say that even if they can clean up the whole of the area which they are now attacking, the Germans would find this victory a decisive one. No gains in the area north of the Caucasus mountains can really solve the Germans' oil problem. If you look at the map, you will note that the great chain of the Caucasus mountains runs straight across from the Black Sea to the Caspian Sea. South of the mountains, on the east side, is the great oil town of Baku. This is the main source of Russian oil, and is one of the most important, if not *the* most important, oil area in the world. That is the German objective and they have got to cross the mountains to reach it. They are already somewhere near Pyatigorsk, which is at the beginning of one of the military roads across the Caucasus, but it is unlikely that they will succeed in fighting their way across the mountains this year, and it is doubtful whether they will try. These mountains are the highest in Europe and intense cold sets in any time from October onwards, so that the risks of beginning a campaign in this area in mid-August are very great. It is more probable that the Germans will try to move down to the Baku area along the coast of the Caspian Sea. This means moving through very narrow passes, which we may count on the Russians to defend with the utmost determination. And in weighing their chances, one has also to take into consideration the possibility of the Germans being faced by an unexpected attack in Western Europe. Whether this will happen, we still cannot predict, but it is at least certain from the tone of their newspapers and wireless that the Germans consider it possible.

Last week, we reported that the Japanese were showing fresh activity in New Guinea, obviously as a prelude to another attack on Port Moresby. However, between now and then, the American and Australian forces forestalled them by an attack of their own. About four days ago, news came that the Americans were attacking Tulagi, in the Solomon Islands. The first reports were only of an air and sea action, but we now know that the Americans have also landed ground troops on three of the islands, and though the reports that have come in are very meagre, it is known that these troops have established themselves on shore, and are holding their ground.[216] We shall probably be able to give a full account of this action, which is almost certainly a very important one, next week. In the meantime, we can only give a bare outline of the facts, and at the same time explain their strategic meaning. All we know is that the Americans have landed troops, that in doing so they have lost a cruiser, and had other vessels damaged, and that they are expecting fairly heavy casualties. It is probable, though not yet officially confirmed, that two important airfields hitherto held by the Japanese have been captured by the Allied Forces. No information can be obtained from the Japanese reports, as these constantly contradict one another, and are obviously only put out for propaganda purposes.[217] It is evident, however, that things are not going altogether well from the Japanese point of view. As to the meaning of this move, it is best understood by looking at the map. The Solomon Islands lie eastward of New Guinea and north-eastward of Australia. From bases here, the Japanese submarines and aeroplanes can attack American ships, bringing supplies to Australia. If the Americans can obtain possession of the Solomon Islands, their supply route to Australia is not only made much safer, but can be shortened, as their ships will not have to make such a wide detour to avoid Japanese submarines. But the purpose of the move is also an offensive one. If the Solomons were in Allied hands, the position of the Japanese in New Guinea would be made much more difficult, and they could probably be forced to withdraw from there. This action, therefore, is probably the first step in an Allied offensive in the South Pacific. We do not predict yet whether it will be successful; it must be remembered that actions of this kind are difficult to carry out, and that it was in attempting something similar that the Japanese lost so heavily at Midway Island. The tone of the American communiqués, however, is confident. While the main

[216] The first Allied offensives in the Pacific were announced in Washington on 12 August. The attacks commenced on 7 August and were still continuing with landings on the islands of Tulagi, Florida and Guadalcanal.

[217] Both the Japanese and German broadcasts for their home audiences proclaimed a great victory for the Japanese, Tokyo radio describing a naval victory 'of historic importance having inflicted grievous losses on the British and American fleets'. The Axis broadcasters in English were more cautious and eventually acknowledged the true position.

operation takes place against the Solomon Islands, Allied aeroplanes from Australia are heavily bombing the Japanese in New Guinea, and have forced them to retreat from the positions which they occupied recently. The object of this move no doubt is to tie down Japanese forces in New Guinea, and prevent them from reinforcing the Solomons. Simultaneously with the attack on the Solomons, the American navy has made another attack on the Japanese in the Aleutian Islands. It is known that damage has been inflicted and several ships sunk.[218] This, however, is a comparatively unimportant action, and it does not appear that any attempt has been made to land troops.

There is little news from Egypt. Both sides are being reinforced, and it is known that American troops have now arrived and are ready to take part side by side with the British in any forthcoming action.[219] In the central Mediterranean there has been an important air and sea battle which has resulted in the island of Malta receiving a large consignment of fresh supplies, including fighter aeroplanes. A British convoy fought its way along the thousand miles between Gibraltar and Malta against continuous attacks by Axis aeroplanes and submarines, and got through to its objective, though with the loss of a cruiser and an old aircraft carrier.[220] We have not yet received full reports of Axis losses, but it is known that they lost two submarines sunk and had two cruisers damaged by torpedoes. The geographical position makes it impossible to reinforce Malta without suffering losses on the way, but these are justified since Malta lies midway between Italy and Africa, and its aeroplanes make constant attacks on Axis supplies crossing to Tripoli. The desperate effort the Axis have made to overwhelm Malta by bombing show how important it is for the Allies to hold on to it.

There have been a number of German air raids on Britain, all of them on a very small scale. It is uncertain whether these raids are made in order to give the German people the impression that their airforce is avenging the British raids on Germany, or whether they are undertaken for reconnaissance, in preparation for heavier attacks to be made later.[221] The RAF continues with its attacks and during this week has

[218] Attacks by both ships and planes took place on 8 August.

[219] It is not clear which American troops Orwell refers to here. There were very considerable quantities of American tanks and other equipment in use.

[220] The Axis radio in reporting these convoys always exaggerated their losses and always maintained that they had been destined for Egypt but prevented from reaching there. Malta was rarely mentioned. The cruiser lost here was HMS *Manchester* and the carrier HMS *Eagle*, an ex-Chilean Navy ship that had been adapted to carry a mere twenty planes – as Orwell says, an old carrier.

[221] A determined attempt by Orwell to play down the significance of German bombing raids. The RAF raids he goes on to mention – Duisburg on 6 August, Mainz on 11-12 August – were part of the continuing bombing policy mentioned before.

made a very heavy raid on Duisburg, and two others on Mainz. In the latter attack, apart from hundreds of tons of explosive bombs, 50,000 incendiary bombs were dropped. The Air Ministry has recently issued exact figures about our bombing of Germany. They show, in the first place, that in June and July 1942 the RAF dropped on Germany more than four times the weight of bombs dropped during the same period of 1940; and also that there have now been about a dozen raids in which the RAF have dropped a far greater load of bombs than the Germans ever dropped in their heaviest raids on Britain. Although raids on this scale cannot be undertaken every day, because the weather is not always suitable, there is no doubt that their number will constantly increase as the American as well as the British air force comes into play.

The news of riots, shootings, guerilla warfare arrests, reprisals and threats against the civilian population comes in almost continuously from all over Europe.[222] It is clear that not only in the Balkans, but even in parts of Western Europe, a state not far removed from civil war has been reached. For example a few days ago the German wireless laconically announced that 93 persons, described as terrorists, had been shot that day, in the single city of Paris. In all areas along the Atlantic coast, the Germans have issued decrees threatening the most savage penalties against anyone who should assist an invading Allied force, and more or less openly admit that the people in the occupied territories are heart and soul for the Allies. When we look back two years, and remember how confidently the Germans boasted that they would make the New Order a success, and eliminate every trace of British and American influence on the Continent, we realise how completely the Germans have lost the political side of the war, even though in a military sense they are still undefeated.

22 August 1942

On Tuesday of this week, the news was released that the British Prime Minister, Mr Churchill, has been in Moscow, to confer with

[222] The Axis propaganda at this time was filled with lurid accounts of the British attempts to put down the insurgents in India activated by the Congress decision to ask for British withdrawal. As Orwell was banned from mentioning these events, he could only answer them by pointing to exactly similar happenings in Axis-occupied Europe, leaving his listeners to draw the conclusion that life under the Japanese would be no better.

Premier Stalin and other leading representatives of the United Nations.[223] No pronouncement has been made yet as to the conclusions reached, but it is known that these were satisfactory, and it can be taken as certain that some important move was decided upon. This is the fourth occasion on which Mr Churchill has travelled halfway round the world to confer with the leader of an Allied nation. Grave though the situation is for the Allies, the comparative ease with which the Allied nations can confer with one another is an index of the real strategic situation, for whereas it is a comparatively simple matter for Mr Churchill to go to Moscow or to Washington, it would be utterly impossible for Hitler to visit Tokyo, unless he travelled by submarine and took perhaps six months over the journey.[224] The United Nations are in full communication with one another, while the Fascist powers control only two separate areas at opposite ends of the world.

Mr Churchill arrived at a critical moment for our Russian allies. During the past week the general direction of the fighting in southern Russia was much as before. The Germans have made further advances on the Caucasus front, and have definitely overrun the important oil centre of Maikop. Before evacuating the town, the Russians removed or destroyed all the machinery and the existing stocks of oil, so that the capture of this area is no direct gain to the Germans, although it is a severe loss to the Russians. At the same time the German attack in this area has fanned out to east and to west, the easterly attack moving towards the other important oil area of Orowey, while the westward one endangers the port of Novorossiysk, the most important Russian naval base on the Black Sea. One column of German troops appears to be trying to cross the Caucasus mountains, but there has been no news of this movement for some days past. Further north Stalingrad, the strategic key to the whole of this campaign, is firmly in Russian hands, though it is menaced by a German attack from the south, as well as from the west. The Germans claim to have overrun the whole territory within the elbow of the Don, at the angle of which lies Stalingrad, but they have not succeeded in crossing the river anywhere in this area. Further north, at Voronezh and in the areas of

[223] The Axis radio stations announced that Churchill was in Moscow on 4 August. Although Churchill did not actually arrive in Moscow until 12 August, the telegram to Stalin announcing his visit was *sent* on 4 August. Clearly the Germans had intercepted this or similar information in some way, but only getting a general picture. There are other examples of Axis propagandists' prescience, notably their knowledge of Cripps's mission to India before he had even returned from Moscow. See above, n.80.

[224] This was the journey made by Subhas Chandra Bose; it did indeed take months. See above, p.14.

Moscow and Leningrad, the Russians have made attacks which have had some success and which are no doubt designed chiefly to draw off the German forces from other fronts. Seeing the whole of this campaign in perspective as well as we can, we may say that though the Germans have had great successes, they are not within sight of securing the decisive victory which they hoped to complete before the onset of winter.

The fighting in the Solomon Islands which we reported last week has resulted in a brilliant success for the Allies, after nearly a fortnight of hard fighting. The American and Australian forces are now in control of three of the islands, including Tulagi which possesses the most important harbour in this area. Yesterday's official report described the Allied forces as 'mopping up' – that is crushing sporadic resistances after defeating the enemy's main force. Guerilla fighting will probably continue for a long time to come, but as long as the Allies hold the landing grounds and the main anchorages they can prevent the Solomon Islands from being used as a base for attacks on shipping coming from America to Australia. The Japanese continue to put out extravagant reports of losses inflicted on the Allies, but they have contradicted themselves over and over again and in the last two days have significantly changed their tune. After several times announcing that they were about to issue a report on the fighting in the Solomon Islands they have suddenly stated that no report will be issued as yet – a certain admission of failure. The Allied success, however, was not achieved without losses. It is known that an American cruiser was sunk, and the Australian cruiser the Canberra was also sunk a few days ago.

A few days back, American troops also landed in the Gilbert Islands, nine hundred miles north-east of the Solomons, and destroyed airfield installations. This, however, was only a raid, and the troops re-embarked again afterwards.

We are now able to give fuller figures of the naval battle in the Mediterranean, as the result of which a British convoy reached Malta with much-needed supplies. The British naval losses were a cruiser, a light cruiser, a destroyer and an old aircraft carrier.[225] The Axis losses were: 2 submarines, between 60 and 70 aeroplanes, and 2 cruisers damaged. It is impossible for the Allies to reinforce Malta without losing ships in the process, because after leaving Gibraltar any convoy has to pass through a thousand miles of sea over which land-based Axis aeroplanes can operate. But such losses are well

[225] In addition to the losses already mentioned above (p.134, n.20), further Admiralty announcements mentioned the loss of the light cruiser HMS *Cairo* and the destroyer HMS *Foresight*. The attacks lasted from 11 to 15 August.

justified, since Malta is an ideal base for bombing Italy and for raiding Axis supplies on their way to Libya. The people of Malta throughout the past two years have gone through a most terrible experience of endless bombing, and fairly severe food shortage, and have behaved with unexampled courage. They are well aware of what would happen to their liberty if the Axis won the war, and Malta passed under Fascist rule, and consequently have suffered their long ordeal without even a murmur, at the moment when food was very short and the island barely possessed any fighter aeroplanes with which to hit back at its attackers. The arrival of the recent convoy will ease Malta's position considerably.

German submarines have recently sunk several Brazilian passenger ships in the most wanton way, drowning a large number of people.[226] This has caused great popular indignation in Brazil, where there have been large demonstrations in favour of the Allies, and the offices of German subsidised newspapers have been wrecked by the crowd. The residents of Brazil have promised that in compensation for the sinking, German ships interned in Brazilian ports will be seized, and the property of Axis nationals in Brazil confiscated. In addition a hundred Germans have been arrested as hostages.[227] The unprovoked sinking of Brazilian ships will have its effect in other South American countries besides Brazil.

More and more the peoples of the South American Republics are coming to realise how important it is that all free nations should stand together against the aggressor states, who are the natural enemies of their independence and their national institutions.

On Wednesday of this week there took place the largest combined operations raid of the war, on Dieppe on the French coast, about sixty miles from the coast of Britain. British, Canadian, Free French and American troops took part, the whole force evidently numbering five or ten thousand men. They remained on shore about ten hours, and successfully destroyed batteries of artillery and other military objectives, before re-embarking. Tanks were successfully landed, and took part in the operations. This is probably the first time in this war that tanks have been landed from small boats on to an open beach. It is known that there were heavy casualties on both sides and very heavy losses of aeroplanes. The Germans are known to have lost about 90 planes destroyed for certain and a large number were reported as

[226] On 16 August Brazil reported that three of her cargo and passenger ships had been sunk by German submarines. They were the *Annibal Benevola*, the *Baependy* and the *Araraquara* with a total loss of 223 lives.

[227] It was formally stated that they were being held as hostages for a number of Brazilian Jews interned in occupied France.

probably destroyed, so that 130 would be a conservative figure for their total loss. The British lost nearly 100 planes.[228] These losses are much more serious for the Germans than for the British, as the great part of the German air force is now on the Russian front, and any large loss of planes means that others have to be brought across Europe to replace them.

When the raid began, the BBC repeatedly broadcast to the French people, warning them this was only a raid and not an invasion of Europe, and that they had better remain in their houses and not join in the fighting. There was good reason for doing this. On a previous occasion, in the raid on Saint Nazaire, the French population, seeing their chance of striking a blow against the Germans who have been oppressing them for two years, rose and fought on the side of the British. Afterwards, when the raid was over and the British troops had re-embarked, the Germans committed fearful atrocities against the local population, and the British Government had no wish that such a thing as this should be repeated, and therefore carefully warned the French population to remain aloof.[229] The broadcasters added, however, 'We shall warn you when the real invasion comes, and then will be your opportunity to get weapons in to your hands and regain your liberty.' Whether or not this raid was a try-out for a full-scale invasion, it has at least demonstrated that the Allies are able to land troops in large numbers on the most strongly defended points of the French shore – a thing which only a few weeks ago the Germans were boastfully declaring to be impossible.

29 August 1942

Stalingrad on the Volga is still in great danger. After many attempts the Germans have succeeded in crossing the Don at the point where

[228] The German radio had in fact only claimed 83 British planes. The Axis propagandists' view of the action was that it had been a serious attempt at an invasion, saying that a very large fleet offshore was obliged to withdraw when the first landings failed. The action was described as a premature one forced on Churchill by Stalin, and the use of Canadian troops was said to be a deliberate action to bring home to the Americans the great dangers of an attempt at a landing without adequate preparation. Orwell here gives the British view of the attempt.

[229] The Axis propagandists could not deny the existence of these broadcasts, which ran counter to their suggestions that the attempt had been at a full-scale invasion; instead they referred to them as a cover designed to conceal the real purposes of the attack if it should fail. As gratitude for the co-operation of the local population, Hitler ordered the release of all French prisoners of war from the Dieppe area.

this river and the Volga pass close to one another, and Stalingrad is menaced by attacks converging from several sides. It has been very heavily bombed. During the last day or two, however, the German attacks have not made much progress, and the Russian forces still west of the Don are counter-attacking strongly in the neighbourhood of Kletsk. [*Censored*: If Stalingrad should definitely fall into German hands it will be difficult to defend Astrakhan, which lies on the north-western shore of the Caspian Sea and is the key point of all the sea and river communications of this area. Should Astrakhan fall, the northern and southern Russian forces will be effectively cut off from one another. How decisive this might be depends upon the quantities of oil, ammunition and other war materials which the Russians have already stored at various strategic points.]

Further south, the Germans claim that some of their troops have reached the mouth of the Kuban river on the Black Sea thus encircling the Russian forces in the neighbourhood of Novorossiysk. They also claim that other detachments have already reached the highest points in the Caucasus mountains.[230] These claims are not confirmed from other sources,[231] and should be treated with caution. Some people doubt whether the Germans will try this year to pass directly across the Caucasus mountains, even if they get control of the northern end of the military road. It may be that they will rather try to obtain possession of Astrakhan and thus reach the oilfields by way of the Caspian Sea. Meanwhile, none of their successes is decisive, since unless they can make an end of the Red Armies as a fighting force – and there is no sign of this happening – they have got another winter in the Russian snow before them. It is important, however, that the Red Army should retain its power of counter-attacking, so that the Germans will be obliged to maintain a large army in Russia throughout the winter and not merely a small force which could be relieved at short intervals. During the past fortnight the Russians have carried out an offensive of their own in the Moscow sector, of which

[230] Orwell can only be referring here to a report noticed by the BBC monitors of the successful climbing of Mt Elbrus: 'Berlin, Transocean correspondent Georg Schroeder: "Captain Heinz Groth ... conquered the Elbrus peak in the Caucasus on 21 August, as he told me with a broad smile on his face in Berlin today. This slim tall Captain with sparkling blue eyes in tanned sharp-cut face just loves jokes and wit ... He is still very enthusiastic about the descent he made on skis from the 5,630 metre high pinnacle together with First Lieutenant Leopold, many times German champion in long distance ski racing. It is the longest descent in the world, 4,000 metres of downhill course in a straight line from a mountain which is 800 metres higher than Mont Blanc." '

[231] A camera team accompanied the group to record the climb and the planting of the German flag on the peak.

full reports have now come in. The Russians have made an advance of thirty miles, killed 45,000 Germans and captured a very large quantity of war materials. Fighting is going on in the outskirts of Rzhev, the chief German stronghold in this area. [*Censored:* This successful attack will have its effect upon events further south, if the Germans have to divert extra force to meet it.]

Another great battle, a sequel to the events which we reported last week, is raging in the Solomon Islands. The Americans have succeeded in landing on three of the islands, and hold the most important harbour and some of the airfields. A few days back, the Japanese made an unsuccessful counter-attack, which was beaten off with heavy casualties. They are now attempting to retrieve the position by means of naval action, and so far as can be gathered from the reports, have sent a very strong fleet to attack the American stronghold. Full reports have not yet come in, but it is known that American bombing planes have already hit and damaged a number of Japanese warships including two plane carriers.[232] In all, 14 Japanese ships have been damaged and 33 Japanese aeroplanes destroyed. Ten days ago the Japanese fleet withdrew, but it has evidently reformed and is making a fresh attack. The results of this have not yet been reported. The Japanese have also made another landing in the south-eastern tip of New Guinea, where fighting is now going on. The object of this may either be to make another attempt against Port Moresby, or to draw the American fleet away from the harbours it has captured in the Solomons. Undoubtedly the Japanese will make very strong efforts to dislodge the Americans from Tulagi, and they will be willing to risk large numbers of warships in doing so. They are now, however, fighting at a disadvantage, since their ships have to meet land-based aircraft. This battle in the South Pacific, so confused and so far away,[233] is of the highest importance for India, because whether or not the Japanese are able to invade India depends partly on their strength in aircraft carriers. Every plane-carrier the Americans destroy makes India a fraction safer. We shall probably be able to give fuller news about the Solomon Islands next week.

Brazil has declared war on Germany.[234] This was the logical result of the wanton sinking of Brazilian ships which German submarines had carried out during past weeks. Brazil is the most important of the

[232] Orwell repeats his earlier report and then goes on to give first reports of a naval battle that reached London on 25 August. The smaller of the two carriers was identified as the *Ryuzyo*; the other was not named.

[233] It was of course very far away in Indian terms, as well as from Orwell's studio in London.

[234] War was declared on 22 August.

South American republics, having a population of about 40 million, and being a country of immense size – roughly the same size as India – and immense natural wealth. From a strategic point of view, it is particularly important, because its many excellent harbours and its small but efficient navy will make the patrolling of the Atlantic easier for the Allies. In addition, Rio de Janeiro, the capital of Brazil, is the point at which the Americans are nearest to the Old World, being in fact within easy flying distance of West Africa. The Axis Powers were undoubtedly scheming sooner or later to invade the American continent by way of Brazil,[235] using Dakar in French West Africa as their jumping-off point. They hoped also to make use of a Fifth Column recruited from the large German population of Brazil. Now that Brazil is definitely at war, all Germans of Nazi sympathies are being rapidly rounded up. In addition, the German and Italian ships interned in Brazil harbours have been seized, and will be a very useful addition to the Allied stocks of shipping.[236] Brazil's action in going to war will have its effects on the other South American republics. Uruguay, Brazil's neighbour to the south, though not formally at war, has declared complete solidarity with Brazil, and Chile, previously somewhat tepid towards the Allied cause, has also declared a state of non-belligerency which will be of benefit to the Allies.

The swing-over of opinion in South America during the past three years is a sign of the political failure of the Axis, and the growing understanding all over the world of the real nature of Fascism. At the beginning of the war, many South American countries were somewhat sympathetic towards Germany, with which they had close economic ties. The considerable colonies of Germans in South America acted as publicity agents for their country[237] and in addition the Germans had bought up a number of South American papers which they used to spread false news in their own interest. It should be remembered that only a minority of the population in most South American countries is of European origin. The majorities almost everywhere are American Indians, with a considerable percentage of Negroes. German, and more particularly Japanese, propaganda has tried to inflame the poorer sections of the population and to stimulate anti-white feeling, rather as

[235] This extraordinary suggestion would seem to be another Orwellian fiction, along the lines of his idea that Japan would invade Russia but on an altogether more imaginative scale.

[236] There were in fact 15 ships with a total displacement of 123,000 tons.

[237] At the outbreak of war between Germany and Brazil there were approximately one million German nationals in Brazil, in addition to some 200,000 Japanese and many persons of Italian descent.

the Japanese have attempted to do in Asia. This failed, largely because the Central and South American countries have strong and growing labour movements and their leaders are well aware that the interests of working people everywhere are bound up together, and are menaced by Fascism, however alluring the promises of Fascist propagandists may be.

The ban has been removed from the *Daily Worker*, the daily paper of the British Communist Party. It will reappear on September 7th. [*Censored:* Although the *Daily Worker* was never a very important paper, having at the best only a circulation of about 100,000, it was influential in certain quarters, and at times its attacks on the Government were damaging.[238] In allowing it to circulate again, the British Government has proved clearly that the British claim to be fighting for freedom of speech and of the press is well founded.]

There is not, as yet, any definite news from Egypt, but it can be taken as certain that there will be large-scale action there in the near future. Both the British and the Germans have succeeded in reinforcing their armies and the present position is unsatisfactory from the point of view of both the British and the German commanders. From the British point of view the Germans are dangerously close to Alexandria and the problem of reinforcements is complicated by a long supply line. The Germans have a shorter line of sea communications, but this is open to heavy attack, and their supplies when once landed have to travel long distances overland before reaching the battle area. During the last few days the Germans have lost several oil tankers[239] and other supply ships in the Mediterranean. Whether the Germans or the British will be the first to attack in Egypt we do not predict, but now that the cooler weather is beginning and it is possible for tanks to move in the desert, we must expect to hear news of large-scale action before many weeks have passed.

5 September 1942

September 3rd was the third anniversary of the outbreak of war. Before giving our usual resumé of the week's news, it may be worth

---

[238] Until the invasion of Russia the *Daily Worker* had adopted a neutral or overtly pro-German stance; immediately after the invasion it swung round to a totally anti-German position, but the ban remained. No doubt representations on the subject had been made to Churchill in Moscow. The other paper banned during the war was the sophomoric production *The Week*, published privately by Claud Cockburn.

[239] The German supply situation was critical; Orwell is referring to an Admiralty release which described the sinking of German tankers by British submarines.

while to look back over the past three years and thus see the present phase of the struggle in its true perspective.

If one looks thus at the whole picture and not merely at one corner of it, the fact which stands out is that after three years of desperate war, Britain is far stronger than she was when the war started. Whereas in the autumn of 1939 the entire British Commonwealth was barely able to mobilise a million trained men, and had only a very small air force and depleted navy, to-day there are several million trained men in Britain alone, putting aside the great armies in the Middle East, in India, and in other places. The RAF has grown till it is more than the equal of the German air force, and the Navy, in spite of heavy losses in the unending and difficult work of convoying war materials to Britain, is much more powerful than at the outbreak of war.

When the German commanders survey the situation the fact that their main enemy, Britain, is merely stronger and not weaker after all their attacks, must be the first to strike them. And behind this is the other immense fact that America now stands behind Britain and is rearming upon an enormous scale and at lightning speed in places where neither the German army nor the German air force can affect the process. The other fact which the German commanders have to take into consideration is the continued resistance of Soviet Russia, the complete failure of the Red Army to disintegrate as it was supposed to do in the autumn of 1941, and the frightful drain on German manpower which the Russian campaign represents, especially with another winter in the snow looming two or three months ahead.

Looking back we see that there have been really three turning points in the war and at each of them a Fascist victory receded further into the distance. The first was the Battle of Britain, in the late summer of 1940. The Germans, confident of a quick victory, hurled their air force against Britain and not only suffered heavy losses to no purpose, but were brought to realise that they could not win the war quickly, but had got in front of them a long and exhausting struggle in which almost inevitably the rest of the world would end by turning against them. The next turning point was in the winter of 1941, when the German advance on Russia petered out and the Russians drove the Germans back from Rostov. The German attack on Russia had been a direct result of the successful British resistance and the British sea blockade. Unable to break out and establish communications with Asia and America, the Germans had planned to conquer Russia at one blow, after which they would have at their disposal an enormous area which could be plundered of almost all the raw materials they needed, while at the same time they would no longer have the Red Army as a perpetual menace to their rear, so that they could devote their whole forces to a renewed attack on Britain. This also failed, and the Germans, in spite of great gains of territory, found themselves in for an exhausting struggle in which they were fighting against tremendous manpower and impossible climatic conditions, while their air force was so heavily engaged that they could not prevent the RAF from pounding the cities of Western Germany. The third turning point was when Germany succeeded in pushing Japan into the war. The Japanese were mainly concerned with the conquest of East Asia, but the plan from the German point of view was to divert the attention of the Americans and prevent them from sending further aid to Britain. Once again the great gamble failed, for though the Japanese won easy victories at the beginning, they too soon found themselves in for a protracted struggle against a superior enemy, and the Americans, while fighting the Japanese in the Pacific, were not diverted for a moment from sending men and supplies to Europe. In spite of successes which look brilliant on a short term view, each of the three great gambles of the Fascist powers has failed, and they are able to see gradually forming against them a vast coalition of nearly four-fifths of humanity with overwhelming resources and unalterable determination to make an end of Fascist aggression once and for all. In 1940, Britain was alone, poorly armed and not by any means certain of being joined by further allies. In 1942, Britain has beside her the Red Army, the enormous American war industries and the 400 million human beings of China. However long the struggle may yet be, its end cannot be in much doubt. That is the picture of the war which we see if we look at it in its broad lines and do not allow yesterday's newspaper to occupy the whole of our attention.

We have occupied most of our time in giving this general review of the war, and we shall therefore give only a short summary of this week's events.

In Egypt, the fresh German attack which we foretold in last week's newsletter has begun.[240] It is however too early to give any worthwhile news of it. We will merely utter a warning that the conditions in Egypt are not easy for the Allies, and the fact that the Germans attacked first suggests that they have been successful in replacing the losses of the battles in June and July. The British, however, have also been reinforced and American troops[241] and

---

[240] Rommel's attack started on the night of 30 August. Orwell's warning that follows was unnecessary, as his earlier report of the sinking of vital tankers was correct and for this and other reasons Rommel's attack did not succeed.

[241] Again it is not clear to which American troops Orwell is referring.

aeroplanes are now beginning to take their place on this front. After making a fairly strong attack with their armoured forces, the Germans are now retreating again, but it is not clear yet whether this is because they found the British defences too strong for them or whether it is some kind of feint or manoeuvre. The Allied air forces have been very active in the Mediterranean and have sunk several Axis ships this week. We shall be able to report more fully on the Egyptian situation next week.

The fighting in the Solomon Islands has been a brilliant success for the Allies. The Americans are now more or less in control of six islands and what was particularly important, on the island of Guadalcanal they captured a large air base which the Japanese had almost completed. About five days back, probably in hopes of driving the American fleet away from the Solomons, the Japanese made a fresh landing at Ellne Bay at the south-eastern tip of New Guinea. The force which they landed there has been almost completely destroyed by the Australian forces, and its remnants are now in process of being mopped up. From the northern side of New Guinea, the Japanese have made a fresh attack in the direction of Port Moresby, but with indecisive results. They also appear to have made a fresh landing on one of the Solomon Islands. We may expect them to make very violent efforts to dislodge the Americans from the Solomons, for so long as the Americans remain in possession of these islands the Japanese position in New Guinea is threatened and their chance of attempting the invasion of Australia is almost negligible. Probably, therefore, there will be further sea and air battles to report. Although it is several thousand miles distant, India should watch these struggles in the South Pacific with interest, for on their outcome partly depends the possibility of the Japanese attacking India. They probably will not do so unless they can gain naval and air superiority round the shores of the Bay of Bengal, and consequently each aeroplane carrier destroyed by the Americans makes India a fraction safer.

The position in Russia is still very grave, but has not altered materially since last week. The Germans are still hurling all their forces against Stalingrad and in the last day or two have gained a certain amount of ground south-west of the city. At this moment the most violent fighting is raging almost within gunshot of Stalingrad and the Germans are throwing all the tanks and aeroplanes which they possess into the attack. But up to date the news is that the Russian defences are holding firm. Further south, the Germans have also gained some ground in the drive towards the Grosny oilfields. On the other two fronts, the Moscow front and the Leningrad front, the Russians themselves are still on the offensive. There have been more heavy air raids on Western Germany, and for the first time in this war Gdynia on the Baltic Sea has been bombed. The fact that a town so far away can be bombed from Britain at this time of year, when the nights are still fairly short, shows the great increase in the striking power of the RAF. The Russian air force has recently bombed Berlin. The various proclamations on the subject of air raids which have been issued by the German press and radio shows how seriously the German people, especially in the big industrial towns, are being shaken by ceaseless bombing.

12 September 1942

Last week we reported that fighting had broken out again in Egypt, and added that we hoped to be able to give fragments of it this week. This particular phase of the Egyptian campaign is already over, and has resulted in a severe setback for the Germans. They made what was evidently a large scale effort to break through the Allied defensive positions and were repulsed with very heavy losses, especially of tanks and other vehicles. The actual number of tanks lost by the Germans has not yet been officially reported, but Mr Wendell Willkie, the American envoy to the Turkish government, who passed through Egypt on his way to Ankara, stated that the Germans had lost a hundred tanks, which represents forty per cent of their full strength in Egypt.[242] Mr Churchill also in his recent speech – to which we refer later – has stated that the result of this battle has been to make Egypt safe for some months to come.

It should be remembered that the Egyptian campaign has not finished, the German forces are not destroyed. The losses they have suffered, however, are undoubtedly serious for them, especially their losses in tanks, because of late they have been finding the sea passage from Italy to Africa very costly. During the past week our submarines alone have sunk or damaged twelve Axis supply vessels, and this is in addition to the damage done by Allied aeroplanes. Now that Malta has been reinforced and has fighter planes to guard its aerodromes, it can again be the base from which British bombers attack Axis shipping and ports in Italy and Sicily. On the whole, therefore, we may say that

[242] Figures later released showed that 38 German and 11 Italian tanks had been lost, as against 67 British. For some reason Wendell Willkie and his journeys about the world particularly annoyed the Axis broadcasters, who made repeated attacks on his veracity and sincerity. For his own account, see Wendell L. Willkie, *One World* (1943).

the situation in Egypt has improved very greatly – more greatly indeed than we thought it safe to prophesy a week ago.

Heavy fighting is still going on in central New Guinea, where the Japanese are trying to advance directly over the mountain range which runs along the centre of the island, and reach Port Moresby. They have made a definite advance within the past two days, and are now only about forty-five miles from their objective. Port Moresby cannot be considered safe as long as there are Japanese anywhere in New Guinea. The Japanese have failed to dislodge the Americans from the islands they have seized in the Solomon Archipelago in spite of the fresh landing attempt which they made three days ago.

During the past few weeks, the Chinese have regained a good deal of territory in the Eastern provinces, and have so far frustrated the efforts which the Japanese are making to complete their railway communications north and south. The other objective which they have in this area is to prevent the Chinese getting or keeping possession of any base from which Japan itself could be bombed. At present several towns in Chekiang province which are potential air bases for use against Japan are in Chinese hands. The Japanese efforts to capture them have failed. However, even if the Chinese hold on these areas can be consolidated. That does not mean that the bombing of Japan can begin immediately, because the building up of an air base with all its numerous staff of mechanics, its buildings, workshops and supplies of oil, ammunition and spare parts for repairs is a long business. Moreover, the transport difficulties are very great since the Burma Road, originally the chief route for war materials entering China, is in Japanese hands. Air transport, however, is being improved and new routes into China from India are being opened up. When these are fully established the advantage of possessing bases within bombing distance of Japan can be exploited.

Following on his return from Moscow, Mr Churchill has made a general statement on the war to the House of Commons.[243] This authoritative statement clears up several points about which information was previously lacking. Perhaps the most important reference Mr Churchill made in his speech was to the Dieppe raid, which he described as being a reconnaissance in force, necessary in order to obtain information for larger operations later. Mr Churchill naturally made no mention of dates or places, but left it quite clear that an invasion of Europe is contemplated and will be undertaken at the appropriate moment. He explained that in his talks with Premier Stalin he had reached complete agreement and had both convinced

[243] On 8 September.

himself of the readiness of the Russian people to go on fighting in no matter what circumstances and of our own readiness to make whatever sacrifices may be necessary to take the pressure off our allies. Mr Churchill added that the Russians felt that they had had to make an unduly great part of the common effort – a feeling which, considering the history of the past year, was not unjustifiable. All they needed from ourselves, however, was an assurance that we would make a diversion when opportunity served, and this assurance they now have. Mr Churchill also made a statement on the Egyptian campaign and gave an assurance about the defence of Egypt which we have mentioned already. He explained that he had separated the command of the Tenth Army in Persia from that of the Eighth Army in Egypt in order to prevent the Commander in Egypt from being overburdened with what might prove to be a double campaign.[244] For Mr Churchill also mentioned the possibility of the British army in Persia being used in direct aid to the Russian armies in the Caucasus area. Mr Churchill also spoke of the recent naval battle in the Mediterranean as a result of which the British convoy reached Malta with much-needed supplies. The arrival of this convoy, he said, had made Malta's position secure for many months and though the naval losses were heavy – an old aircraft carrier, two cruisers, one of which was a new one, and a destroyer – this price was not unduly high since the effect was to keep Malta in being as an air and submarine base. The Axis losses in aeroplanes and U-boats destroyed and warships damaged were in any case heavy.

Mr Churchill was also able to disclose that the sea war on which both the food and the armaments of Britain finally depend had taken a decided turn for the better during the past three months. The rate at which Americans are building ships is now decidedly higher than the rate at which Axis submarines are sinking them, and the submarines themselves are being harassed so successfully that there is hardly a day on which the news of a submarine being either sunk or damaged does not come in. Our bombing raids on Western Germany, on the ports in which the submarines are built, also have an indirect beneficial effect on the sea war.

[244] Orwell skates very rapidly here over changes that would not have sounded well to an Indian audience. In particular, General Auchinleck was the most highly regarded Indian Army man in the Middle East and yet he had been removed from overall command and had declined the command of the Tenth Army. The double campaign would have been the fighting on two fronts, inevitable if the Germans had succeeded in crossing the Caucasus.

19 September 1942

British sea, air and land forces have carried out a daring raid at Tobruk more than a hundred miles behind the enemy's lines in Egypt.[245] Although the full results have not yet been disclosed, it is known that the British raiding party lost two destroyers,[246] and probably some prisoners and that they did very heavy damage. Tobruk is now the principal port used by the Germans to bring war materials from Greece or even from Italy, and the object of the raid was to supplement the damage already done by the bombing planes of the RAF. [It is outside the range of any but heavy bombers, and the object of a commando raid on such a place would be to carry out more accurate destruction than could be achieved from the air.][247]

We may be sure that there will be further large-scale operations in Egypt and the advantage will lie with whichever side can get ready to strike first. This is largely a matter of bringing war materials over sea. Raids of this type if successfully carried out might upset the German plans almost as effectively as sinking their ships in transit.

The fighting in New Guinea appears to be stationary for the time being and we may hope that the Japanese advance towards Port Moresby has been stopped, though they are certain to make fresh attacks in this direction. During the past week there has been very heavy fighting on the island of Guadalcanal where the Japanese have succeeded in landing fresh troops. The Americans hold the main port of the island and the airfield, and the Japanese efforts to dislodge them have failed. Reports coming from China, however, suggest that a large Japanese fleet is approaching the Solomon Islands and we must expect them to make the most desperate efforts to recapture these islands, which so long as they are in American hands, endanger their whole position in the South Pacific. The Americans express themselves confident of being able to hold on and to use the Solomon Islands as a base for further advances.

The Germans are still concentrating every man, tank and aeroplane

[245] Known as Operation Daffodil, it was unsuccessful, though whether Orwell would have known that is doubtful. Reports in the British press from MOI releases were very misleading, saying that the troops had withdrawn in good order. The Axis broadcasters' reports of a débacle with large numbers of prisoners taken and three destroyers lost was close to the truth. They compared the action to that at Dieppe.

[246] There were in fact three destroyers lost, *Sikh*, *Zulu* and *Coventry*.

[247] This passage was deleted by Orwell himself before censorship.

they can muster upon the attack on Stalingrad. Since last week they have advanced in certain sectors and in places they have even penetrated into the town where street fighting is said to be going on. Both sides have been reinforced within the past few days. On this front, the Germans have a considerable preponderance of aeroplanes, especially dive bombers, which they are using in immense numbers. The Russians are resisting with the utmost courage and obstinacy but the situation of Stalingrad must be regarded as extremely grave and it is becoming harder and harder to reinforce it. We do not care to prophesy one way or the other as to whether Stalingrad will hold out. If it does not, the Germans probably cannot be prevented from reaching the Caspian Sea, and the Volga ceases to be of any use as a means of communication. If the Germans reached Astrakhan, the Caspian Sea itself would cease to be at any rate a safe route for the transport of oil and other supplies, as almost its whole area could be ranged by German aeroplanes.[248] On the other hand it is already the middle of September and there is no sign as yet that the Germans are within sight of getting across the Caucasus mountains and reaching the Baku oilfields, which are their real objective. Novorossiysk on the Black Sea has fallen into German hands and they may possibly attempt to bypass the mountains by moving down the coast of the Black Sea. On the other Russian fronts the Germans are either making no progress or the Russians themselves are taking the offensive. They have just launched another offensive in the Voronezh area. It is significant that the Germans are already making preparations for a winter campaign, are building fortified positions well behind their lines in Russia and are scouring the whole of Europe for furs and other warm clothes.[249] They probably expect, therefore, to have to keep a large army on the Russian fronts, including the northern fronts, throughout the winter, in which case they will inevitably lose great numbers of men from the cold, though their preparations to meet it may be better this winter than last. The importance of the battle now being fought round Stalingrad lies in the fact that if the Germans do not take Stalingrad, they cannot avoid forcing millions of their soldiers to spend the winter in the Russian snow. If they do take Stalingrad, they hope that the northern Russian armies may be unable to get their supplies of oil, in which case the

[248] Orwell had in fact implied this in his warning earlier about having to fight a double battle. The British Military Attaché in Moscow at the time thought that the Caucasus would be crossed within a month of the beginning of the campaign, and this was a widely held belief.

[249] German broadcasts for the home audience at this time were filled with appeals for warm clothing of all sorts, giving detailed instructions on delivery points and so on.

Germans could hold these fronts with comparatively few men who could be relieved at short intervals. We do not yet know whether this is the case, because naturally we do not know what stocks of oil and other war materials the Russians have stored at Moscow, Leningrad and other places in the north. The preparations which the Germans are making for a winter war suggest that they have reason to think that the Russians will be by no means incapable of making another offensive this winter.

The operations in Madagascar are proceeding smoothly and the seaports which were the principal objective are already in British hands. The British forces are still fifty or a hundred miles from the capital Antananarivo, but are likely to reach it within the next few days. Two days ago a report was put out that the French Government of the island asked for an armistice. This has since been denied and it is probable that the Vichy Government has put heavy pressure on the French authorities to put up a pretence of resistance. In fact, however, resistance has been negligible and it is quite clear that the Vichy regime has not much support from the French population and little or none from the indigenous population. The shouts of anger which have gone forth from the German radio over the British occupation of Madagascar demonstrate that the Germans rightly regard this island as being of great strategic importance. Points on its coast line were in fact being used for refuelling Axis submarines, and the elimination of this danger will appreciably ease the Allied shipping situation.[250] The local officials are carrying on their work under the British military authorities and there is not likely to be any interruption to the food supplies or the life of the island generally.

It is reported that Axis agents have made an unsuccessful attempt to assassinate the President of Nicaragua.[251] Brazil, the latest ally of the United Nations, is increasing its armed forces. From Argentina comes the news of big popular demonstrations of solidarity with Brazil, making it clear that the common people of the country are much more friendly to the Allied cause than the government of the moment.

The British bombing raids on Western Germany continue and are now too frequent to be enumerated individually. The RAF are now dropping bombs which weigh no less than 8,000 pounds or $3\frac{1}{2}$ tons. These bombs do not penetrate into the ground but burst on the surface, devastating the houses for hundreds of yards round. Aerial photographs of Karlsruhe, Düsseldorf and other places show whole

[250] There was no evidence for this apparently, and Orwell is merely repeating an MOI propaganda line.

[251] The Axis propagandists did not claim responsibility for the attempt, but reported it instead as an attempted Nationalist Putsch.

areas of hundreds of acres where there is scarcely a house with its roof intact. Neutral travellers arriving from Germany have reported that morale in Western Germany is suffering considerably under the continuous raid to which the German air force seems able to make no reply.

Four days ago, September 15th, was celebrated throughout this country and the world as the second anniversary of the Battle of Britain. Between August and October 1940, after the fall of France, the Germans made an all-out effort to conquer Britain by air and loudly boasted that they would be able to do so within a few weeks. They started off in August and September with daylight raids aimed at destroying the Royal Air Force, and when this had evidently failed, switched over to night raids directed chiefly at the working-class areas in the East End of London, aiming at terrorising the civilian population.[252] The whole manoeuvre however was a failure and in about two months of air warfare the Germans lost between two and three thousand planes, with some thousands of irreplaceable airmen. September 15th is celebrated as the anniversary because on that day the Royal Air Force shot down no less than 185 German planes, and it was about that date that the failure of the Germans to overwhelm the British defences by daylight bombing became apparent. Now that we can look back and see the events in better perspective it is becoming clear that the Battle of Britain ranks in importance with Trafalgar, Salamis, the defeat of the Spanish Armada and other battles of the past in which the invading forces of a seemingly invincible monarch or dictator have been beaten back and which have formed a turning point in history.

26 September 1942

The situation at Stalingrad is better than we felt ready to predict a week ago. During this week, the Germans have been making desperate efforts to fight their way into the heart of the city and literally every yard of ground has had to be bought with many lives. The Germans, however, have made very little progress and during the past few days the Russians have won back some of the ground which they lost earlier. The Stalingrad battle has no doubt already been a severe

---

[252] The beginnings of another propaganda line in answer to the German protests at the Allied bombing of exclusively civilian targets. The Indian audiences would not know, of course, that the East End of London also meant the docks.

drain on German manpower as in this type of fighting it is impossible to gain any objective without heavy loss of life and the advantage is usually with the defenders.[253] The situation is still extremely grave, but even if the Germans were to gain full possession of Stalingrad tomorrow, it would still have held them up for about six weeks longer than they expected.

The announcements of the German wireless have now ceased, not only promising an early end to the war but even promising the early capture of Stalingrad. On the contrary, all the emphasis in the Axis broadcasts is on the extreme difficulty of the present battle and on the necessity of the German people preparing themselves for a long war. During the past few days one or two of the German broadcasters have begun to suggest that, after all, Stalingrad is not very important, and that its capture <? is therefore not important> is a direct contradiction of what the Germans themselves were saying a few days earlier, and suggests that they are now beginning to be doubtful whether Stalingrad will, in fact, ever fall into their hands. We may be certain that they will make further desperate efforts to take it, for if this part of their campaign should fail they will have to retreat to a shorter line for the winter. This would mean relinquishing some of the territory they have won during the summer, and it would then be difficult to prevent the German people from asking why so much blood had been shed in vain. There are some significant signs of restlessness among the minor partners in the Axis. Rumania, Bulgaria and Hungary are hardly likely to get any solid gains from the war in the event of an Axis victory, and the common people in these countries, at any rate Bulgaria and Rumania, are strongly pro-Russian in sentiment.[254] They are doubtless beginning to realise that the Germans are simply using them as cannon fodder and that the prospects which their leaders thought a little while back they had before them of seizing large territories without having to fight for them were illusory. Budapest, the capital of Hungary, was recently bombed by the Red Air Force. No doubt this will be repeated and the fact that war is a serious business and not simply a matter of easy looting of defenceless peoples will be brought home more and more to the petty dictators who follow in Hitler's train.

Simultaneously with the attack on Tobruk which took place more than a week ago it is now learned that British land-forces made a most

[253] A direct reference to Orwell's experience of street fighting in the Spanish Civil War.

[254] Orwell's first mention of the other troops fighting on the Russian front. The suggestion that the average Romanian was pro-Russian would have been questioned by any citizen of Sebastopol.

daring raid five hundred miles or more in the rear of the Axis armies. Reports of this were only released three days ago. It now appears that the British land forces raided Benghazi,[255] the main Axis port in Libya, and destroyed thirty aircraft on the ground, made a similar attack on the port of Barce while another force seized the desert oasis of Jalo, held it for two days and destroyed the ammunition dumps and other war materials before returning to their base. It is too early to say whether these raids are the prelude to further large-scale operations in Egypt. But their effect must be to force the Germans to use more troops in guarding their lines of communication and thus weaken their main striking force. Reports which have come in suggest that the German commander in Egypt has already begun to regroup his forces.

In the Solomon Islands the Japanese efforts to recapture the port and airfield on the island of Guadalcanal have failed. There have been several reports of powerful Japanese forces approaching the islands, and during the past week there have been two engagements between Japanese ships and American bombing planes.[256] For the moment it appears that the Japanese naval force has been obliged to retreat. There are indications, however, that the Japanese are going to make another strong effort to recapture the Solomons, and from what they have lost already we must assume that they regard these islands as so important as to be worth very heavy losses. Probably, therefore, there will be more fighting to report from this area during the next week. In the island of New Guinea the Japanese advance towards Port Moresby has been brought to a halt. The Japanese forces which landed at Milne Bay, at the eastern end of the island, have now been completely annihilated.[257]

During the past few weeks several distinguished politicians have succeeded in escaping from France and reaching Britain. This is very important for two reasons. In the first place, it indicates the almost

---

[255] This was Operation Snowdrop, an SAS operation commanded by David Stirling; it too was something less than a success. The raid had become known to the Germans in the minutest detail through lax security. No planes were destroyed, and the force suffered heavy losses. The raid on Barce, Operation Hyacinth, was carried out by the Long Range Desert Group with some results. It was there, in fact, that the planes were destroyed. Jalo, the intended first staging-post on the escape route, was in fact never captured and those arriving from Benghazi merely joined in the fighting en route.

[256] The US Navy had announced hits on three transport ships near Shortland Island on 24 September and other general attacks.

[257] The Japanese landing at Milne Bay, under cover of darkness, had taken place on 29 August. General MacArthur had announced the expulsion of the force by Australian troops under Major-General C.A. Clowes on 31 August, some weeks before Orwell's broadcast reference here. There may have been some delay before the full press release reached the MOI.

complete lack of popular support for the puppet regime of Vichy, and secondly, through these fresh arrivals we can get first-hand and up to date information about internal conditions in both Occupied and Unoccupied France. There can be no doubt even on the evidence of the Germans themselves that resentment against the German occupation is growing stronger and stronger. For example, only the other day the Germans announced that they had just executed no less than 160 people[258] in the single town of Paris. This tale of reprisals and executions is repeated over and over all through occupied Europe, not to mention those areas like Jugoslavia where a state amounting to civil war exists. What we learn, however, from the new arrivals from France, is of the formation of a new political alliance between all patriotic sections in the occupied countries. Political parties which previously regarded one another as deadly enemies are now completely united in their opposition to the invader. The most distinguished political figure to reach England in recent weeks was M.André Philip, the French socialist. He has been followed by several other socialists, but more recently by M.Charles Vallin, who was previously one of the leading figures of the Croix de Feu – a French Fascist organisation. This Fascist party of course favoured collaboration with the German invader. It now appears, however, that the cruelty and exactions of German rule have become so unbearable[259] that even some of the French Fascists are beginning to revolt and to throw in their lot with the parties of the Left. M.Vallin has come to England to help organise common resistance. All this resistance in the occupied countries, of course, has to go on in secret, but the Germans have been quite unable to prevent it or even to prevent the appearance of secretly printed newspapers, of which great numbers, some of them with circulations of many thousands, are appearing in France and throughout Western Europe.

It was announced during this week that another big convoy of Allied ships carrying war materials has arrived safely in northern Russian ports. Some ships were lost on the way but the great majority

---

[258] In fact 116, no doubt a literal mistake in transcribing the monitors' report. The executions were announced by General Stulpnagel on 18 September as a reprisal for Resistance murders of French civilians.

[259] Orwell for some reason does not mention here the specific grounds for the rapid and widespread sense of outrage among all people in France, viz. the treatment of the Jews. There was a joint protest by the Catholic cardinals and bishops in the occupied zone, and in Vichy France a major rift developed between the Catholic hierarchy and the Vichy Government over the question, several Jesuit priests being imprisoned for refusing to hand over Jewish children who had been entrusted to their care. These feelings were shared by many who had acquiesced until this point in the German presence.

got through and only one of the naval vessels escorting the convoy, a destroyer, was lost. The Germans lost at least ten aeroplanes besides several submarines. This route by which war materials are carried to the northern Russian armies is the most dangerous of all because the convoys have to skirt the Norwegian coasts where they can be attacked and observed all the way by land-based aircraft. Nevertheless a steady supply of materials has continued to reach our Russian allies by this route and the successful defence of Leningrad can no doubt be partly attributed to these supplies.

British troops have occupied Antananarivo, capital of Madagascar. They were cheered by all sections of the population when they entered the town, and the administration is functioning smoothly. The Vichy Governor has fled and declares his intention of keeping up resistance,[260] but it is evident that such opposition as was put up by the French garrison of the island is at an end.

3 October 1942

The battle for Stalingrad continues. Since last week the Germans have made a little progress in their direct attacks on the city and savage house-to-house fighting is still going on. Meanwhile the Russians have launched a counter-attack to the north-west of Stalingrad which has made progress and must have the effect of drawing off some of the German reserves.

It is still uncertain whether or not Stalingrad can hold out. In a recent speech the notorious Ribbentrop, onetime ambassador to Britain and signatory to the Russo-German pact, was allowed to state that Stalingrad would soon be in German hands.[261] Hitler made the same boast in his speech which was broadcast on September 10th. Elsewhere, however, there has been a marked note of pessimism in German pronouncements and a constant emphasis on the need for the German people to prepare themselves for a hard winter and for an indefinite continuation of the war.

In this connection the report recently given to *The Times*[262] by a neutral who had just left Germany and has also been in the occupied parts of Russia, is of great interest. The picture as he paints it is something like this. The Germans have now occupied enormous areas

[260] M. Annet had retreated to Fort Dauphin.
[261] The speech referred to is one made on 27 September on the Tripartite Pact.
[262] For 30 September.

which contain almost all that they need in the way of food and raw materials but are barely able to exploit them because they have been unable to obtain the co-operation of the conquered peoples. This neutral visitor describes seeing farms in the Ukraine being worked by German gang labour including boys as young as fourteen. The intention the Germans previously had of setting up puppet regimes in the occupied parts of Russia appears to have been abandoned. It would be impossible for them to set up any quisling administration that could gain the obedience of the population and they are consequently obliged to rely on direct military rule. As to Germany's internal condition, this visitor considered that the morale of the German army is still good and that the people are still ready for great sacrifices but that there has been a great falling off in confidence. The failure of the Russian campaign to bring about any decisive result has disappointed all expectations and so also has the failure of the German Army in Africa to overrun Egypt and capture the Suez Canal. Meanwhile the RAF raids make life in Western Germany less and less bearable, and it is generally recognised that these are only a foretaste of what is coming when the British and American air forces have reached their full expansion. Corroborating what this neutral observer says, we may notice that German home propaganda during recent months has concentrated more and more on terrifying the German population with stories of what will happen to them should they be defeated.[263] The old fables about an international Jewish conspiracy are brought forth again and the Germans are told that should the war go against them, they have nothing to hope for except slavery. This of course is a lie, but it is exceedingly significant that the German Government should consider it a lie worth telling. For two years ago, or even a year ago, the possibility of defeat was not even envisaged. The tune played on the radio was not 'What will happen to us if we lose', but 'What we shall do after we have won'.

In general the present situation has considerable parallels with the situation in 1918. At that time the Germans had overrun most of the

[263] The main story was that German children would be removed from their parents and brought up in an entirely un-Germanic environment with no knowledge of their ancestry. The story originated partly in reports in the neutral press but also in a well-known case of some 5,000 Spanish children who had been taken to Russia at the end of the Spanish Civil War. Broadcasts from the Spanish Blue Division fighting on the Russian Front made references to the fate of these children as one of the main reasons for their fighting, and some of these 5,000 had been found fighting in the Russian ranks. The fate the Germans themselves had imposed on the children of Lidice and elsewhere cannot have been far from their minds. The other stories referred to by Orwell had been in circulation continuously, as a glance at the speeches of Hitler and the others will show.

territories they have overrun now, and though it is true that they had not got possession of France or Norway, and had not got Italy on their side, on the other hand they could draw on the vast resources of the Turkish Empire with territories stretching right down to the borders of Egypt. But then as now it was impossible for them to make the conquered territories into a paying concern,[264] and for precisely the same reasons, that the behaviour of the invaders roused such hatred that it was impossible to make the conquered populations work. In the Ukraine the peasants either left the land uncultivated or hid their grain, and the attempt to set up a quisling was a miserable failure. The reactions of the population at home were also very similar. They had had many victories and yet never seemed any nearer to final victory. And meanwhile the lists of casualties mounted into millions and the food situation got steadily worse. As all the world knows, the German armies suddenly collapsed in the late summer of 1918 only a few months after winning what had appeared to be their greatest victory. We do not predict that a similar collapse will take place before the Germans have received a decisive defeat on land, but we do point out how the general situation has deteriorated from the German point of view and how ominous it must seem to ordinary thinking Germans to see the repetition of events very similar to those which last time led to disaster.

From other fronts than the Russian one there is not a great deal to report. The most important news this week is that the Australian forces in New Guinea have launched a small-scale offensive and made some progress. They have already pushed the Japanese off the central ridge of the mountains that ran from end to end of the island,[265] and the latest news is that the advance was continuing. The success of the Australian attack appears to have been largely due to superiority in the air. It should be remembered, however, that the whole of this operation is on a small scale, and it is too early to say whether it will have any decisive results. The Japanese claim to have occupied some more small islands lying between New Guinea and the Australian mainland. This claim has not yet been confirmed from Allied sources and should be treated with suspicion. As long as Port Moresby remains in Allied hands the Japanese are not likely to make any serious attempt on the mainland of Australia and they probably would not make a landing on islands which are in an isolated position and liable to heavy bombing from the air.

[264] A strange phrase for Orwell to use, probably calculated to annoy his Axis counterparts who despised the profit motive and what they called 'plutocrats'.

[265] The Australian attack was launched on 28 September, and by the following day they had occupied Ioribaiwa ridge and were continuing their assault.

During the past forty-eight hours the British have launched a successful attack in Egypt, straightening out a small salient and driving the enemy back several miles.[266] At this moment fighting is probably still going on. This appears to be only a local action and too much should not be expected of it. We may be able to give a fuller report next week.

The position of the Germans in Egypt has probably been much weakened by the successful attacks made on their supply routes by Allied aircraft and submarines. It was recently revealed[267] that during the past four or five months the amount of Axis shipping sunk in the Mediterranean by RAF planes alone was more than 60,000 tons. This is in addition to the sinkings by Allied submarines which during the past week have sunk five Axis supply ships in this area. The effect of these Allied successes is to prevent the Germans from effectively using the port of Tobruk and make them bring their supplies by the comparatively short sea journey from Sicily to Benghazi, which imposes much delay and compels the Germans to feed their armies by a thin supply line running along the coast, where it is subject to constant bombing.

Hitler's latest speech was broadcast on September 30th.[268] Although it mostly consisted of wild boasting and threats, it made a surprising contrast with the speeches of a year ago. Gone were the promises of an early victory, and gone also the claims, made more than a year ago, to have annihilated the Russian armies. Instead all the emphasis was on Germany's ability to withstand a long war. Here for example are some of Hitler's earlier broadcast statements: On the 3rd September 1941: 'Russia is already broken and will never rise again.' On the 3rd October 1941: 'The Russians have lost at least 8 to 10 million men. No army can recover from such losses.' He also boasted at the same time of the imminent fall of Moscow. That was a year ago. And now, on 30th September, the final boast upon which Hitler ended his speech was: 'Germany will never capitulate.' It seems strange to look back and remember how short a while ago the Germans were declaring, not that they would never capitulate, but that they would make everyone else capitulate. Hitler also uttered threats against saboteurs, a tacit admission that the German home front is no longer entirely reliable.

M. Herriot, onetime President of the French Republic, has been

---

[266] This was an attack on 30 September by the 131st Brigade of 44 Division led by Lt.-Gen. Brian Horrocks. It was not an entire success, being called off a day later, with important lessons learned for the future Battle of El Alamein.

[267] I have not been able to locate Orwell's source for these figures.

[268] This was Hitler's speech at the Sportspalast.

arrested by the Vichy authorities because of his courageous stand against the policy of 'collaboration' with the German invader.[269] The arrest of so popular and deeply respected a man is simply one more confession of the political failure of the Vichy regime, and the contempt and hatred in which all decent Frenchmen hold the small clique of so-called collaborators.

10 October 1942

Stalingrad is holding firm, and there is even some reason to think that the Germans may have abandoned the hope of taking it. Both Hitler and Ribbentrop, in their recent speeches, spoke of Stalingrad as though it were about to fall, but more recently the German High Command have issued a statement to the effect that they were going to abandon direct assaults on the town and attempt to reduce it by artillery bombardment.[270] This may mean that they believe that they can blast the remaining defenders out of Stalingrad by using the heavy artillery with which they reduced Sebastopol, but it may on the other hand mean that they have given up hope of crossing the Volga at this point and are doing their best to save face with the German home public.

The battle for Stalingrad has now been going on for nearly two months, and must certainly have cost the Germans some tens of thousands of men, without any corresponding gain. This is now the beginning of October, and we may say that in spite of the large territories which the Germans have overrun, and even if Stalingrad should fall, the German campaign this year has not quite attained its object, missing it by a narrow margin, as did the campaign of 1941. We may be certain that the German objective this year was to reach the Caspian Sea and to cross the Caucasus Mountains, after which Germany's oil problem would have been a comparatively simple matter. We are safe now in saying that it is too late for the Germans to complete this programme, and in addition the prolonged defence of Stalingrad has given time for the northern Russian armies to be

[269] M. Herriot was formerly President of the Chamber of Deputies but was removed when that post was abolished by Pétain and Laval in a decree of 26 August. He was arrested on 2 October and confined to his residence.

[270] This statement has not been found in the monitors' reports, but a restatement of it appears in a broadcast to Spain which Orwell may well have seen as it is placed in the Summary of World Broadcasts immediately before the section relating to Axis broadcasts to India.

reinforced and to receive fresh supplies. Even if the Germans should capture Stalingrad, cross the Volga River and thus, in effect, cut the Russian front into two halves, this probably will not reduce the fighting power of the Russian armies as it would have done a couple of months ago. We may conclude that the German dream of driving the Russians back behind the Ural Mountains and reducing them to mere guerilla activity will have to be abandoned .

We mentioned last week the speech made by Hitler in which a decidedly different tone was apparent from that of his triumphant speeches of a year or two earlier. This has been followed by a rather similar speech by Goering,[271] and from this and other indications we can probably infer the new plan of campaign which has been forced on the Germans by their failure to conquer either Britain or Russia.

Both Goering and Hitler dropped the claims made earlier to have destroyed the Soviet armies once and for all. They merely claimed to have driven the Russians far enough back to prevent an invasion of Europe, and at the same time dwelt upon the wealth of the territories they had conquered. Both declared that Germany is ready for a long war and Goering in his speech made it abundantly clear that Germany's new plan is to plunder Europe in order to keep the German war machine going. He said that the British blockade did not affect Germany since the whole of Europe is at Germany's disposal, and added bluntly that whoever went hungry in Europe, it would not be the Germans. We can see, therefore, that the specious talk of a year ago about the New Order, and about Europe, freed from British and American influence, raising its standard of living under German guidance, has been dropped. Instead, the Germans come forward quite undisguisedly as a nation of slave-masters[272] who are going to keep the other European races in subjection and plunder them of their food and other goods in order to sustain the attacks of the United Nations. This is an important development because it means that the Germans are more or less throwing away their opportunities of winning the real allegiance of the countries they have overrun. Quite possibly these speeches are the prelude to some kind of peace offer in which the Germans would claim that they have no wish for further expansion, that the war has consequently lost any meaning. Similar speeches made recently in Tokyo suggest that the Japanese may be contemplating a similar strategy. The United Nations, however, are not likely to be deceived, and the chance of any premature peace which

[271] The Harvest Thanksgiving Day speech given by Goering to an assembly of German farm workers and their families on 4 October.

[272] This is an allusion to part of Goering's speech referring to 6 million foreign workers in Germany and 5 million prisoners of war, all of whom had to be fed.

would allow the Fascist Powers to renew their aggressions after a year or two can be written off.

In New Guinea, the Australian advance is continuing and little opposition is being encountered, though the advance is necessarily slow because of the difficult nature of the country. The Allies still have air superiority in this area. The Japanese retreat from the position which they had reached quite near to Port Moresby is capable of several interpretations, and we do not care to comment on it at this stage. There is still serious fighting on the island of Guadalcanal, where the Japanese have several times landed fresh troops under cover of darkness and are attempting to win back the port and airfields captured by the Americans. Further north, at another island in the Solomons group, American planes have made another successful raid and damaged several Japanese warships.

The Americans have occupied fresh islands in the Aleutian Archipelago and are establishing airfields there. As a result, the Japanese-held island of Kiska is already being bombed by land-based American planes.[273] So far as can be discovered by air reconnaissance, the Japanese have now abandoned the other islands they had occupied in the Aleutian Archipelago and are only holding on to the island of Kiska.

British bombing raids on Germany continue. Now that the nights are longer the bombers can go further east, and several parts of the Baltic Sea have been bombed during the past week or two. More and more American planes are now taking part in the RAF raids. Yesterday, the biggest daylight raid of the war was carried out over northern France. About 600 Allied planes took part and only four failed to return. This may be compared with the biggest daylight raid carried out by the Germans, on September 15th, 1940, when 500 or 600 German planes came over Britain and 185 were shot down.

There have also been successful raids on German bases in occupied Norway. In these raids a new British light bomber, the Mosquito, has played a conspicuous part. The full details of the Mosquito have not yet been released for publication, but it is evident that it is a very light and very fast bombing plane, especially suited to daylight raids. We shall probably be able to give further particulars about it later.

[273] Reports reaching London on 5 October said that the first of these raids took place on 1-2 October. The islands Orwell goes on to refer to were the Andreanos group.

The British and United States Governments have just announced[274] that they are relinquishing all extra-territorial rights in China. This applies to Free China immediately, and will apply to the whole of China after the war. For about a century past various European nations have had concessions in Shanghai, Tientsin and other Chinese cities, and they were not subject to Chinese law, and also had the power to station their own troops in China and to enjoy various other privileges. This is now coming to an end as the result of an agreement between the British, American and Chinese Governments. This step not only demonstrates the mutual trust and friendship between China and the rest of the United Nations, but marks the final emergence of China as a modern nation on an equality with the western powers. It is a fitting tribute for today's anniversary of the Chinese revolution.[275]

Yesterday it was announced that Abyssinia is entering into full alliance with the United Nations.[276] Abyssinia was the first country to be overwhelmed by Fascist aggression, and also the first to be liberated. The Abyssinians are now ready to place their military and economic resources at the disposal of those who helped to set them free. In these two events we see how the world-wide struggle of the free peoples against aggression is growing steadily stronger.

17 October 1942

After a lull of some days the German attacks on Stalingrad have been resumed and appear to have made some progress. The German High Command seem to have realised that they cannot take the town by direct infantry assault, and to have been waiting until they could bring up more artillery and dive-bombers in order to make a preliminary bombardment. Evidently they are now using the very big guns which they used in the capture of Sebastopol. The effect of

[274] The announcement came in the form of notes delivered to the Chinese Chargé d'Affaires in London and Washington expressing Britain and America's intention to submit a treaty to this effect to the Chinese Government at some time in the not too distant future.

[275] Axis propaganda described the proposals as meaningless and pointed out that the British had just granted to American troops in the United Kingdom the same privileges that they were now renouncing in China – trial by their own rather than British Courts, and so on.

[276] President Roosevelt made the announcement on 9 October by acknowledging a letter from Emperor Haile Selassie requesting permission to join the United Nations.

artillery such as this is worse even than air bombing and the heroic defenders of Stalingrad may have before them an even more terrible ordeal than that of the last two months. On the other hand, two facts should be mentioned which justify some degree of optimism. The first is that the Russian defenders of Stalingrad are in a very much better position than those of Sebastopol since they have not got their backs to the sea and can fairly easily be supplied and reinforced. The other is the fact demonstrated in the last war that it is difficult even for the heaviest concentration of artillery fire to drive out defenders who have had time, as the Russians have had in this case, to fortify their position thoroughly. It is possible that Stalingrad may yet fall, but the German change of plan so late in the year is a confession of at least partial failure.

Evidence accumulates that the Germans are now thinking in terms of a merely limited victory. They are talking of their impregnable position on the Atlantic coast and of the power Europe has to be self-sufficient in food and raw materials when scientifically organised. The picture which is being drawn by German journalists and broadcasters is of Europe as a vast fortress containing in itself all the necessities of life and invulnerable to any attack from outside. Within this fortress, of course, the German people will be the master race, and the other European peoples will be reduced to varying degrees of serfdom. No doubt, the main object of this new turn in German propaganda is to reconcile the German people to a prospect of endless war[277] and at the same time to persuade the Allies that further attacks are useless. It must be admitted, however, that the picture of Europe as a huge self-contained slave camp is not altogether fanciful. Such an arrangement could be made to work, always provided that it were not assailed from the outside and that there were no serious resistance within. But the ever-increasing British air attacks, the growing strength of the Allied Armies and the increasing discontent and sabotage among the conquered peoples suggest that both these expectations will be disappointed. During this week there has been news of fresh trouble for the German invaders in France, Norway and Jugoslavia. In the latter country guerilla fighting is continuous and all attempts to crush the Serbian patriot forces under General Mihailovitch[278] have failed. In Norway, the quisling administration

[277] The concept of super powers in an endless state of war, hot or cold, which Orwell developed in *Nineteen Eighty-Four* is clearly seen here.

[278] Orwell does not refer here to Tito. The exact position of the different anti-German groups in Yugoslavia then was obscure, and the passage of time has only thrown a limited amount of light on the question. It has been suggested that Mihailovitch also accepted assistance from the Italians.

has been a miserable failure and it is hardly even pretended that it represents the will of the people. In France, the attempt to get together a large draft of volunteers to work in Germany has also failed; the Germans demanded 150,000 men, and though as a bribe they offered to release a corresponding number of war prisoners, only a few thousands have volunteered.[279] The conquered people of Europe have by this time fully grasped the hollowness of the so-called 'New Order', and though the Germans may still hold millions of men as slaves, they have probably lost all chance of obtaining their willing cooperation.

As we foretold earlier the Japanese are making very determined efforts to recapture the islands in the Solomons occupied by the Americans. They are directing their attacks particularly against the island of Guadalcanal, where the Americans hold a port and an airfield from which they can attack Japanese shipping with land-based aeroplanes. During the past week the Japanese have landed various detachments of men on the south side of Guadalcanal under cover of darkness. Four days ago they attempted a landing on a large scale and received very severe damage in a naval action.[280] A Japanese cruiser and four destroyers were sunk. Other warships were damaged and the United States losses were only one destroyer. On the following day the sinking of another Japanese cruiser by submarine action was announced. Since then, however, the Japanese have made a fresh landing and appear to have succeeded in bringing artillery ashore. Fierce attacks both from land and sea are being made on the American-held airfields. The Americans expect to be able to hold their positions, but do not disguise the fact that there is a hard struggle ahead. The Australian advance in Central New Guinea is still continuing and for some time past little opposition has been met with. No one knows why, but it is thought possible that the Japanese are withdrawing troops from this area in order to use them in the Solomons. The Americans meanwhile have occupied two more small islands in the Solomons group. So long as the Americans are there, the Japanese position in New Guinea and indeed their whole position in the Southern Pacific, is in great danger and we must therefore expect further heavy fighting in this area. The Americans have also occupied

[279] The figures claimed by the Axis broadcasters were substantially greater than this. From the German point of view exchanges were of great benefit, for they replaced prisoners of war with men who would be working for the food they were eating and at the same time showed German confidence in the 'New Order' in Europe by releasing into their home communities fully trained French soldiers.

[280] The landing had been followed by a naval battle on the night of 11-12 October which Orwell describes direct from the US Navy Department briefing. The subsequent landing was on 15 October.

another island in the Aleutian Archipelago, without encountering opposition.[281]

The Germans have renewed their heavy air attacks on Malta, and during the past week no less than 103 German planes have been shot down there. The probable reason for this renewal of the attacks on Malta is that the successful work of the RAF and the Allied submarines in the Eastern Mediterranean makes it difficult for the Germans to use the ports of Tobruk and Benghazi. They are once again compelled to bring their supplies from Italy to Tripoli and it is necessary from their point of view that Malta should be immobilised if possible. The fact that they are willing to lose aeroplanes at the present rate suggests that they are bringing, or are about to bring, large reinforcements to Africa.[282] In any case a renewal of fighting on the Egyptian front is to be expected in the near future. Three Axis supply ships have been sunk in the Mediterranean during the past week, and several others damaged.

Nine hundred and fifty French soldiers from the garrison of Madagascar have joined General de Gaulle. Those taken prisoner were given the alternative of joining de Gaulle or of being repatriated to Vichy France. Only a very few chose the latter alternative, the great majority preferring to continue the fight at the side of the Allies. This is yet another sign of the contempt and loathing in which the Vichy regime is held by nearly all classes of Frenchmen.[283]

German propagandists in the press and on the wireless are putting out persistent rumours that the British and Americans are about to attack Dakar in French West Africa. The Vichy wireless has just announced that the commander of the French air forces at Dakar has been killed, probably in a reconnaissance flight over British territory. These rumours should not be altogether ignored, because they probably mean that the Germans are seeking a further pretext for aggressive action against French West Africa, on which they have had designs for years past.[284]

[281] A further island in the Adrianos group.

[282] The main concern was to get fuel to Rommel's armies whose recent attacks had all failed when petrol supplies had run short.

[283] As a propaganda point this simplification by Orwell shows him at his weakest. The fighting in Madagascar was still going on and was regularly featured in Indian papers and Axis broadcasts; so the Indian audience would have seen little sign of this contempt and loathing in the nearest French colony to them.

[284] The rumours which Orwell refers to here have not been found in the monitors' reports. Since the American invasion of North-West Africa was imminent it seems likely that this was a propaganda smoke-screen which Orwell had been instructed to put up. The suggestion that the Germans were thinking of invading French West Africa is akin to the alleged threats of Japanese use of Madagascar.

24 October 1942

The battle for Stalingrad has now lasted for more than two months and the issue is still uncertain. During all this period the fighting has never slackened for more than a few days, and though accurate figures are hard to obtain, the Russian High Command considers that the German casualties in this battle alone exceed a quarter of a million. During the past week the German attacks have not made much progress, and the latest reports seem to indicate that the Germans have again abandoned direct infantry assault and are relying on artillery bombardment. There has been heavy rain, and the mud has no doubt slowed down the German tanks. From the other Russian fronts there is not much to report.

On the island of Guadalcanal in the Solomon Islands, the Japanese have made no new attacks on the American airfield during the past four or five days, but they are known to have powerful naval forces in the neighbourhood and heavy fighting must be expected in the near future. The Americans have also been reinforced on land and on sea, and their commanders speak confidently about the forthcoming struggle although admitting that it is certain to be a hard one. At present it is largely a struggle of air power against sea power. The Americans have superiority in the air and have the advantage of possessing the Guadalcanal airfield, but storms and foggy weather have aided the Japanese warships, which are awaiting their opportunity to cover another Japanese landing. The latest news is that American Flying Fortresses have scored hits on ten Japanese warships and are believed to have sunk a cruiser and a destroyer. The Americans themselves have lost two destroyers during the current week.[285] In New Guinea, the Allied advance has continued, though slowly because of the difficult nature of the mountain and jungle country through which our troops are moving. The Australian forces are now not far from Kokoda, the last Japanese stronghold before their sea and air bases on the coast of New Guinea.

October 21st was the anniversary of the battle of Trafalgar. This battle 137 years ago occupied rather the same place in the Napoleonic War as the Battle of Britain in 1940 occupied in the present one. The French Emperor, Napoleon, a man who had many points in common

---

[285] The US Navy Department gave the names of these ships as USS *Meredith* and USS *O'Brien*.

with Hitler,[286] had assembled a powerful invasion army at Boulogne opposite the coast of Britain. Could he have got his army across the Channel he would almost certainly have conquered Britain, in which case the other European nations would in all probability not have gone on fighting. Europe would have been given over to military dictatorship[287] and its development would have been set back by many years. However, it was impossible for Napoleon to bring his army across without obtaining command of the sea, and the fleet with which he had tried to lure away and destroy the British navy was utterly destroyed off Cape Trafalgar on the coast of Spain. Thereafter, the danger of invasion hardly existed, and though it took another ten years to win the war, it was at any rate certain that Britain could not be conquered at one blow. In just the same way in 1940 the Germans only needed command of the air to attempt the invasion of Britain, and with their defeat in a battle which lasted several weeks and in which they lost between two and three thousand aeroplanes, the danger of invasion passed, at any rate for the time being.

We draw attention to the anniversary of Trafalgar because the naval side of the war is ultimately the most important, though it is the most easily forgotten. The whole struggle of the Allied Nations in the Far East, in Australia, in Africa and even on the plains of Russia, is finally dependent on the command of the sea which allows men and materials to be freely sent to and fro. Very appropriately, the Admiralty marked the anniversary of Trafalgar by announcing that two new battleships of the King George V class have been put into commission.[288] These ships, which are each of 35,000 tons, are about the most powerful vessels now afloat. This makes five new battleships Britain has launched since the outbreak of war, of which one, the *Prince of Wales*, has been lost. In almost all classes of warship, the British Navy is stronger than it was at the outbreak of war and the long, slow struggle against the Axis submarines is being gradually won. During the past week, two facts which gave great encouragement in this connection have been revealed. One is that convoys crossing the Atlantic can now by means of a series of patrols be given air protection the whole way. The other fact revealed in a statement made

[286] In one of his radio talks Orwell also compares Hitler with Macbeth (see *OWB*, p.160f).

[287] In *Nineteen Eighty-Four* Europe is given over to a military dictatorship, with Russia, as the superpower Eurasia.

[288] Orwell goes on to mention the increase of British strength since war broke out; it is interesting to note that of these two ships HMS *Anson* was laid down in July 1937 and HMS *Howe* in June 1937. The Japanese in fact had two battleships of over 70,000 tons.

a few days ago by the First Lord of the Admiralty is that since the outbreak of war the British and Americans have sunk or damaged no less than 530 Axis submarines.[289] This is in addition to any submarines sunk or damaged by the Russians. This achievement is important not so much because of the submarines destroyed – for submarines can be fairly rapidly built – but because their crews are highly trained men whom it is difficult to replace. In the last war, the struggle at sea took a rather similar course for a long time: the German submarines enjoyed great success and there was a period in 1917-1918 when the shipping situation of the Allies was desperate. In the long run, however, the German naval effort was worn down by the killing or capture of their best submarine crews and in the later months of the war it deteriorated quite suddenly so that towards the end the Allied convoys could sail almost unmolested.

On October 17th, a very heavy daylight raid was carried out by British bombers on the Schneider arms factories in Occupied France. After Krupps factories at Essen, these are probably the biggest arms works in Europe, and it is known that they were working at full pressure for the Germans. Ninety-four of the heaviest British bombers, each of which can carry eight tons of bombs, made an attack and only one bomber failed to return. The damage is known to have been tremendous. This is the second big raid within about ten days that Allied forces have carried out in daylight. Two days ago, British bombers also carried out a heavy raid on Genoa[290] in Italy. This involved a flight of fifteen hundred miles, and it also involved flying over the Alps, which are almost as high as the Himalayas. At present the Germans are only countering the British raids in a very petty way by single raiders or small groups which machine-gun civilians somewhere near the coast and hurriedly make off again. Their bombing fleet is too busy on the Russian front to do more than this, and the success of the British and American daylight raids suggests that the Germans no longer have sufficient fighter planes to guard every corner of their territories.[291]

The struggle of Laval, the French quisling, to force Frenchmen to work for Germany is continuing, without much success. The Germans

[289] Announced by A.V. Alexander, First Lord of the Admiralty, on 20 October. The figures also excluded those sunk by the French navy before June 1940.

[290] This raid, led by Wing-Commander L.C. Slee, was described as the largest unescorted daylight attack of the war. The planes, Lancaster bombers, flew at zero feet there and back. For the significance of this raid, see Orwell's broadcast on 31 October.

[291] After the initial air raids were over there was a break in German bombing largely for the reasons Orwell mentions. This situation changed dramatically with the coming of the 'doodlebug', or flying bomb.

want 150,000 workers and have held out the bribe that a corresponding number of war prisoners will be released. In spite of this, it is known that not more than 30,000 volunteers at most have come forward,[292] and the time-limit for enrolment has had to be extended several times. It is of course in the power of the Germans to apply compulsion, but that is not very satisfactory from their point of view; it means dropping once and for all the pretence that the New Order has been willingly accepted by the peoples of Europe. Almost simultaneously with this the German 'protector',[293] as he is called, of Czechoslovakia has announced that reprisals are going to be taken against the relatives of Czech exiles in Britain and also that the Czech universities which were closed for a period of three years in 1939 are not going to be reopened. The reason, he said, was that the Czech intelligentsia have shown themselves irreconcilable. Many similar events could be reported from other parts of Europe and indeed they are a weekly occurrence. We could if we wished completely fill this newsletter every week with news of civil war, rioting, sabotage, strikes and executions from occupied Europe.[294] But we merely pick out from time to time one or two instances to remind our listeners of the utter failure of the New Order and the growing understanding among the European peoples of the evil nature of Fascism.

Field-Marshal Smuts, President of the Union of South Africa, spoke on October 21st in London to a gathering of the members of both Houses of Parliament. His speech excited great interest and has been broadcast and published all over the world.[295] General Smuts

[292] Orwell here repeats his previous week's statement almost word for word; there was a battle of figures between the propagandists on the issue which was still continuing. The MOI at this time circulated a figure of 18,000 to the British press; Vichy radio announced that the 80,000th man had just volunteered; Orwell provides his own average.

[293] Karl Frank, successor to Heydrich, had been incensed by a radio broadcast by President Benes from London. On 18 October he ordered that relatives of the government in exile in London be sent to concentration camps. The universities had originally been closed after student massacres on 17 November 1939.

[294] The Axis propagandists were of course filling their channels with news of British atrocities in India, and Orwell, unable to mention these, is again pointing to the other side of the fence and saying that things are no different there. At this time there was an outbreak of terrorism in India by Dacoits of the sort which has occurred from time immemorial to the present day and which had, of course, to be put down. Coming on top of the Congress actions, it would not have made it any the easier for Orwell to interpret what was going on in India had he been allowed to try. The authorities knew, however, that these Dacoit attacks were understood in India for what they were.

[295] One of the relatively few major public speeches by Allied leaders, in contrast to the continuous stream of lengthy harangues which were a central element in the Axis propaganda programmes.

reviewed the progress of the war up to date and paid high tribute to the gallant peoples of Russia and China, both references being loudly cheered by the audience. He also said that we must never forget the year during which Britain fought alone and probably saved the world by doing so. Although preferring not to discuss future military operations, he said that the time had now come when the United Nations were able to take the offensive, and emphasised the fact that our strength was constantly growing while that of our enemies was beginning to decline. After the war he looked forward to a more stable society in which poverty and political oppression would be abolished and internationalism would be a reality. General Smuts, who is now aged 72, fought with distinction against the British in the South African War of forty years ago. He afterwards became completely reconciled to Britain and was one of the most brilliant and influential members of the British War Cabinet in the war of 1914-1918. Few modern statesmen are more respected in Britain. His speech was wound up by Mr Churchill and introduced by his former chief, David Lloyd George.

31 October 1942

A week ago the Allied forces in Egypt opened up a large-scale attack, and since then fighting has been almost continuous. In the opening stages of the attack, the Allies broke into the enemy positions and took considerable numbers of prisoners. The Germans then counter-attacked and there were some clashes between armoured formations, but the ground gained was all successfully held. This morning's news is that the Allies have made a further advance and taken another large batch of prisoners. It is worth noting that the prisoners taken in this second advance are mostly Germans – a sure sign that the Axis forces are doing their best to hold to their positions, as it is usual to put Germans rather than Italians in any place when hard fighting is expected.

As yet we prefer not to predict the outcome of the battle in Egypt,[296] but we can point to one or two factors likely to govern it. One is that

---

[296] This must be one of the most low-key announcements of a great victory ever to come from a propaganda department. Orwell is talking here of the Battle of El Alamein, and the tone he adopts shows more than anything else he broadcast the extent to which he and his colleagues had become inured to so much seemingly good news turning out to have a dark side to it. The impact of the victory was correspondingly great and Orwell's scripts reflect this over the next weeks and months.

any advance in the area where the fighting is now going on is likely to be slow. The battle area is a narrow space between the sea and the Qattara Depression, a marshy area, where tanks cannot operate. Consequently the only method of advance is direct frontal attack, which is a slow process since it means assaulting a series of strongly fortified positions and carefully clearing minefields, without which the tanks cannot advance. In this sort of fighting, therefore, an advance of two thousand yards, such as that reported this morning, means more than an advance of many miles in the open desert. Secondly, the outcome of such a battle is largely a question of supplies, and the fact of the Allies having attacked first is probably a good sign. Arms and reinforcements for the Allied army in Egypt have to travel much further than those destined for the Axis forces, but the Axis line of communications from Italy to Tripoli and thence up the coast to the Egyptian front is liable to sea or air attack almost the whole way. During recent weeks the Axis losses on this supply route have been very heavy, and a recent Admiralty statement revealed that during this year the Axis have had no less than 600,000 tons of shipping sunk or damaged in the Mediterranean. This is the background of the present fighting in Egypt in which both sides fight under considerable difficulties. It is evident that the Allies are stronger in the air. Which side is stronger in tanks and other fighting vehicles we cannot yet say. The main body of our troops comes from Britain, but Australian, South African, New Zealand, Indian, Free French and Greek[297] troops are all taking part. We shall be able to report more fully on the Egyptian campaign next week. It is now evident that the heavy RAF raids on Genoa and Milan in Northern Italy, the first of which we reported last week, were a preliminary to the attack in Egypt. Axis supplies and reinforcements for the Egyptian front are largely despatched from Genoa, and the disorganisation caused by these raids will make itself felt on the battlefield.

During the past week there has been heavy fighting in the Solomon Islands and some anxious moments for the Allies. It was clear that the Japanese had a powerful fleet in the neighbourhood of Guadalcanal, and they had also been able to land enough troops on the island to outnumber the Americans who hold the all-important airfields. The Americans were being shelled by warships every night besides having to beat off land attacks by forces which included tanks. At the same time there were a number of sea and air engagements in which both sides had ships sunk and damaged. However, this morning's news is

[297] It had been announced on 18 October that a new Greek Army under General Katsotas was in action in the desert war.

that the Japanese fleet has retired again and that all the land attacks have been successfully resisted. Colonel Knox, the United States Navy Secretary, has just announced that the Americans still hold all the territory which they captured from the Japanese at the beginning of August.[298] This does not mean, however, that the fighting in the Solomons has ended. The Japanese are certain to renew their attacks, partly because of the importance of the Guadalcanal airfield, partly because of the loss of face if they fail to drive the Americans out after promising confidently to do so. As Colonel Knox put it, the first round has gone to the Americans but the defenders of Guadalcanal are waiting for the second round to start.

The battle for Stalingrad continues and both sides have suffered heavy casualties during this week. The German attacks have made little or no progress. It is now more than a month since the speeches in which Hitler and Ribbentrop promised the capture of Stalingrad within a few days. As yet, apparently, the German people cannot be allowed to learn what enormous numbers of their sons and brothers have gone to their deaths in vain attacks on Stalingrad. But such facts cannot be kept secret for ever, and the heavy and more or less futile casualties of this year's campaign are likely to have their effects on morale, later in the winter.

News was released a few days ago that the new military road known as the Alaska High Road has been opened.[299] This road runs from the United States through Canada and Alaska and makes it possible to supply any force operating in the Aleutian Islands much more rapidly than could be done before. The Aleutian Islands are the point at which Allied territory is nearest to Japan, and also the point at which America is nearest to Soviet Russia. The strategic importance of this new road is therefore very great. It was completed in an astonishingly short time, although for much of the way it runs through virgin forests which had previously hardly been explored.

We are able to give a few more details about the new British bombing plane, the Mosquito, which made its first official appearance two or three weeks ago. This was the first front line plane in this war to be built entirely of wood. Its body is therefore easily manufactured and is probably cheap. Its great feature is its extremely high speed, which rivals that of fighter planes. It is also powerfully armed, carrying 20-millimetre cannons as well as machine-guns. It has been used very

[298] He was quoted as saying, on 30 October: 'The first round is over. We are in as complete control of the situation in Guadalcanal as we have ever been.'

[299] US War Secretary Stimson announced the completion of the 1670-mile-long road on 29 October. It was not opened officially until the following month, on 21 November, at a ceremony on the Canada-Alaska border.

successfully for several daylight raids on the continent.

We will end by giving an extract from *The Times* of two days ago, which has some up-to-date information about the behaviour of the Japanese in Java.[300]

A young Dutch officer who escaped from Java several weeks ago and is now in Australia reports that the attitude of the people in Java towards the Japanese invaders is one of passive hostility. During the early days of the occupation the Japanese took cruel measures against looters. Dead Malays were often seen hanging from trees in Batavia. The Japanese military police still habitually beat up persons from whom they want information. These repressive measures have cowed the Javanese people, who, though sympathetic towards Europeans, are afraid of offending their temporary military masters.

All the sympathy they may feel towards the Europeans is really suppressed by the fear, so it is quiet sympathy.

The production of rubber, tea, tobacco, and other commodities in which Java is so rich has been drastically curtailed. There is a great deal of unemployment in the country.

Groups of Allied soldiers are still at large in the mountains, but they are unable to maintain any effective resistance. Wounded Japanese soldiers from those regions are still brought occasionally to hospitals in Batavia.

7 November 1942

The Battle of Egypt has developed into a great victory for the United Nations.[301] The Axis forces are not yet destroyed, but they are in great danger, and for three days they have been in disorderly retreat, with wave after wave of Allied bombers attacking them as they go. Something over three hundred Axis tanks have been destroyed or captured. Prisoners taken by our forces amounted yesterday to 15,000

[300] The paragraphs that follow are taken verbatim from a report on page 4 of *The Times* for 29 October. Orwell did not repeat the entire piece, for it ended with the sentence: 'Japanese military discipline has been good and no cases reported of white women being molested.' This would, perhaps, have contrasted too strongly with the reports Orwell had made previously of Japanese behaviour at Hong Kong (see above, p.63); Orwell rarely suppresses information to better his story, but here we must conclude that he did.

[301] The phrase 'The Battle of Egypt' speedily fell from use, the more popular 'El Alamein' being universally adopted. The Africa Corps Commander referred to overleaf was General Ritter von Thoma.

– but there will be many more within the next few days. The commander of the Africa Corps has been taken prisoner, together with a number of other German and Italian senior officers.

It is clear from the reports that have come in during the last two days that when once the Axis positions in the narrow neck of land between the sea and the Qattara Depression had been broken, the enemy had no choice but to fall back as rapidly as possible and attempt to make another stand somewhere in the neighbourhood of the Egyptian frontier. We do not care to predict as yet whether they will be able to do this. Now that the minefields round El Alamein have been cleared, the Allied tanks have raced ahead, and together with the RAF are pounding the retreating Axis columns along the coastal road. It is clear that the Allies possess almost complete supremacy in the air, and the retreating enemy must be losing all the time in tanks, transport, and men. Nevertheless, the German commander may be able to extricate sufficient tanks and anti-tank guns to make a stand in the strong positions at Halfaya and Salum, on the border between Libya and Egypt. The most recent news is that our forces have captured the airfield at Puka, seventy miles west of El Alamein, and fighting is taking place at Mersa Matruh, another fifty miles to the west. Large numbers of Axis troops, chiefly Italians, have been left behind in the southern part of the battlefield, and these will be almost entirely destroyed or captured. Six Axis supply ships have been sunk by our submarines in the Mediterranean during the past few days.[302]

It is certain that by next week we shall have further news to report about the Egyptian campaign, and possibly sensational news. Meanwhile it is too early to say that the Axis armies in North Africa have been destroyed, but it can at least be said that the threat to Egypt has been removed.

The Japanese landed some reinforcements on the island of Guadalcanal, in the Solomons, four days ago, but have not renewed their attack. There has been some land-fighting, in which the Americans have gained a little ground. The Japanese are certain to make further efforts to recapture Guadalcanal, but for the moment they have evidently lost too many planes and warships to continue without a pause for refitting. On the island of New Guinea, the Australian forces have made another advance and captured the

---

[302] This information was taken from a news statement issued in Cairo on 5 November – it was also said that no oil tanker had reached Rommel's armies in six weeks.

Japanese held village of Kokoda,[303] with its airfield.

Throughout most of the week there has been heavy fighting at Stalingrad but little or no change in position. In the south of the Caucasus area the Germans have made an advance within the last few days. They appear to be trying to get possession of the northern approaches of the main roads over the Caucasus mountains. At this time of year, to cross the mountains is probably not practicable, but they may be thinking of the spring, as well as of securing defensible positions for the winter. In Ukrainia, the Germans are making great efforts to organise the captured territories and exploit them in order to feed their home population. In the German press and on the radio, it has been explained in the frankest way that the Germans intend to plunder these territories for their own advantage, without regard to the interests of the inhabitants, and that they intend to break up the collective farms which the Russian peasants had built for themselves, and hand the land over to individual German owners.[304] It is clear, however, that this process is not proceeding so smoothly as the Germans would like to pretend. The farming of this important cornland depended almost entirely on oil-driven tractors, and when the Russians retreated they took care to destroy such machinery as they could not rescue. It is impossible for the Germans to supply fresh agricultural machinery in anything like the quantities required, and it will probably be difficult for them even to muster sufficient labour. During the last war, it will be remembered, the Germans also had possession of the Ukraine, and tried then, as now, to plunder it for their own benefit, but in fact they got very little out of it. It looks very much as though the same story were going to be repeated this time.

Premier Stalin broadcast to the Soviet people last night on the eve of the twenty-eighth birthday of the USSR. The keynote of his speech was his confidence in the complete victory of the United Nations. Although, he said, the Germans had been able to take the offensive this year because of the absence of a second front in Western Europe, and the Red Army had had to face the onslaught of 240 German divisions, the main strategy of the Germans had failed. They had sought to outflank Moscow from the south and then capture it, and simultaneously to capture the oilfields of Baku. Both dreams had failed to materialise.

[303] The capture of Kokoda announced on 2 November was the result of a five-week campaign. It was somewhat more than a village in real terms. It had an airfield and was the last Japanese base in the Owen Stanley range.

[304] There were, for example, Axis broadcasts such as 'Talk for rural youth: "Work in the German East" ' which were purely neo-colonial in character, like Victorian appeals to young men to go to the colonies.

Stalin contrasted the aims of the Fascist nations, who attempt to exterminate and subjugate other peoples, with those of the Allies, who have no wish to subjugate anybody and are fighting only to destroy the so-called New Order and kill off the comparatively small cliques of people responsible for it. He also ridiculed the idea that political and economic differences were any obstacle to collaboration between Britain, Soviet Russia and the United States. In the fight against slavery, he said, it is possible even for nations with very different ideologies to have a common programme, and the events of the past year prove conclusively that the members of this great coalition are coming nearer and nearer to one another.

The hostilities in the island of Madagascar have been brought to a close, the French Governor-General having asked for and received an Armistice.[305] Although the campaign in Madagascar was only a side-show and involved little fighting, it has had its importance as the possession of Madagascar was necessary for the command of the sea approaches to Egypt, and the Middle East. The victory in Egypt has only been made possible by the fact that the Allies were able to build up there a substantial force of tanks and aeroplanes, which they could not have done unless the sea routes round Africa were reasonably safe. At a press conference two days ago, President Roosevelt disclosed that only a minority of the armaments used in Egypt were of American manufacture, the great bulk of them being British. It has taken a long time and continuous journies by great fleets of ships to build up this force, and the seizure of Madagascar and consequent cutting off of Axis submarine bases – which existed or were always liable to exist while Vichy remained in control of this island – has played its part in the campaign.[306]

[305] The Armistice was signed by M. Annet on 5 November. The Allied news agencies reported that 3000 French and Malagasy prisoners had been taken. However, the Vichy radio, from the first outbreak of hostilities, had put the number of Vichy troops on the island at no more than 1500 white and coloured.

[306] As has already been pointed out, there were no Axis submarine bases or any Japanese presence, which Orwell seems now to have realised by his use of the word 'liable'. The campaign did none the less have a great effect in France, where the Vichy authorities had given extensive coverage to the campaign, exhorting M. Annet and his garrison to resist to the last man. The defeat left an impression entirely out of proportion to the number of troops involved.

28 November 1942[307]

At the end of my commentary last week, I promised that this time I might be able to give some news from the other fronts, particularly the Russian front. Well, the news has come, and it is just as sensational as the African move of a week or two earlier.

Six days ago, the Russians opened an offensive north-west and south of Stalingrad. Almost immediately there was news that the northern attacking forces had broken through, made a fifty-mile advance and captured 13,000 prisoners. Since then, however, it has gone very much further. The attacking Russian army has circled round to the south and captured in all something over 60,000 prisoners and an enormous amount of material. The latest Russian reports speak of driving the enemy eastward over the Don, which can only mean that they have circled right round to the rear of the enemy forces and that a very much larger body of Germans than those taken prisoner already is in danger of being cut off if they don't get out quickly. Even in the German communiqués it is possible to deduce the fact that the present position of the German army before Stalingrad is very shaky, and I think in any case we are safe in saying that the long siege of Stalingrad has now been definitely raised.

I don't care as yet to predict too much about the result of this Russian offensive. If the German position is as precarious as it looks on the map they may not only have to lose very much more heavily in men and material, but they may even have to make a big retreat and go back to somewhere about the line they occupied last winter. But however that may be, I want to emphasise two facts about the Russian offensive. The first is its probable effect on German morale and Axis morale in general. It will now be very hard indeed to conceal from the German people the fact that the Germans' campaign in Russia in 1942 has been a failure. The objectives of that campaign were first of all to get to Baku and the oilfields, secondly in all probability to capture Moscow by an encircling movement from the south, and thirdly quite certainly to get to Astrakhan on the Caspian Sea and thus cut the Russian communications running north and south. Well, not one of those objectives has been achieved, and the prime cause of the failure has been the heroic Russian defence of Stalingrad. It is impossible that

[307] This is the first surviving script broadcast by Orwell in his own name (for the change, see *OWB*, p.242f.). Note that from now on he uses the first person singular.

the German common people should not recognise how important Stalingrad is, because it has been in the news for too long.[308] Indeed, so long as they felt confident of taking it the German military spokesmen emphasised the importance of Stalingrad for all they were worth. It is now something over three months since the siege began, and something over two months since Hitler solemnly promised that it would be taken. A month or so later, when Stalingrad hadn't been taken, Hitler explained that after all, it was not of very great importance because even if the Russians were still in possession of the city itself or what was left of it, the Germans were in a position to prevent Russian traffic moving up and down the Volga. Well, now that almost certainly the Germans will be forced to retreat from Stalingrad even that claim can't be made any longer. The German propagandists, therefore, will be in the unenviable position of having to admit that their military commanders have poured out lives and material on an enormous scale for an objective which finally wasn't achieved. The effects even on German morale must be bad, and on Germany's so-called allies they may be disastrous. The war has already lost most of its meaning from the Italian point of view, and it will not make the Italians any happier to know that tens of thousands of their sons are being frozen in Russia for absolutely nothing, at the same time as their African Empire is slipping away from them and their cities are being bombed to pieces.

The other thing I would like to point out about this Russian campaign is its correlation with the North African campaign. Through a great part of this year the Russians have had to fight almost alone against the biggest army in the world. Now Russia's allies have managed to stage a diversion elsewhere and the effects make themselves felt almost immediately on the Russian front. For there cannot be much doubt that the Russian success is partly due to the Germans having to withdraw part of their air strength in order to rush as many planes as possible south in hopes of retrieving the situation in Africa.[309]

Since last week French West Africa has fallen into line with the other French colonies and entered into collaboration with the

[308] Orwell does not make the obvious point that the previous very lengthy siege of this type had been at Sebastopol and that the final result there, after many setbacks, had been victory. The failure of the campaign at Stalingrad was therefore even greater by contrast. No doubt the example of the ultimate success at Sebastopol led Hitler to continue the siege of Stalingrad long after the great danger there became obvious.

[309] While this was a good propaganda point to make to the Russians, the fact seems to be that few German troops or planes were diverted to North Africa until the American invasion, which began on 8 November, was well under way.

Allies.[310] The only bit of French African territory still nominally neutral is French Somaliland with the port of Djibouti, which no doubt will come over in the near future. French West Africa coming into the Allied sphere of influence is not merely important because of the valuable products – raw rubber, vegetable oils and various foodstuffs – which we shall now be able to get from these territories. It is also important because of the great naval base of Dakar which has docks big enough to take battleships and which is only 1600 miles from Brazil. With nearly the whole of the West African coastline under our control it is much easier to deal with the U-boats in the South Atlantic, and also with the ports further north which we now hold we have a much safer supply route to the Central Mediterranean than we have had hitherto. There is road and rail communication all the way from Casablanca almost to Tunis and if the North African campaign succeeds completely it will be possible to travel from Gibraltar to Suez by a comparatively short route without once entering in the range of the Axis aeroplanes. French West Africa came over quite amicably without any fighting and is under the general control of Admiral Darlan. I repeat what I said last week, that we must regard the present political setup in French Africa as merely temporary and likely to come up for revision when the military part of the campaign is settled. We may not like the past record of some of the Vichy commanders who have now come over to our side, but the fact of their coming is at any rate a good symptom – it means that with their much greater inside knowledge of events in Europe than we ourselves can possess at present – they have decided that the Nazi ship is sinking.[311]

There hasn't been a great deal of development on the two battle-fronts in Libya and Tunisia. The Eighth Army entered Benghazi almost a week ago – in all probability this will be the third Christmas they have spent there – and they have also occupied Jedabya, fifty miles south on the coastal road, and are in contact with the enemy near El Agheila. Probably the Germans intend to make a stand here and it may take the Eighth Army some days more to get their heavy equipment into position for a fresh attack. If the Germans decide not to stand at El Agheila, they will probably have to go back to Masurata, another two hundred miles along the Libyan coast. The

---

[310] Axis announcements of this were bitter, referring to 'the traitor Darlan'.

[311] It is difficult to speculate here on what Orwell's real opinion might have been of the situation that was developing in North Africa. He seems to be making the best case that his conscience would allow, but others in the BBC felt acutely the hypocrisy of accepting Darlan's position. The Free French officer seconded to the BBC who wrote the newsletter for France equivalent to Orwell's for India refused to broadcast as long as Darlan was kept in his position.

Allies have also occupied the Jalo oasis, two hundred miles south in the desert, which safeguards them against any outflanking movement. On the other side, in Tunisia, the First Army is evidently getting into position for a direct assault on Tunis or Bizerta. Their movement has been slowed up no doubt partly by the fact that much of their material still has to come all the way from Casablanca, but partly also by the evident fact that the Axis are for the time being stronger in the air on this front.[312] It isn't easy for the Germans to reinforce their army in Tunisia on any big scale with men or heavy equipment, but they can reinforce their air strength more quickly than we can, and this advantage may remain with them for some days to come. In the long run, however, it is unlikely that the Germans will get the better of the air battle, even on this front, because the total air strength of the Allies is now greater and is getting increasingly more so. In any case, any air reinforcements they send to Tunisia is weakening some other front, especially the Russian front. Meanwhile, their air losses have already been heavy and even if they successfully fight a delaying action which allows the bulk of Rommel's army to escape by sea, they may turn out not to have gained much in the process.

There is not very much news from the South Pacific. The Japanese succeeded in bringing their forces at Buna some small reinforcements by sea, but it is not expected that they will be able to hold on to Buna much longer. The Allies have captured Gona,[313] a few miles along the coast, and the Japanese are being heavily bombed besides being attacked on the ground. If they are driven out altogether from the Eastern part of New Guinea, this, along with the stronger American hold on the Solomons after their naval victory, will make it possible to launch an attack on Kabaul which is the most important Japanese base in this area.

Hitler has broken his pledge to Marshal Pétain and occupied Toulon. The French commanders have scuttled the French fleet and destroyed the naval arsenal and ammunition dumps. Hitler has ordered the demobilisation of what is left of the French army. I give these items of news very baldly because it is too early to comment on them adequately. We don't know yet whether any of the French ships

---

[312] Axis planes landed at Tunisia, despite Laval's protests made on a visit to Hitler at Berchtesgaden, and the availability of the facilities at the airports after the occupation of Vichy France were of considerable help.

[313] In the MOI release the fighting was described as fierce, and in fact the news of the capture seems to have been premature. Gona's capture was announced again on 6 December.

escaped to join the Allies,[314] though we do know that none of importance have fallen into the hands of the Germans. I hope to comment on this next week. Meanwhile, just let me point out two things. One is that this marks the end – and from our point of view the successful end – of Hitler's two and a half years of intrigues to get hold of the French fleet. The other is that it is the final death blow to the New Order. Any chance of French collaboration with the Nazis has now gone for good.

12 December 1942

Since last week both the Russian offensives have slowed down somewhat, owing to stiffening German resistance and also, on the southern front, to the soft snow that has been falling. We can't, I imagine, expect any further big move on this front for the time being, and this week the chief interest has centred in North Africa, where it has become even clearer than before that there's a hard struggle ahead.

It is just a week since the Germans counter-attacked west of Tunis and retook Tebourba and Jedeida, the two points which it is necessary for the Allies to control before they assault Tunis itself. The Germans have delivered another attack since, but they don't appear to have got any further, and our main positions round the Tunis-Bizerta area stand firm. It has become clear from the reports that are coming in that the Germans are stronger in the air and are likely to remain so for some time to come.[315] They possess the airfields of Bizerta and Tunis, besides having their air bases in Sicily and Sardinia only a hundred miles away, while the Allies don't at present hold any airfield nearer than Bone, 120 miles away along the Algerian coast. They can and, of course, will prepare landing grounds in the forward area, but this takes time, especially as equipment, ground staff and probably even labour have to be brought from places far to the west, over poor roads and one ill-equipped railway. At present, therefore, the strategic picture in

[314] The fleet was scuttled on 27 November. Orwell's hopes, echoing his earlier statements about the French navy, were unfounded. Admiral Laborde, Commander of the French High Seas Fleet, was very anti-British and would not have obeyed Darlan's broadcast order to defect with the fleet. He did, however, scuttle the fleet rather than let it fall into German hands, waiting until the Germans had actually entered the dock area before doing so.

[315] Realisation of the actual arrival of the German air force on Vichy airfields had by now sunk in. Churchill lamented the fact in *The Second World War* (vol.4, p.560).

Tunisia is something like this. The Allies, whose ultimate strength is much greater, are building up a striking force as fast as they can, but they have to do it in the face of dive-bombing and with insufficient cover from fighter planes. The Germans, who probably have only about 20,000 men in Tunisia and not a great supply of heavy tanks or large-calibre guns, but who possess temporary air superiority, are doing their best to slow up the Allied concentration and to build up their own forces in Tunisia by air and sea. Further south, in the neighbourhood of Sfax and Gabes on the Tunisian coast, another struggle is going on for the control of the coastal road which leads southward in the direction of Tripoli. There isn't at present much news from this area, where the fighting seems to have been chiefly between parachutists and air-borne troops from both sides;[316] but it doesn't appear that any Allied force has yet reached the sea. All in all, the Germans only control the eastern strip of Tunisia, but they are in a strong position so long as they can keep up the stream of supplies from Sicily and Sardinia.

However, the air superiority of the Germans is likely to be a wasting asset. The reserves they have near at hand aren't inexhaustible, and the ultimate source of supply is Germany itself, which is a long way away and is connected with the battle area by railway communications which are none too good. It is here that the RAF bombing of northern Italy, through which all supplies for the African fronts have to pass, is important. The RAF have delivered very heavy raids on Italy during the last week – Turin for instance was heavily bombed twice in twenty-four hours[317] – and have evidently done very severe damage. One can infer this from the broadcasts of the Italians themselves. All this adds to the difficulties of the Germans, who are already fighting a long way from their main base on a front they didn't willingly choose. Moreover, the more they strive to build up their force in Tunisia, the harder it is for them to reinforce another army in Libya – and it is there, in all probability, that the next big move will come.

During the last week there have only been reports of patrol activity at El Agheila, west of Benghazi, but it looks as though the new British attack were about to start. I should expect it to have started before I broadcast my next news commentary – and once again my reason for saying this is the Axis radio propagandists, who are already talking

[316] News reports on 10 December described frequent parachute landings, some behind enemy lines. Earlier in November British and American paratroops had been used at Bone and elsewhere.

[317] On the nights of 8 and 9 December. On the second night fires still burning from the earlier raid were augmented to such an extent that they were seen from the Alpine peaks.

about the forthcoming British attack and don't sound over-hopeful about the possibility of General Rommel holding on. Long before the British Eighth Army got to Benghazi it could be foreseen that the Afrika Corps would make its next stand at El Agheila, which is a naturally strong position – a neck of land with the sea on one side and impassable marshes on the other – rather like the position it formerly occupied at El Alamein. Before General Montgomery could make a new attack he had to bring up his heavy equipment – over a distance of hundreds of miles, remember, and with in effect only one road. The last few weeks, therefore, have been a race to bring up supplies – the British bringing them from Egypt, the Germans from Tripoli. At El Agheila the Germans are actually further from their nearest port of supply – that is Tripoli – than they were at El Alamein in Egypt, when they could use Tobruk. It looks from the German communiqués as though the British have been winning the race for supplies, and the Germans expect to have to fall back again to avoid destruction. They appear to be preparing German public opinion for something of this kind, as they are beginning to claim that Rommel's army in Libya was never intended to do more than create a diversion. It is only three or four months since Rommel himself was announcing in Berlin[318] that he had come to Africa to conquer Egypt and that he already had Egypt in his grasp. But perhaps the German public have forgotten that – or at least the official broadcasters hope they have. If the fresh British offensive at El Agheila takes place and is successful, it won't have an immediate repercussion on the Tunisia front, but it must do so within a few weeks.

An agreement has now been signed between the United States Government and General Boisson, the French commander at Dakar in French West Africa, for the use of the port and airfields at Dakar by the Allies.[319] That will be of great value in dealing with the U-boats in the South Atlantic. There is still much that is unexplained about the precise political situation in North Africa and the relation between General [sic] Darlan and ourselves. This matter has now been debated in Parliament[320] and I think we may expect an official pronouncement on it in the not too distant future. [*Censored:* Here I will mention only

[318] Rommel had returned to Germany for medical reasons. He was present at the Sportspalast when Hitler spoke and made the announcements that Orwell refers to then.

[319] This agreement had been signed weeks before on 24 November. As Orwell went on to say, there was a great deal that needed explaining about the political events of that time.

[320] Stafford Cripps made some observations on Darlan's position in answer to questions in the House of Commons in a debate on 17 November.

two relevant facts. General Catroux, the Free French leader, has uttered a protest against the tie-up between the United States military commanders and General Darlan, which has been given a good deal of publicity in this country. Mr Cordell Hull, the American Foreign Secretary, has given his opinion that by entering into agreement with Admiral Darlan, and thus taking over North Africa peacefully, the United States saved the lives of about 20,000 men.]

Japanese aeroplanes attacked a convoy in the Bay of Bengal about a week ago, and two days ago they carried out a small bombing raid on Chittagong[321] – the first bombs to fall on Indian soil for many months. It is too early to say what this means, but one can say now that a Japanese invasion of India, which seemed so likely a year or six months ago, is now very improbable. The Japanese have been so hard hit in the Southern Pacific that they have in all probability lost their chance of gaining naval control of the Bay of Bengal. During this week, on the anniversary of the Japanese attack on Pearl Harbor, the United States Government published the first full account of the attack and its after-effects, and gave some revealing figures of their own and the Japanese shipping losses during the year. It now appears that the unexpected Japanese attack was very damaging indeed – no less than eight battleships were damaged in varying degrees – but that all except one of the ships damaged has since been put back into service or is in process of being so.[322] Ever since then the Japanese losses at sea have been very much higher than those of the Allies. In the Solomons area alone they have lost 135 ships, warships and merchant ships, sunk or damaged, and over 600 airplanes. The Japanese are very much less able to bear these losses than the Allies, because their industrial capacity is very much less. They are also at least as dependent on seaborne supplies as the British Isles are. Meanwhile during the current year the Americans have turned out over 40,000 aeroplanes of all types, and built 8 million tons of merchant shipping. The American ship-building programme called for 8 million tons in 1942 and 15 million tons in 1943, and the 1942 construction at any rate is up to schedule. They have also built large numbers of warships, including a new battleship of over 50,000 tons launched during this week.[323] Add

[321] Japanese bombers with fighter escort raided Chittagong on 10 December; there was a previous attack on 5 December which had been mentioned in the monitors' reports. Presumably Orwell missed the item.

[322] The figures had been published at the time, or shortly after, and there were no further references on the occasion of the anniversary of the event in the major British national papers. It may well be that the censor had prevented mention of the actual figures of losses until this time.

[323] The USS *New Jersey*, 52,000 tons. The other figures Orwell has taken from US Navy Department press releases.

to all this the fact that the Japanese have lost certainly four and probably six of their largest aircraft carriers sunk, and it becomes clear why they aren't likely after all to attempt the invasion of India. They appear to have given up, at any rate for the time being, their attempts to drive the Americans off Guadalcanal in the Solomon Islands. At Buna, on the coast of New Guinea, they are still holding on to a small area and have fought with great courage, but they are not expected to hold their position there much longer. The threat to Port Moresby, and hence to Darwin in Australia, which seemed so imminent a few months ago, is probably at an end. Mr Curtin, the Australian Prime Minister, however has warned his countrymen that the Japanese might make an attempt further west on the North Australian coast, using the island of Timor as their jumping-off place.[324]

The Polish Government has just published the full facts about the systematic massacre of the Jews in German-occupied Poland.[325] The Polish Government's statement is not propaganda. It is verified from many sources, including the pronouncements of the Nazi leaders themselves. For instance, in March of this year Himmler, the head of the Gestapo, issued a decree calling for the 'liquidation' – remember that in totalitarian language[326] liquidation is a polite name for murder – of fifty per cent of the surviving Polish Jews. It seems as if his programme is being carried out successfully. The Polish Government's figures show that of something over 3 million Jews living in Poland before the war, well over a third – that is, well over one million human beings – have been killed in cold blood or died of starvation and general misery. Many thousands of them, men, women and children, have been deported to Russian territory, sealed up in cattle trucks without food or water for journeys that may take weeks, so that when the trucks are opened sometimes half the people inside are dead. This policy, which Hitler himself has proclaimed over and over again as his chosen one in speeches both before and after the war, is carried out wherever the Germans are in control. Already, now that they have taken over the whole of France, they are putting the anti-Jewish laws into operation there and French Jews are being deported to the

[324] In a broadcast on 6 December.

[325] In a note given by Count Edward Raczynski, Polish Ambassador in London to the Allied Governments. The note described in detail the fate of innumerable Jews. For the background to this note, see Martin Gilbert, *Auschwitz and the Allies* (1981).

[326] In *Nineteen Eighty-Four* Orwell forged the perfect totalitarian language 'Newspeak', but somehow it never acquires the cold horror that Orwell warns people about here.

East.[327] And France, be it remembered, is the country where for a hundred and fifty years – ever since the Great Revolution – there have been no legal disabilities against Jews whatever. I don't mention this persecution of the Jews simply for the sake of repeating horror stories, but because this kind of cold-blooded, systematic cruelty, utterly different from the violences committed in battle, brings home to us the nature of Fascism, the thing we are fighting against.[328]

17 December 1942

During this week there hasn't been much news from any front except the North African one. In Russia both the Russian offensives and the attempted German counter-attacks have slowed down, no doubt chiefly because of the weather. There is bound to be a sort of pause on the Russian fronts at about this time of year, when the snow is falling but hasn't yet frozen hard. But the position of the German armies before Stalingrad and in Rzhev, on the Moscow front, isn't enviable, and the Russians have reported impressive captures of war materials during this week [*censored:* and it looks as though the Germans can hold their present position if they want to.] Down in the South Pacific the Japanese have succeeded in landing a few men – it is not known exactly how many, probably a few hundreds – north-west of Buna in New Guinea. The object, probably, is to bar the way to an Allied advance westward when Buna itself has been mopped up by the Allies. The Japanese lost heavily in men and landing craft.[329] They haven't yet renewed their attempts to drive the Americans out of Guadalcanal in the Solomon Islands. Japanese planes have, however, again bombed Chittagong, the second time in about ten days.[330] It is too early yet to be quite certain what this means, but it's not impossible that the Allies

[327] Orwell now reveals the situation in France that was known to him from the monitors' reports months before. The reference to anti-Jewish laws is to a broadcast by the French Commissioner General for Jewish Affairs, newly appointed, who announced that the Jewish question would be studied 'scientifically in the German manner'.

[328] One must accept the fact, mentioned earlier, that Orwell and others knew nothing of the fire-storm bombing techniques that were being used by the Allies against the German civilian population.

[329] The Japanese attempted a night landing on 13 December. General MacArthur's Headquarters reported that about 250 troops had landed of whom the majority were killed.

[330] This was the third raid on Chittagong. See above, p. 186, n.321.

are contemplating some fresh move in the area of the India-Burma frontier. The main news of this week has been the fighting in Africa, and it's that that I want to devote most of my commentary to.

Last week I suggested that there would be renewed activity very shortly on the Libyan front, and sure enough, it has happened. Five days ago the news broke that the Germans had abandoned their strong defensive position at El Agheila, fifty miles west of Benghazi, and were retreating rapidly westward. Evidently the German plan was to get their main force away as rapidly as possible, while holding up the pursuit of the British Eighth Army by small rearguard actions and by sowing anti-tank mines. However, there has evidently been a hitch in the plan already. The day before yesterday the news came in that an advance detachment of the Eighth Army had made a big outflanking movement, circling round through the desert and then reaching the sea again at a place called Matratin, about sixty miles west of El Agheila. The Axis rearguard was cut off and attacked from both sides, and appears to have been scattered.[331] How many men are involved is not yet known, but it is probable that the Axis force which was cut off included considerable numbers of tanks and guns. To see the full significance of this one has got to relate it to the probable German plan, and to the North African campaign as a whole.

It doesn't appear as though the Germans intend making another stand in Libya, except perhaps in defence of Tripoli itself. Having abandoned El Agheila, the most natural place to make another stand would be at Misurata, about a hundred and fifty miles east of Tripoli. This is another natural defensive position, with the road leading up to it flanked on one side by desert and on the other by a marshy area probably lending itself to ambushes, and with several streams forming natural obstacles. Misurata also has a small seaport and is within fairly easy road distance of Tripoli. However, the tone of the German communiqués rather suggests that their plan is to abandon Libya altogether and transfer Rommel's army to Tunisia, or, possibly, to get it away by sea. For the first few days the Axis radio commentators refused to admit that any retreat was going on. Then they suddenly changed their tone and switched over to claiming that the retreat was a clever prearranged manoeuvre which had completely thrown the British strategy out of gear. To read the German communiqués of this moment you would think that retreating was the whole art of war, and certainly some of their phrases are most ingenious. We have all heard

---

[331] Orwell's account is an optimistic one, reflecting MOI briefings. In fact Rommel's retreat was completed and the anti-personnel mines, combined with booby traps, greatly delayed the Eighth Army pursuit. The outflanking movement was largely unsuccessful.

of 'strategic withdrawals' and 'elastic defence', but the German commentators have thought of better ones than that. Their best phrase to describe a rapid retreat is 'We have successfully increased the distance between ourselves and the enemy'; another is 'We have compelled the British to advance westward' – also, of course, that by choosing to retreat General Rommel 'retains the initiative'. You will have noticed that when a dog is chasing a rabbit, the rabbit retains the initiative. But this phraseology is worth noticing, because it makes clear that the Germans are preparing their home public for bad news.[332] They don't, in all probability, expect to be able to turn the tables this time, and the best they can hope is to slow down the British advance while the other Axis force consolidates its position in Tunisia.

That is where the importance of the defeat of the Axis rearguard comes in. At best it is difficult for the Eighth Army to advance rapidly, because the distances to be covered are enormous, and moreover they are now entering the desert of Sirte, which is about two hundred miles wide. Most of their water will have to be brought from the rear, either by road or in barges along the coast. The function of the Axis rearguard was to hold up the Allied advance by destroying such wells as exist, and by anti-tank mines. When these are buried in the ground they blow up any vehicle which passes over them, and the army as a whole can't advance till special troops have gone ahead and dealt with the mines, which often take a long time to find.[333] The outflanking move which has cut off the Axis rearguard will probably have disrupted these delaying tactics considerably. Meanwhile the main enemy force is being pursued westward, along a narrow coast where it is difficult for them to disperse to avoid air attacks. All the reports that have come in show that the Allies are greatly superior in the air on the front.

But now look at the Libyan front in relation to the other front in Tunisia. There the Allied attack on Tunis and Bizerta is still held up, and evidently by the same cause as before – German superiority in the air. The Germans are still better supplied in the matter of airfields, and probably they are being fairly rapidly reinforced – in men, that is – by air from Sicily and Sardinia. They have not, however, been successful in their new attacks since their capture of Tebourba and Jedeida. The British First Army is still holding on to Medjes el Bab, west of Tunis,

---

[332] Preparing people for bad news was another essential aspect of propaganda that Orwell refers to here, and also in *Nineteen Eighty-Four*.

[333] Orwell's detailed explanation here, repeating earlier references, illustrates the difficulty he had in ensuring that his Indian audience understood him. He actually commissioned a series of talks to explain such things, writing one himself on 'Sabotage' (see *OWB*, p.77ff.).

in spite of several German attacks. The main Allied position, behind which they are building up their striking force, has not been breached. If the Eighth Army gets to Tripoli or thereabouts, that will weaken the German position in Tunisia just as much as heavy reinforcements on the other side. The Germans will be subjected to air attack from both east and west, and also from Malta, which it has already been possible to reinforce. It is probably safe to say that with the Allies both in Tripoli and in Algiers the Germans could not hold on in Tunisia, though from the amount of reinforcements they have thrown in already it looks as if they mean to gamble on it – perhaps partly for prestige reasons.

Admiral Darlan has issued a fresh statement[334] in his capacity as High Commissioner for French North and West Africa. He has said that the French warships at the various African ports will operate on the side of the Allies. These include the warships which were at Dakar and Casablanca, and also those which were interned in Alexandria when France went out of the war. These will make a big addition to the Allied fleets, though perhaps not an immediate one. Besides several heavy cruisers and a number of destroyers and smaller vessels, they include two battleships, both of them at present damaged, the *Richelieu*, which was hit by a British torpedo soon after the armistice in 1940, and the *Jean Bart*, which was more heavily damaged in the fighting at Casablanca. These will take time to repair, and the vessels which were interned were partly disarmed. But the smaller ships, it is thought, will be able to start in service almost immediately. The fate of the French fleet is now finally settled, after more than two years of uncertainty, and the Allies have come immensely better out of the bargain than the Germans.

[*Censored:* Certain points about Admiral Darlan's position have still not been made clear. In his statement to the press, however, he said two things which have caused widespread satisfaction. One was that all Frenchmen in North Africa who had been interned or imprisoned by the Vichy authorities for activities against the Axis are to be released, just as President Roosevelt requested. It isn't absolutely clear whether this covers the various other anti-Fascist refugees, chiefly Germans and Spaniards, who had been shut up in concentration camps under the Vichy regime. We may hope it does – at any rate it should be possible to get confirmation on this point in the near future.[335] The other thing Admiral Darlan announced – this

---

[334] At a press conference on 16 December published from the Allies' General Headquarters.

[335] Darlan granted full amnesty to all 'against whom any action had been taken because of their sympathy with the Allies'.

had also been requested by President Roosevelt – was that the anti-Jew laws in North Africa, which had been forced on Vichy by the Germans, are to be abolished.]

I spoke last week about the fresh German persecution and massacre of the Jews in Poland. Even after three years of war, when people inevitably grow callous, this has caused the most profound horror all over the world. I believe there is not a newspaper in this country that has not commented on it with indignation. It has been debated in both houses of Parliament, and many intercession services have been held in which Jews and Christians have taken part together. Mr Anthony Eden has given a solemn promise on behalf of the British Government that after the war those responsible for these cold-blooded massacres will be punished – and not merely the little clique at the top of the Nazi party, but also those who have actually carried out their orders.[336] The International Federation of Trade Unions has called on the German working class to demonstrate, before it is too late, that they are not at one with those who rule them.[337] Until the war is won that is about all that it is possible to do. There is, however, just a slight chance that something positive can be done even now to save at any rate some of the victims of persecution. A move is on foot to evacuate Jewish children from German-occupied Europe under the supervision of some neutral power. It may not come to anything, but on the other hand it is just possible that it may. The Germans have shown that they are not more merciful to children than to adults, but because of their food problem it might seem to them worthwhile to get rid of some of their unwanted population. Even so there are many and obvious difficulties in the way of such a scheme. But we may earnestly hope that it will be put into operation, and the fact that it is at least put forward and receives popular support shows that the people of this country have not forgotten what cause they are fighting for.[338]

[336] In a statement in the House of Commons on 17 December; an identical statement was issued in Washington and Moscow.

[337] An interesting political point for Orwell to try to make. The National Socialists in Germany looked for their strongest support to ordinary working men and women, particularly those in skilled occupations.

[338] The principal barrier to such emigration of children, if they could have been got out, was the reluctance of the British authorities in Palestine to admit them. A request had been made for 'Palestine certificates' for 870 Hungarian and Romanian Jewish children on 23 March 1942, but Sir Harold MacMichael, High Commissioner in Palestine, felt obliged to refuse it, for fear of establishing a precedent. Within the British Civil Service there were those who simply did not believe the cases of atrocity reported to them. J.S. Bennett, a Colonial Officer, stated: 'What is disturbing is the apparent readiness of the new Colonial Secretary to take Jewish Agency "sob-stuff" at

26 December 1942

I said in earlier commentaries that before long there would be some official pronouncement defining the position of Admiral Darlan, High Commissioner for French North and West Africa. Well, it so happens that his position has been defined in another way. He is dead. He was assassinated two days ago. The assassin was captured and tried by a French court martial. He was due to be executed this morning. That is all we know at present, except that General Giraud has taken over Darlan's position as commander of the French forces in North and West Africa for the time being. The administration is proceeding as before.[339]

[*Censored:* I said in recent news commentaries that before long the British and United States Governments were likely to issue some official statement defining the position of Admiral Darlan, the High Commissioner for French North and West Africa. Well, it so happens that his position has been defined in another way. He is dead, having been assassinated in Algiers the day before yesterday. The assassin was captured, but we don't yet know who he is or what his motives were.[340] No doubt the world will be enlightened on those points within the next few days. Meanwhile I should like to emphasise that Darlan's death makes no difference to the general situation. The stability of the regime in French Africa did not depend upon him, and there is no reason to think that the loyalty to the United Nations of the French troops in Africa will be in any way affected. For the moment

its face value. As a political manoeuvre this will establish a good precedent which the Agency will no doubt exploit' (quoted by Martin Gilbert, op.cit., p. 99). Orwell could have known nothing of this at the time, except by rumours.

[339] This paragraph was written by Orwell after the original opening that follows in brackets had been censored. The last line of the new version was deleted by the censor on re-submission.

[340] He was Bonnier de la Chapelle, 20, described in Churchill's *The Second World War*, vol.4, p.577f., as 'connected with Henri d'Astier'. Vichy propaganda blamed the British and American secret service, adding for good measure that the assassin's wife was Jewish. Since Vichy had referred to Darlan in bitter terms as a traitor, it would have been at least as likely that the blame lay at their door.

General Giraud, who escaped recently from Germany[341] and reached Africa via Vichy France, has taken over the command of the French forces in Africa. A successor to Darlan will no doubt be appointed shortly. During the past week or two a great deal of evidence had accumulated as to Darlan's unpopularity with the French North African population, who presumably didn't forget his record as a 'collaborator' in the Vichy Government, and didn't feel that his having changed sides a second time necessarily wiped out the first time. The cause of the United Nations will be a lot better off if as successor to Darlan we get someone who has been less conspicuously associated with the policy of surrender to the Nazis.]

Apart from the assassination of Admiral Darlan, the chief development this week on the North African front has been the continued and rapid retreat of the Germans in Libya. At the time when I delivered my commentary last week the rearguard of General Rommel's army had just been cut off west of El Agheila and seemed likely to be completely destroyed. Most of that rearguard ultimately got away,[342] though not without losing fairly heavily in guns and other material, besides a few hundreds of prisoners. But the retreat has gone on, and our advance patrols are now in contact with the Germans somewhere near Sirte, about a hundred and fifty miles west of El Agheila. It looks as though the Germans are about to abandon Sirte, and ultimately, in all probability, the whole of Libya, though no doubt they will fight a delaying action in defence of Tripoli. They are still doing their best to slow up the Eighth Army's advance by sowing anti-tank mines, and by ploughing up the airfields they have to abandon; when this is done it is some days before the airfields can be used by Allied planes. Also, within the last few days German airplanes have begun to reappear on the Libyan front, after about a week in which almost the only air activity had been that of the Allies. No doubt the German commander hopes to hold up the Eighth Army till the bulk of the German forces have got away, probably into Tunisia or, possibly, back to Sicily by sea.

From the German point of view the complete abandonment of Libya has the disadvantage that it means giving up the last scrap of the Italian Empire and thus robbing the Italians of any motive they may still have for continuing the war. There is much evidence that morale in Italy is

[341] Giraud escaped from the fortress of Königstein in mid April; he was reported in Switzerland between 21 and 25 April and arrived in Vichy France at the beginning of May. At the time of the invasion of North Africa he was brought by an Allied submarine to General Eisenhower's Headquarters, arriving there by 20 December.

[342] A communiqué, issued at Cairo on 17 December, said that 'some tanks and infantry had escaped', but see above, p.189, n.331.

already low, the food situation is bad, and the British air raids have caused much panic and disorganisation. There has even been serious talk of declaring Rome an open city to save it from being bombed. If this is done it will be a tremendous blow to Axis prestige and an open admission that Italian morale is shaky. The Germans, however, are not likely to be affected by any concern for Italian feelings. However much the Italian people may hate the war they are not in a position to make any anti-war move while the German army is quartered upon them. And for the Germans to abandon Libya altogether and concentrate on holding on to Tunisia would have considerable advantages. If they could hold Tunisia permanently – which, however, isn't likely – they could completely bar the passage through the Mediterranean to Allied shipping. But even if they can only hold it for a while they can cut their losses and get out of Africa less disastrously than if they risked having a whole army destroyed in Libya. Also their supply problem in Bizerta and Tunis is very much simpler than it is in Tripoli. To supply Tripoli means a constant loss of ships and transport planes. Throughout the present operations the Axis have been losing on an average a ship a day – far more than they can afford with their limited amount of shipping. So my forecast for North Africa would be that the Germans are likely to defend Bizerta and Tunis as long as possible, but not to make an all-out effort to defend Tripoli.

Since last week the Russians have opened up fresh offensives, this time on the middle Don, north-west of Stalingrad and also in the Caucasus. They broke through the German defensive positions almost immediately and in just over a week they have made an advance of about a hundred miles and claim 50,000 prisoners, besides great captures of war material.[343] The advance the Russians have made in a south-westerly direction makes it still harder for the German army before Stalingrad to get out of its uncomfortable position. How decisive this Russian victory will be we can't yet say. A feature of the winter fighting in Russia is the difficulty either side has of making any prolonged offensive, owing to the severe weather conditions and consequent break-down of communications. But the series of limited offensives which the Russians have now made at widely-separated points along the front have added greatly to the Germans' problems. The Russians are now in several places across the railway connecting Voronezh with Rostov, which makes lateral communication much harder for the Germans. If you look at the map of the Russian front, from Leningrad down to the Caucasus, you will notice that the line

---

[343] The offensive had in fact begun on 16 December. The figures Orwell quotes were from a Russian communiqué issued the same day as Orwell's broadcast.

occupied by the German armies is roughly twice as long as it need be, owing to the huge salients in it. The Germans could shorten it by means of a general retreat, but considerations of prestige make that difficult for them.[344] And the Germans have again failed to capture large cities in which to winter their troops. Last year thousands of Germans – we do not know how many thousands – were frozen to death because of the failure to capture Moscow and Leningrad. This year thousands more will die of cold because of the failure to capture Stalingrad and to get across the Caucasus Mountains. And the more activity the Red Army can keep up during the winter months, the harder for the Germans to rest their armies and get ready for the Anglo-American offensive next year.

Last week I suggested that the Japanese bombing of Chittagong might mean that the Allies intended some move in the area of the India-Burma frontier. This has been confirmed by the advance that British and Indian forces have made into Burma in the direction of Akyab. The fact that the Japanese have three times bombed Calcutta suggests that they take this move seriously. We ought not, however, to expect any immediate great results from the Allied advance. It is probably only a reconnaissance to test Japanese strength and also to make contact with the Burmese and discover their reactions to the Japanese occupation. Akyab is not of itself an objective worth fighting a serious battle for.[345] There is only one really important objective in Burma, and that is Rangoon, the only port of entry through which war materials could once again be sent to the Burma Road. The Allies would have to capture Rangoon to make any campaign in Burma worth while. A more significant bit of news, which has attracted less attention, is the air raid on the island of Sumatra by British planes which must have come from an aircraft carrier.[346] This is significant because it shows how the balance of naval power is shifting *against* Japan. This is the first action the Allies have taken against Sumatra since March of this year, and till a few months ago no Allied aircraft carrier could possibly have got near Sumatra. Japanese naval

[344] An amusing propagandist way of saying that the Russians had as yet failed to force the Germans to retreat.

[345] This advance, the first against the Japanese in Burma, was reported to have begun on 21 December and the first contact with Japanese troops to have occurred on 26 December. It would seem that Orwell was being disingenuous in saying that Akyab was not worth fighting for. Its aerodrome dominated the airspace as far as Rangoon and its capture was seen as essential.

[346] The Japanese base at Sabang, Sumatra, was raided on 20 December by planes from the British Eastern Fleet.

superiority is waning even on the eastern side of the Bay of Bengal, thanks to the heavy losses they have had in the South Pacific and the much faster rate of Allied construction in ships and planes. The British raid on Sumatra is a demonstration of this, but it must have had some direct military purpose as well, and it may have been connected with the advance into Burma. It would be worth keeping an eye on the Andaman Islands, which lie south-west of Burma and command the approaches to Rangoon and Singapore.

This is the fourth Christmas of war, and in the minute or two remaining to me I should like to glance back, as I have sometimes done in earlier commentaries, and say something about the development of the war as a whole. Look back two years, to the Christmas of 1940. Britain was alone, fighting desperately with her back to the wall, and London and other British cities were being bombed to pieces. America was neutral, Soviet Russia also neutral and only very doubtfully friendly. An Italian army had been destroyed in Cyrenaica and the air battle over Britain had been won, but the Germans had conquered the whole of Western Europe and there was no kind of certainty that the New Order would not be a success. Now look back one year, to the Christmas of 1941, when too the outlook was black enough. Hong Kong had just fallen, an unannounced attack had temporarily crippled the American fleet at Pearl Harbor, and the Japanese had started on their career of conquest which – so it appeared at the time – was certain to lead on to the invasion of India and of Australia. But there were compensations there had not been the year before. Russia and the United States were in the war, the attempt to knock out Russia at one blow had visibly failed, and the German army was still breaking its teeth on Moscow. Moreover Britain's strength, in arms and trained men, had grown enormously in the intervening year. And now look at the situation as it now stands. In Russia the Germans have suffered huge losses for no corresponding gain, and they have another winter in the snow ahead of them. The Japanese are where they stood seven months ago, they have lost scores of irreplaceable warships, and in the South Pacific the struggle has begun to turn against them. Most of Libya has been lost to the Axis, and the whole north-west corner of Africa, with its good ports and airfields and its important raw materials, has passed into Allied control. Both American and British arms production have got into full swing. As for the New Order, even the Germans themselves have almost stopped pretending that it is a success. There have been moments even during 1942 – especially during the middle of the summer – when things looked dark enough, but we can see now with certainty that the tide has turned. Just at what moment it turned is disputable. It might have been the Battle of Britain in 1940, or the failure of the Germans before Moscow in 1941, or the Anglo-American invasion of North Africa in 1942 – but it has turned, and one can tell even from the speeches of the Axis leaders themselves that they know very well it won't flow their way again.

9 January 1943

This week there is little fresh news except from the Russian front, and I propose to devote most of my commentary to that. But I would like first to summarise shortly the news from the other fronts, so as to get the Russian front into its proper perspective.

In North Africa there have hardly been any fresh developments. In Tunisia the struggle see-saws to and fro, neither side gaining or losing much ground and both sides are evidently building up their forces for the big battle yet to come. The Germans in Tunisia have evidently been reinforced in tanks as well as men, in spite of their losses at sea, which continue to be serious. Malta has been reinforced now that the naval position in the Mediterranean has shifted in favour of the Allies and air activity based on Malta is increasing.[347]

Free French forces moving northward across the desert from Lake Tchad in equatorial Africa, have driven in the Axis outposts in the Libyan desert and captured an important oasis about four hundred miles south of Tripoli.[348] This manoeuvre has meant a march of about a thousand miles largely over desert. An attack coming from this direction is an added threat to the Axis positions, both in Tripolitania and in Tunisia, but it is very difficult to move large numbers of men or vehicles across the desert, not only because of the lack of water but because of the time taken in building up petrol dumps. That is about all the news from North Africa.

In Eastern New Guinea, Japanese resistance at Buna has been finally overcome. The only Japanese forces now left in this part of the island are at Sanananda, about fifty miles to the west, where they were landed a few weeks ago. The Allies are now regrouping for the final attack on Sanananda. The Japanese loss of Eastern New Guinea,

[347] Admiral Harwood, Commander-in-Chief Mediterranean, had outlined the changed position of Malta as a result of the Eighth Army advances in a press conference at Alexandria on 26 December.

[348] Oum-el-Arameb, the main Axis outpost in the Fessan, was reported captured by the Free French on 6 January.

and of Guadalcanal in the Solomon Islands, will have upset their plans in the South Pacific, but it does not look as though they have yet given up all hope of attacking Australia. Air reconnaissance shows that they have assembled another big fleet of warships and transports in Rabaul, in New Britain, and some observers report that this is the biggest fleet which they have yet assembled. We do not yet know what operation they are intending, but it has been suggested that they might make another effort at invading Australia somewhere on the northwest coast.[349] They would probably have another try at retrieving the situation in New Guinea and the Solomons before doing so. This threat is taken seriously in Australia where conscription, both for the armed forces and for war industries, is being extended.

British and American air raids along the coast of Burma have been increasing in volume and they have ranged all the way from the Aoikan coast to Pagoda Point and as far inland as Mandalay. We have not at present very much evidence of how things are going for the Japanese in their occupied territories but what evidence there is all shows that local resistance is increasing everywhere. The latest bit of news is the announcement by the Japanese wireless that they have just executed a number of Burmese for sabotage and destruction and also two Indians on the charge of sabotaging railways. The Japanese have also issued orders that the people of Burma are forbidden to listen in to foreign broadcasting stations – a sure sign that Allied broadcasts are attracting attention.[350] We are probably safe in guessing that the Burmese are already beginning to find out the real nature of the Japanese New Order.

I don't think that during this week there have been any other events on the Asiatic fronts on which I can significantly comment.

Now as to the Russian front. The Russians have followed up the capture of Veliki Luki[351] near the Latvian border, by capturing Mozdok and Nalchik on the Caucasus front, hundreds of miles to the south. The loss of Nalchik puts the seal on the failure of the German Caucasus campaign. If you look at a map of Russia on which the present approximate position of the armies is marked, you will see that the German army in the Caucasus is doing nothing except to maintain

[349] This convoy was first sighted on 6 January and repeatedly attacked on its way to Loe, which it reached on 8 January. Many of the ships and their escorting planes were reported destroyed.

[350] The monitor source for these statements has not been found, but the prohibition on pain of death was a widely adopted course when radio propaganda was beginning to have an effect. In some cases the receivers were mechanically fixed on 'friendly' channels when jamming was not possible.

[351] An important German strongpoint that fell on 1 January 1943 after bitter fighting.

a huge salient which has no direct value. When the Germans advanced southward in the summer they expected, and a good deal of the rest of the world expected, too, that they would cross the Caucasus Mountains[352] and get to the Baku oilfields before the winter. At the least it was expected that they would remain in possession of the key towns, commanding the passes over the Caucasus Mountains, and would be able to renew their offensive early in the spring. Now they are being driven back and are evidently retreating rapidly. They can hardly make another stand before they get to the Kuma river and may have to go much further back than that, for, at the same time as the German army in the south has lost its footing, the Russian armies west of Stalingrad are still advancing along the Don. They are now thought to be only about seventy-five miles from Roztov. If they should reach Roztov, which is not impossible, the whole German army in the Caucasus area will either have to retreat hurriedly or run the risk of being completely cut off. Undoubtedly the right thing to do would be to retreat now, but German strategy is not governed altogether by military considerations. The Germans have had huge and useless losses because Hitler did not care to abandon Stalingrad after boasting that he would take it, and the same story may be repeated in the south.

Meanwhile, the German public is apparently being prepared for bad news. If one studies the German wireless and newspapers, one notices two propaganda tricks constantly employed. One is that place names are mentioned as seldom as possible, the commentators merely stating that fighting is in progress in such and such an area and by not mentioning names avoiding stating whether the German armies are retreating or advancing. The other device is to dwell on the immense difficulties of the Russian campaign and especially the severity of the Russian winter. It is also admitted, however, by some German commentators, that the Russian troops are fighting well and are not short of tanks and weapons generally.[353] There are even some quite detailed accounts of the special methods the Russians use to overcome the difficulty of moving over deep snow. All this suggests that the Germans are contemplating a big retreat and are trying in advance to make this acceptable to the public. The articles in the German press and on the wireless emphasising the strength and numbers of the Red

---

[352] See above, p.151, n.248.

[353] The point was worth making as Axis propagandists were frequently saying that the Russians were being reduced to the use of cavalry and other techniques from an earlier age, and that captured Russian officers were often not able to read or write. In answer, the Russians proudly described their cavalry actions in detail as late as September 1942.

Army do not fit in very well with the official statement of more than a year ago that the Red Army had been destroyed once and for all, but the people in totalitarian countries are expected to have short memories.[354] At present it looks as though the Nazi leaders can see no good news ahead, at any rate on the Russian front, and are excusing this as best they can by implying that the task before them is superhuman.

President Roosevelt's speech on January 6th, when he addressed the United States Congress, has already had a lot of publicity, but I should like to re-emphasise two points in it because a speech of this kind is in itself an event and can be just as important as anything that happens on the battlefield.[355]

In the first place the President added some more figures of American war production to the ones I was able to give you last week. For instance, he revealed that during 1942 the United States has produced 48,000 military aeroplanes, which is more than the production of Germany, Italy and Japan put together. By December the United States was producing aeroplanes at the rate of over 60,000 a year. Again, in 1942, the United States produced 56,000 fighting vehicles, such as tanks or self-propelling artillery. Again during the past year the United States armed forces have grown from a strength of 2 million men to over 7 million men. Now it is no use reading out long lists of figures which after a little while only become confusing, but the upshot is that during the past year the whole of America's war production has enormously increased, sometimes by an increase of several hundred per cent over 1941 and still is increasing rapidly. American food production has increased as well.

The other outstanding point in the President's speech was the complete and uncompromising break he made with isolationism.[356] He said quite clearly and at considerable length that Americans realised more clearly than ever before that the whole world is now potentially one unit and that no nation can stand aloof, either from the job of preventing aggression or from the job of supplying the wants of the common people everywhere. 'We cannot,' he said, 'make America an island in either a military or economic sense. Victory in this war is the first and greatest goal before us. Victory in the peace is the next. That means striving towards the enlargement of the security of men here and throughout the world, and finally striving for freedom from

[354] The destruction of the past, of memory, by totalitarian regimes is of course a central theme of *Nineteen Eighty-Four*.

[355] A speech given to Congress after the elections of 3 January.

[356] Axis radio made great play of the success of a number of isolationist candidates during the election.

fear.' 'The United Nations,' he added, 'are the mightiest military coalition in history. Bound together in solemn agreement that they themselves will not commit acts of aggression or conquest, the United Nations can and must remain united for the maintenance of peace by preventing any attempt to rearm in Germany, in Japan and in Italy. There are cynics and sceptics who say it cannot be done. The American people and all freedom-loving peoples of this earth are now demanding that it must be done and the will of these peoples shall prevail.' This is a great step forward from the isolationism and the purely nationalistic conception of security and prosperity with which the United States, as well as some other nations, ended the last war.

16 January 1943

During this week there have been only two events of major importance and I should like to devote most of my commentary, as I do from time to time, to giving a general survey of the war as it now stands. But first let me just mention those two events which I spoke of as important – one of them military, the other political.

The important military news is that the Russian offensives on four separate parts of the front are all continuing and making headway. I said last week that the Germans retreating in the Caucasus might make another stand on the Kuma river about Georgievsk, and already Georgievsk is in Russian hands and the Russians are well over the Kuma river and are still advancing. The advance along the Don towards Stalingrad is also continuing, though less rapidly. It is important not to expect Rostov itself to fall at all rapidly or easily. The Germans are now falling back on Rostov from all directions and are certain to defend it obstinately. If they should lose it, their whole Caucasus campaign will have gone for nothing and in all probability a large body of men further south would be cut off with only a rather slender chance of escaping by sea.

The other important event of this week is the final signature of the treaty between China, Great Britain and the United States.[357] By this treaty extraterritorial rights in China are formally relinquished. One hundred years ago treaties were made with the [*censored:* imposed on the unwilling] Chinese by which the nationals of various countries enjoyed privileges in China's territory which were not compatible with

[357] The Treaty was signed on 11 January and ratified in a formal exchange of documents at Chungking on 20 May.

China's existence as a sovereign state. They were exempt from China's law and payment of taxes and their warships had the right to navigate in Chinese rivers. All this has now been signed away once and for all by the British and American Governments. The Japanese, [*censored: not to be outdone on the propaganda front,*] are making a pretence of some similar arrangement, but as they are in actual possession of about a quarter of China, with the status of conquerors, their claims cannot be taken very seriously. Simultaneously with this, the Japanese have ordered the so-called government of Nanking to declare war on the United Nations.[358] This is not of very great importance, as the Nanking Government has no real existence, being merely a marionette show put on by Japan, and in any case the few Chinese who have sided with the Japanese were for all intents and purposes at war with the United Nations already. The Anglo-Chinese treaty has caused great satisfaction in this country, perhaps almost as great as it has caused in China. It is one of those events like the settlement with Abyssinia which shows that the claim of the United Nations to be fighting for liberty and against aggression and tyranny is not simply a show of words. Incidentally, it is rather interesting to couple with this the results of a survey of public opinion[359] taken recently in Britain on the question of feeding Europe after the war. A representative cross-section of the British public were asked if it were necessary in order to prevent starvation in Europe would they be ready to continue with food rationing in Britain when the war was over. Eighty per cent answered 'Yes' and only seven per cent answered with a definite 'No'. Things like this tell one more about the real reasons for which the ordinary man is fighting than declarations of war aims expressed in high-sounding and general terms.

I said I was going to attempt a general survey of the war situation at the beginning of 1943. The first point which would be conceded, even by our enemies, is that the situation is enormously better for the Allies than it was at the beginning of 1942. Even Dr Goebbels, in his weekly article in the newspaper *Das Reich*[360] warns the German public that their position is more difficult and dangerous now than it was at the beginning of the war. If one looks at the past year, in spite of the many

[358] The Japanese had somehow got wind of the announcement and published their own Sino-Japanese agreement with the National Government of China at Nanking which, at the same time, declared war on the British Empire and the United States.

[359] Surveys of public opinion were far less common at this time than they are now. Orwell was in close contact with Tom Harrison, the founder and Director of the best known survey, Mass Observation (see *OWB*, p.31ff.).

[360] Goebbels's articles in *Das Reich* were also broadcast and were reproduced in the monitors' reports.

and brilliant successes of the Axis, there are three main facts which stand out. These facts are, first the failure of the Japanese to keep up the initial impetus of their attack against the United Nations. The second the failure of the German campaign in Russia to gain any of its major objectives. The third is the quite obviously growing strength of Britain and the United States, by means of which the danger to Egypt and the Suez Canal has been removed and a whole corner of Africa, larger than Europe in area, has passed into the control of the Allies. The most immediately important of these three events is the German failure in Russia with all its damaging effects, present and to come, in losses of men, materials and prestige, and it is important when one assesses this to remember that the successes the Russians have had, though chiefly due to their own courage and energy, also owes a great deal to the less obvious efforts of Great Britain and the United States. We hear less about the convoys to Murmansk than we hear about the Russian battlefields, but it is important to remember that the British supply of war materials to Russia has never flagged, even in the face of the greatest difficulties and even when the need for arms on other fronts was most acute. For example, Britain has already delivered for Russian use 3,000 aeroplanes, 4,000 tanks and many thousands of tons of war materials of all descriptions, including medical supplies.[361] The United States has similarly contributed and has also sent Russia a good deal of food, but the chief help which Britain and America have brought to their ally has been indirect. By the threat to invade Western Europe, which it is known will be carried out sooner or later, they have forced the Germans to keep at least thirty-five divisions in Western Europe, and consequently, to deplete their strength on the Russian front to that extent. The British army in Libya keeps another ten or more Axis divisions busy, and this diversion becomes more serious owing to the German effort to hold on to Tunisia. During this year the Germans will probably find it necessary to hold and fortify the whole of Southern Europe on the same scale as Western Europe, with a corresponding drainage on their manpower. The peculiar features of the New Order have ensured that the German manpower problem is now serious. If the Germans had kept the various promises to the European peoples with which they started the war, they might possibly have had, by this time, a large reliable European army fighting on their side, and a huge fluid labour force. The whole of European industry might have been working at top speed for their benefit. As it

[361] Orwell's source for these figures has not been found. In a speech in the House of Lords on 3 February Lord Portal gave the figures to 31 December 1942 as 2,480 planes under the Anglo-Russian Agreement (3,000 including those outside it) and 2,974 tanks.

is, they have no ally in Europe whom they can really rely upon, for even Italy is almost as much a liability as an asset, and though they have been able to force the European peoples to work, they have not been able to make them work with the speed and willingness which total war demands.

A year ago, when the Japanese offensive was at its height, it was possible to outline the grand strategy on which the Axis powers based their plans. It was evident that Germany and Japan had a rendezvous somewhere in the neighbourhood of the Persian Gulf. The Japanese were to dominate the Indian Ocean and probably India itself, and the Germans were to cross the Caucasus mountains from the north and break through to Suez from the west. The United Nations would then be separated from one another – Soviet Russia would be isolated and its armies would probably have to retreat behind the Ural mountains, while China would be completely cut off and could be destroyed at leisure. After this, Britain could be attacked with the full weight of the German war machine and if Britain was conquered America could be dealt with at some time in the future. That was the Axis grand strategy. It was possible to discern it both from what the Axis military commanders were doing and from what their propagandists were saying. It should hardly be necessary to point out that this has failed completely, and however hard the struggle ahead may be, it is never likely to come so near success again. The Japanese are involved in a difficult struggle in the South Pacific in which they are losing ships and planes far faster than they can replace them, and the defences of India have been so strengthened that no attempted invasion is now likely. Japanese naval supremacy which once threatened to cover the whole Eastern part of the Indian Ocean has now receded to the Western Pacific. The Germans have failed to reach the Caucasus Mountains and have lost enormously in a vain effort to reach the Caspian Sea. British strength is just about reaching its peak and American strength will do so some time during next year.

That is the picture as it appears at the beginning of 1943, and we ought to keep that picture in mind when we consider the less visible aspects of war. Probably the best card which the Germans have left is the U-boat warfare which still, without any question, causes the Allies heavy losses in shipping and reduces their offensive capacity. For about a year past, the Government has adopted the practice of not publishing shipping losses regularly, and this practice is probably justified, since it keeps the enemy guessing about the truth of the shipping situation.[362]

---

[362] The Germans, on the other hand, published a regular weekly listing of the Allied shipping losses. Its accuracy was annoying to British propagandists, but they adopted the practice Orwell talks of here rather than fabricate inaccurate figures.

The Germans were caught napping by the Anglo-American move into North Africa and this was partly because they had underrated our true shipping capacity. I don't care to offer an opinion on something which is an official secret, but I may add that we have a clue to the shipping situation in the fact that the food rations have not altered in Britain during the past year. The German propagandists are making the most they can of the U-boat warfare, because at the present they have not much else with which to comfort the German home public. In general, we can say this much of the situation as it now stands: the end is not in sight and we cannot safely prophesy that any of the Axis powers will be out of the war before 1943 is ended,[363] but we can safely prophesy that 1943 will be the year in which the United Nations will hold the initiative and will be strong enough to pass over from mere self-defence to an aggressive strategy.

                                                    20 February 1943

Since the Japanese evacuated Guadalcanal there has been no very big event in the Far Eastern end of the war and this week I would like to talk chiefly about the Russian and North African fronts and also to say something about Madame Chiang Kai-Shek's visit to Washington and about the debates on the Beveridge Social Insurance scheme in this country.

I don't need to tell you what are the big events of the week. Anyone who is listening to this broadcast will have heard of the capture by the Red Army of Rostov and Kharkov.[364] This is a very great victory, probably the most important single event in the whole course of the Russo-German war. The capture of Kharkov, which the Russians failed to achieve last winter, is even more important than the recapture of Rostov. Kharkov is not only a great industrial city[365] but a great railway junction at which all the communications of the Ukraine cross. The Germans have not only lost heavily in territory, men and materials, but they are going to lose more, for one army is all but cut off on the shores of the Sea of Azov and another somewhere in the rear

[363] Despite the successes of the year, Orwell maintains a cautious outlook; there is no repetition of Stalin's threat early in 1942 (see above, p.44).

[364] Moscow announced the capture of Rostov on 14 February; at the same time she announced that 10 Italian Divisions, 13 Hungarian Divisions and 20 Romanian Divisions had been 'wiped out'. Kharkov was recaptured on 16 February.

[365] It was described in official communiqués as the third largest city in Russia and the second most important railway junction.

of Rostov is threatened by the same fate. The Russians are not only driving westward from Rostov but another column has struck southward from the neighbourhood of Krasnoarmeisk and is moving more or less in the direction of Mariupol on the northern shore of the Sea of Azov.

The Germans in that area will have to get out quickly if they are not going to suffer the same destruction as has already happened to the German Sixth Army at Stalingrad and threatens the army which is isolated in the Caucasus. Last year, when the Russians retook Rostov, they did not get further westward than Taganrog, about 50 miles from the west, and the Germans were able to hold on to the Crimean Peninsula. This year, the Russian offensive is much more far-reaching in its effects and it is generally believed that the Germans will have to go back to the line of the Dnieper, thus leaving themselves in a position considerably worse than they were before their 1942 campaign started. Some observers, including Dr Benes, President of Czechoslovakia, even think that they will retreat as far as the River Dniester, which means standing on the borders of Poland and Rumania and abandoning the whole of the Russian territory which they have overrun.[366] This may be an over-optimistic forecast, but at any rate enough has happened already to make it undisguisably clear to the German man in the street that the 1942 campaign, with all its enormous losses, has been fought for exactly nothing.

You can imagine, even if you have not read, the sort of dope that is being handed out to the German masses to explain away the mistakes of their leaders. Hitler himself has been silent and apparently in retirement for some weeks past but his underlings, particularly Goebbels, have been very active. What Goebbels says to the German people is not of great importance to us, but it is important to examine the propaganda line which is being handed out to the world at large because this propaganda is intended to deceive and weaken us and it is as well to be armed against it in advance.

Briefly, the main line now being followed is the Bolshevik bogey. It is being put out crudely by the German propagandists and somewhat more subtly by those of Italy and other satellite states. According to Goebbels's broadcasts, Europe is now faced with the fearful danger of a

---

[366] Orwell is referring here to a radio broadcast made by Benes on 13 February. It began, 'We have passed into the final period of the war, the period of inevitable military catastrophe for Germany', and went on in the same vein. Within a few hours of the transmission of his speech, BBC monitors picked up a broadcast from Prague giving details of reprisals that had been taken, with named colleagues of Benes being arrested and sent to concentration camps. (See also above, p.171, n.293.) This perhaps is why Orwell does not refer to Benes's broadcast directly.

Communist invasion, which will not stop at its Eastern borders but sweep as far as the English channel and beyond, engulfing Britain as well as the other European countries. The Germans, it now appears, only took up arms in order to defend Europe from this Bolshevik peril, and by allying themselves with the Bolsheviks, Britain and the United States have betrayed European civilisation. All the talk which the Germans were uttering about the need for living space, or 'Lebensraum' as it is called, and the divine right of Germany to rule the world, appears to have been forgotten for the time being. Germany's war is purely defensive, so Dr Goebbels says. It can be seen, quite clearly, of course, that the real drift of these speeches is to appeal to those sections in Britain and America who are frightened of seeing Soviet Russia become too powerful and might be willing to consider a compromise peace. This is augmented by the Italian publicists, who are openly talking about a compromise, and the duty of Britain to collaborate with the Axis powers against the Bolshevik danger.

All this is foredoomed to failure because the anti-Russian sentiment on which the Axis propagandists seem to be playing is almost non-existent in the Anglo-Saxon countries. So far as Britain is concerned, Soviet Russia was never more popular than at this moment.[367] But we ought not to underrate the danger of Fascist propaganda which has scored such great triumphs in the past. Even if the anti-Bolshevik line of thought does not achieve much in Britain, it may find listeners among the wealthier classes all over Europe and in addition the hints which have been dropped by the Italian propagandists may be followed up later by very attractive-sounding peace offers. Towards India, of course, German propaganda will take a different line. The talk about defending Western civilisation is only for European consumption. To India the propaganda line will be that Soviet Russia is the ally of Great Britain and therefore shares the responsibility for any grievances which the Indian Nationalists have, or believe they have.[368] We can best deal with these propaganda campaigns if we start with the knowledge that they are, in essence, simply strategic manoeuvres and take no more account of the truth than a military commander does when he disposes his army so as to deceive the enemy.

---

[367] This is an honest expression of the state of public opinion in Britain at the time. However, Orwell himself viewed the increasing influence of Russia with dread.

[368] Perhaps the closest Orwell gets to pure sophistry. He knew that most of the Congress leaders were in prison or some other form of detention, but he must also have known that, at the behest of Stalin, members of the Indian Communist Party had been set free.

In Tunisia, the Germans have had a considerable local success during this week.[369] It probably won't affect the final outcome, but unquestionably the Axis Forces in Tunisia have turned out to be stronger in armoured vehicles and in the air than had been anticipated. During this week the Germans have attacked westward in Southern Tunisia, driven back the American troops opposing them, and captured several advance airfields. The main object of this manoeuvre is probably to drive a wedge between the British First Army in Tunisia and the British Eighth Army which is advancing from Tripoli. The British Eighth Army has now reached the outposts of the Mareth Line, the fortified area which guards the approaches to Gabes. We cannot expect their progress to be rapid, for communications hardly exist in this area, and the Eighth Army is now a long way from its base. Probably the nearest seaport it can make full use of is Benghazi. Also the North African rainy season is still on, which makes the movement of heavy vehicles difficult. However, it is unlikely that the Germans will be able to hang on in Tunisia indefinitely, and some observers on the spot believe that they do not intend to do so. Quite possibly, they are only fighting a delaying action in the hope of getting as many as possible of their forces away by sea. General Catroux, the Fighting French Commander, has given his opinion that the Germans will be out of Tunisia in two months.

The Beveridge scheme of social security[370] is still under debate. The government has already proposed the adoption of the greater part of it, but a Labour amendment in the House of Commons demanding the adoption of the scheme in its entirety received as many as 117 votes. I have spoken of the Beveridge scheme in earlier news commentaries[371] and don't want to detail its provisions again. I merely mention the debate now taking place in order to emphasise two things. One is, that whatever else goes through, family allowances are certain to be adopted though it is not yet certain on what scale. The other is that the principle of social insurance has come to stay and even the most reactionary thinkers in Great Britain would now hardly dare

[369] On 14 February Rommel had counter-attacked at the Faed Pass, and at the Kasserine and other passes on the day following. The American Second Corps took the brunt of this attack.

[370] Sir William Beveridge's Report, *Social Insurance and Allied Services*, which laid the basis of the post-war British welfare state, was published on 1 December 1942 (Cmnd.6404). It had given rise to extensive discussion and the House of Commons debated it on 16-18 February.

[371] There is no trace of these earlier mentions. Presumably Orwell is referring to daily announcements on the same channel or other programmes whose scripts have not survived.

to oppose this.[372] The Beveridge scheme may ultimately be adopted in the somewhat mutilated form, but it is something of an achievement even to be debating such a thing in the middle of a desperate war in which we are still fighting for survival.

Madame Chiang Kai-Shek, the wife of the Generalissimo, who has been staying in Washington as the guest of President and Mrs Roosevelt, has addressed both of the American Houses of Congress.[373] She was cheered when she warned the United Nations against the danger of allowing Japan to remain as a potential threat after the war is won, and also when she pleaded for a peace settlement which would not be either vindictive or nationalistic in concept. China, she said, was ready to co-operate in laying the foundations of a sane world society. She also, speaking out of her own experience, warned the Americans against underrating the strength of the Japanese, whose power will grow if they are left too long in possession of the territories they have overrun. Parts of Madame Chiang Kai-Shek's speech were re-broadcast in this country and aroused great interest. It is recognised in this country that the Chinese who have now been fighting in the common struggle for five and a half years have suffered far more than any of the other of the United Nations, and can hardly be blamed if they now complain that their Western allies have done very little to help them. Madame Chiang Kai-Shek's visit to the United States will have done a great deal to promote good relations between China and the rest of the United Nations.

27 February 1943

During this week the only major military developments have been in Tunisia and on the southern part of the Russian front, near the shores of the Sea of Azov. There have also been heavy bombing of Japanese concentrations of shipping in the Solomons and New Britain, and a British sea-borne raid on the coast of Burma,[374] but so far as the

[372] The 'Right Wing' National Socialists in Germany pointed out in repeated broadcasts that they had introduced most of these reforms themselves years before. They also pointed to their laws requiring two workers to be on the board of every public company, a suggestion that was not in the realm of practical politics in Britain.

[373] Madame Chiang Kai-Shek arrived in Washington 18 February and made her address the following day.

[374] The Royal Indian Navy landed a commando force at the Japanese-occupied village of Myebon in a successful raid on 22 February. There had been almost continuous bombing over the previous week by American planes.

eastern end of the war is concerned one cannot say that the military situation has changed. I should like to spend my time this week in discussing the Russian and North African fronts and then to say something about the speech which Hitler composed but failed to deliver three days ago.

In Southern Tunisia there has been a dramatic change during the past three days and the situation which looked threatening a week ago has probably, though not absolutely certainly, been restored. The Germans were attacking westward through the Kasserine Pass, almost the only pass through the Atlas mountains in this area. They not only captured three airfields but they came within a very few miles of capturing the town of Thala, which is an important spot from the point of view of communications. However, the Allied commander on the spot seems to have thrown in all his aircraft in a heavy attack and the Germans were driven back through the pass with considerable losses of men and material. Evidently both the Germans and the Allies have lost heavily in tanks. It is too early to say with absolute certainty that the situation is restored, because the airfields they have captured give the Germans a local air superiority in central Tunisia and also because we do not know what reserves of tanks they possess. We do know that they are now using a new mark of heavy tank, weighing 55 tons and carrying an 88mm gun which has not made its appearance before. However, the Minister for War has just stated in Parliament that the armour of this tank has been successfully pierced by our six pounder guns,[375] and also that the new British tank, the latest model of the Churchill tank is now in action in Tunisia in large numbers.

Both the Allies and the Germans in North Africa are fighting against time. It is important for the Allies to clear the North African coast as rapidly as possible and it is also important for the German commander, if he can manage it, to drive the British First Army back into Algeria before the Eighth Army arrives in his rear. The Eighth Army has now occupied Medenine, one of the chief outposts of the Mareth Line, and also Djerba, which is so placed that it might make a very valuable airfield or a jumping-off place for sea-borne attacks against the coast.

During this week there has been a considerable revival of the

---

[375] In answer to a parliamentary question about the 'Tiger' tank described here by Orwell, Sir James Grigg maintained that one of them had been 'penetrated four or five times by a six-pounder gun'.

rumour that the Germans are going to invade Spain.[376] They are, so it is said, rushing troops in very large numbers to the Spanish border at the eastern end of the Pyrenees. We have no way of confirming this and we ought to remember that a German invasion of Spain has been one of the recurrent rumours of this war and in some cases has been put about by the Germans themselves. At the same time a German invasion of Spain is by no means impossible and we ought always to keep it in mind because it is one method by which the Germans might hope to retrieve the situation in North Africa and so stall off an Allied invasion of Europe. If the Germans could cross Spain rapidly and then get across the Straits of Gibraltar into Spanish Morocco they would then present a tremendous threat to the whole Allied position in Africa and the Allies would have to scrap the idea of any offensive operations until they had driven the Germans out again. The Germans could, of course, only bring this off if they could capture Gibraltar on the way. Gibraltar is not a mere naval base like Singapore. It is an immensely powerful fortress,[377] which has been strengthened through three years of war, and it is probably the strength of Gibraltar rather than any consideration for international law which has prevented the Germans from invading Spain much earlier than this.

The political situation in North Africa appears to have improved somewhat and a military mission representing General de Gaulle and the Fighting French is expected to arrive shortly and confer with General Giraud, the High Commissioner of French North Africa. Probably it will be headed by General Catroux. We may hope, therefore, that an agreement between the two main groups of Frenchmen outside France will be arrived at before long.

Since last week the Russian advance has continued, but it has slowed down somewhat, partly owing to the weather, partly to the stiffening of German resistance. The whole of this winter has been abnormally mild and great areas in the Ukraine, which would usually be frozen hard at this time of the year, are now a sea of mud, which makes it difficult for armoured vehicles to move. But the Germans

---

[376] To those of a post-war generation the invasion of Franco's Spain by Hitler's Germany seems an unthinkable possibility, both being seen as the epitome of 'right wing fascists', in the language of the popular left. Although a large number of Spanish volunteers in the Blue Division fought with conspicuous success and gallantry, according to broadcasts from the Eastern front, Hitler only made one attempt to come to terms with Franco, which ended in failure. Rather than repeat the meeting, Hitler is quoted as saying that he would rather have had three teeth removed. From then on the invasion of Spain for strategic reasons was always a possibility.

[377] It is perhaps an irony of Orwell's that these were the exact words he used to describe Singapore earlier, just before it fell.

have also been resisting more successfully, and during the past two days the tone of their communiqués has been somewhat less pessimistic. I mentioned last week that on the southern front, north-west of Rostov, the Russians were moving southward in the direction of Mariupol and the whole German forces in that area were menaced with encirclement. It is here that the Germans have counter-attacked.[378] They claim to have recaptured two towns east of Stalino. This is not confirmed but it does appear that the Germans have managed to slow down the Russian advance and that the German troops, who are still in the neighbourhood of Rostov, may get away. Further north, on the central front, Orel, which is one of the key points of the whole German line, is in very great danger and its communications are cut in every direction except towards the west. In general the news from the Russian front is less resounding that it was last week, but the tide is still flowing strongly against the Germans.

The anniversary celebrations of the foundation of the Nazi party took place three days ago. Hitler has always spoken on these occasions and this time he did emerge from his retirement to the extent of sending a written speech which was read out by somebody else.[379] The pretext given was that Hitler is too busy directing the war on the Eastern Front to be able to spare time to come to the microphone. It will be noticed that since things began to go wrong in Russia, Hitler has not shown himself publicly, nor made a speech in his own voice. In this speech he made absolutely no reference to the disaster of Stalingrad or to his own promise that Stalingrad should be captured nor any admission whatever of being responsible for the way things have turned out. This, although Hitler publicly assumed supreme command of the German armies some months ago.[380] It is worth remembering that when Singapore fell, the British public first learned the fact from Mr Churchill himself, who came straight to the

[378] Official communiqués from the MOI at the time were filled with details of extensive counter-attacks by the Germans in the Donetz basin. As always with news from the Russian front, Orwell can only speak in general terms.

[379] Herman Esser, Secretary of State and an old Bavarian comrade of Hitler's, read the speech on 24 February, at Munich. It was indeed, as Orwell goes on to say, a virulent display of all Hitler's prejudices with emphasis on the world peril posed by the activities of the Jewish-Masonic banking communities of Britain and America and the Jewish Communists in Moscow (see below, n.381). In this penultimate news broadcast he dwells on the one major aspect of Hitler's Germany that sums up all that he and the Allies were fighting against.

[380] Hitler had assumed Supreme Command of the German Army on 21 December 1941. Rumours were circulating that he was about to give up the position, and it may be to denials of these rumours that Orwell refers here.

microphone to deliver the news. This makes something of a contrast with Hitler, who grabs any credit that may be available when things are going well, but disappears into retirement and leaves the explanations to other people when things go badly. However, that is not of great importance. What is of more interest is to notice the content of Hitler's speech and its probable bearing on German policy. The speech was addressed ostensibly, at any rate, to the members of the Nazi Party, rather than to the German people as a whole, and it consisted almost entirely of ravings against the Jews, the Bolsheviks and the traitors and saboteurs, who are alleged to be still numerous in Germany itself. Hitler made two quite plain undisguised threats. One was, that he intended to kill off every Jew in Europe – he said this quite plainly[381] – and the other was that in the moment of danger Germany could not afford to be overscrupulous in her treatment of what he called 'aliens'. This remark was somewhat less clear than the threats against the Jews, but translated into plainer terms it means more forced labour and lower rations for the subject European populations. Hitler also uttered threats against traitors, saboteurs and idlers. This agrees with the general tone of German public announcements recently and with the huge extension in the ages of people in Germany now liable for military service or compulsory labour. All this points to the serious shortage of German manpower which was bound to arise sooner or later and which is now almost certainly beginning to become acute. On the other hand the shouting against the Jews and Bolsheviks was more probably directed

---

[381] This statement is crucial evidence for Hitler's knowledge of and responsibility for the Holocaust. Here are the relevant passages of the speech. 'I am still in the East and so cannot be amongst you. The German Army has fought excellently this winter, as it has done since the beginning of the war. It is engaged in a fierce struggle against the world peril conspired by the banking houses of New York and London together with the Jews in Moscow. However large the coalition of Germany's enemies may be, it is smaller than the strength of the alliance of the people who are facing the Bolshevik-plutocratic destruction. We shall break and smash the might of the Jewish world coalition, and mankind, struggling for its freedom, will win the final victory of this struggle. As in the period of my struggle for power, every onslaught of our enemies and every one of their apparent successes made me grit my teeth even more firmly and become even more determined never to stray from the way which leads, sooner or later, to my aim. Today, too, I am inspired by the same will-power to resolve, to the last consequence, the task which fate has entrusted to me ... This struggle will not end, as our enemies plan, with the annihilation of the Aryan part of humanity, but with the extinction of Jewry in Europe. Our ideas will become the common property of all peoples, even our enemies, through this struggle. One state after another will be increasingly compelled to resort to National Socialist theses in the conduct of the war they have provoked. Realisation of the criminal and accursed activity of Jewry will thus be spread by this very war amongst all people. The Jews believe they are at the gates of their millennium, but this year, like the last, they will experience a horrible disillusionment.'

at Western Europe and seems to bear out what I said last week that the Germans are going to play the Bolshevik bogey for all it is worth in hopes of stimulating the fear of Communism in Britain and America and thus paving the way for a compromise peace. I pointed out last week how vain this German manoeuvre is and the celebrations in London of the twenty-fifth anniversary of the Red Army have underlined this. Soviet Russia is more popular in Britain than any foreign country except possibly China. All in all, Hitler's most recent speech and the inferences which can be legitimately drawn from it should be encouraging to all the enemies of Fascism.

13 March 1943

As this is the last news commentary that I shall do in this series I would like to end up with a summary of the world situation rather than a survey of the war fronts. As a matter of fact there has not been a great deal that is new to comment on this week. The big events of the week have been the Russian capture of Vyasma, on the central front, the German counter-attack against Kharkov on the southern front and the unsuccessful German attack in the southern part of Tunisia, but the situation has not fundamentally changed. Even the Red Army's capture of Vyasma, important though it is, could be foreseen as probable when Rghev fell. So, let me use my time, this week, in trying to give a comprehensive picture of the whole war and trying to predict in very general outlines what is likely to happen.

If you look at the war, as a whole, there are six factors which really count, four of them military and two political. Of course they are not separable from one another, but one can see the situation more clearly by listing them separately. The first factor is the failure of the Germans to carry out their full plans in Russia. The second factor is the coming Anglo-American attack on Continental Europe. The third factor is the war of the German U-boats against the United Nations lines of supply. The fourth factor is the Japanese offensive in the Far East and its slowing down for reasons which we are not quite sure about. The fifth factor is the failure of the Nazi New Order in Europe, and the sixth is the attempt of the Japanese in the Far East to set up a New Order designed to benefit only themselves, like that of the Germans in Europe.

The first of these factors is the most important, because Germany is the main enemy and the Japanese cannot really continue to fight alone if

Germany goes out – they might manage to prolong the war for several years.[382] If you look at the map of Russia you can see that, however much territory they have overrun, the Germans have totally failed in what was probably their most urgent war aim and are likely to fail in their secondary one. Thier primary war aim was to capture the oilfields of the Caucasus. It was for this reason that the Germans decided to attack Soviet Russia, probably as far back as the winter of 1940. Since Britain had failed to collapse like France, they saw they were in for a long war, and it was absolutely necessary for them to have bigger supplies of oil than they could get from European sources and from synthetic production. Secondly, they had to have food, which meant that they had to have the fertile lands of the Ukraine. Europe is capable, or nearly capable, of feeding itself, but not if a large proportion of its manpower is making weapons of war for the German army instead of producing food. In peacetime Europe could import food from the Americas, but with Britain blockading Germany at sea the Ukraine was an absolute necessity for the German war machine. As everybody knows, the Germans have failed to get to the Caucasus, but they still hold the greater part of Ukrainia. It is probably a mistake, in spite of the defeats they have had in the last few months, to imagine that they will give this up without fighting. They would probably regard the Dnieper River and a line containing the whole of Poland and the Baltic States as the last frontier to which they could afford to retreat. Probably they will try to stand on the defensive on this line and muster their forces to meet the Allied attack in the West, but this strategy puts them in a dilemma. If they give up the Ukraine they have not the food resources to carry on the war indefinitely. If they hold on to it they are defending an immensely long frontier, inevitably tying up a bigger army than they can afford to use. We don't really know what the German casualties have been in the two Russian winters, but certainly they have been large and the total mobilisation orders in Germany, together with endless attempts to make the European population work harder, shows that the German manpower position is becoming serious. Broadly, one can say that by provoking both Britain and Soviet Russia and the United States against them the Germans have made sure that they cannot win and can only hope at best for a stalemate. We may expect them, therefore, during this year, to make violent political offensives aimed at sowing dissension among the United Nations. They will try to play on American fear of Bolshevism, Russian suspicion of Western Capitalism, and Anglo-American jealousy, and they probably calculate

---

[382] Orwell's analysis has proved remarkably accurate. In the case of Japan, however, Orwell of course could not foresee the atom bomb.

that they have better chances along those lines than on purely military action.

The second and third factors, the Anglo-American attack on Europe, and the submarine war, cannot be considered separately. Much the best chance the Germans have of staving off an attack from the West is to sink so many ships that the United Nations not only cannot transport a big force overseas but, what is more important, keep it supplied. When one realises that one infantry soldier needs about seven tons of supplies, one realises what an attack against Europe means in terms of shipping. Even if the Germans could not stave off an attack from the West altogether they might keep the United Nations embarrassed until the attack started too late to finish the war this year.[383] In that case the stalemate the Germans are probably hoping for will become more likely of attainment. The campaign in Tunisia really has the same object, that is to keep a big Allied army tied up in Africa and prevent it crossing the sea to Europe. I don't care to predict too much about the result of these German delaying tactics because there are two things we don't yet know. First of all, naturally, we don't know what the Allied plan of attack is. Secondly, we don't know the real facts about the shipping situation because the governments of the United Nations, probably justifiably, don't publish figures of shipping losses. But we do know certain facts from which inferences can be drawn and on the whole they are hopeful. The first is that the United Nations succeeded in transporting a large army to Africa, evidently to the surprise of the Germans, and are transporting an American Army, which grows every day, across the Atlantic to Britain. The second is that the food situation, which is probably an index of the shipping situation, has not deteriorated in Britain during the past two years. The third is the enormous expansion of the American shipbuilding industry and the fourth the growing improvement in the methods – surface ships, aeroplanes and bombing of bases – of dealing with the submarine. U-boats have been the Germans' strongest card hitherto, but there is no strong reason for thinking that they will be able to slow down the Allied preparations indefinitely.

We don't know enough about Japanese strategy to be certain whether they have been seriously crippled by the blows they have had in the past eight months, or whether they have slowed down their campaigns according to some definite plan. All we know is that a year ago they overran very rapidly the countries bordering the South-West Pacific, and since then they have made no progress, but on the contrary they

[383] The landing in Europe did not take place until 1944; no doubt the impact of the U-boat war played some part in the delay. Orwell shows a double optimism, however, looking both for the Second Front and for victory in Europe in 1943.

have lost some valuable bases and an enormous amount of war material. Japan's weakest spot, like that of Britain, is that of shipping. They have certainly lost an immense quantity, both warships and merchant ships, at a time when they need ships more and more in order to keep their island possessions running. Moreover, they have nothing like the power of replacement of the highly industrialised states. It is safe to say that the United States can build more ships in a month than Japan can in a year. And in aeroplane construction the margin is even greater. It seems likely, therefore, that if the Japanese did not go on to attack India and Australia, as everyone expected, it was not because they did not want to but because they could not. On the other hand, we ought not to assume that they will collapse quickly when Germany is finished with. The Japanese cannot afford to retreat from the mainland of Asia any more than the Germans can afford to give up Eastern Europe. If they did so their industrial and military power would decline rapidly. We may expect, therefore, that the Japanese will defend every inch of what they have got and in the past months they have shown how obstinately they can fight. But probably the Japanese grand strategy, like that of Germany, is now aiming at a stalemate. They perhaps calculate if they can consolidate their position as they are the United Nations will be too war weary to go on fighting when Germany is defeated, and might be willing to make terms on the basis of everyone keeping what he has got. Of course the real object of this would be to renew the war at the first favourable opportunity[384] and we ought to be on our guard against Japanese peace-talk, no less than against German.

As to the political factors there is no need to talk any longer about the failure of the Nazi New Order in Europe. By this time it stinks in the nose of the world. But it is important to realise that Japanese aims and methods are essentially similar, and that the Japanese New Order or, as they call it, the Greater East Asia Co-Prosperity Sphere, will have the same appearance when the necessary time-lag has elapsed. The Japanese are plundering the lands under their control and it does not make very much difference if in one place they plunder by naked violence and in another by means of a faked paper money which will not buy anything. They must plunder Asia, even if they did not wish to do so, because they cannot afford to do otherwise. They must have the food and raw materials of the occupied countries and they cannot give anything of corresponding value in return. In order to pay for the goods they seize they would have to turn their factories over to producing cheap consumption goods which would be impossible without slowing

[384] Of course Japan did not do so, but instead went on to produce cheap consumer goods, as Orwell in the next paragraph suggests.

down their war industries. The same essential situation exists in Europe, but less crudely because the countries overrun by the Germans are more industrialised. It is as certain as anything can well be that within a fairly short time the Malays, Burmese and other peoples under Japanese rule will find out all about their so-called protectors and realise that these people who were making such grand promises a year ago are simply a horde of locusts eating their countries naked. But just how soon that will happen is a more difficult question and I do not intend to be able [sic] to answer it exactly. At present comparatively little news comes to us from Japanese occupied territories, but we have one great and unimpeachable source of evidence and that is China. The war in China began nearly five years before it began in the rest of Asia and there are innumerable eye-witness accounts of the way the Japanese have behaved. By almost universal agreement it is a regime of naked robbery with all the horrors of massacre and rape [*two words illegible*] that. The same will happen, or has already happened, to all the lands unfortunate enough to fall under Japanese rule. Perhaps the best answer to the propaganda which the Japanese put out to India and other places is simply the three words LOOK AT CHINA. And since I am now bringing these weekly commentaries to an end I believe those three words LOOK AT CHINA are the best final message I can deliver to India.[385]

[385] Orwell's delivery of a 'final message' shows his realisation that, whatever else he might do for the BBC, direct propaganda was not going to be part of it. It demonstrates how strongly he believed in what he was doing and how deep and genuine were his fears for India if she should fall into Japanese hands.

A P P E N D I X

Selected Axis propaganda broadcasts

The texts that follow are transcribed from the BBC monitors' daily reports known as the 'Summary of World Broadcasts'. (Words in parenthesis preceded by a question mark are the monitors'.) These roneoed texts were very extensive, drawing on the output of all radio stations known, from whatever political background. For the period that Orwell was with the BBC alone they number many millions of words. A complete picture of what was put out must await a thorough analysis of this vast quantity of material, which is at present uncatalogued and unindexed. The reports have been closely examined in the areas relating to Orwell's commentaries, the Indian clandestine stations and the German radio stations aimed at India. Three key speeches by Subhas Chandra Bose are included below (nos. 2, 8 and 13), together with a selection of propaganda news releases about Anglo-Indian relations and the racial question in general. Some broadcasts of particular historical significance have also been included, such as the contemporary German account of the Battle of El Alamein (no. 16).

1. India's opportunity for freedom   *1 January 1942*

The Russians have been so soundly defeated by Germany that Europe has nothing more to fear from them, and in this destruction the small nations of Europe took an active part with Germany. Rumania with confidence sent her young men to fight on the side of Germany. Volunteers from practically every part of Europe fought. The Conference of Small Nations held at Berlin showed that Europe is fully prepared for a New Order. Japan's entry into the war has turned the eyes of the world towards the New Order. The world is divided in two parts, one containing the healthy advancing nations of the world, and the other containing the idle, boastful and wealthy. Only those who are prepared to sacrifice their lives unstintingly will be victorious. The price of freedom is sacrifice. Japan has shown India that the wealthy and strong British are after all not very strong. Not only India, but all the other countries who have been oppressed by the British were shown the way to freedom in 1941. All those Indians who have lived in exile because of British oppression are now prepared to sacrifice their lives for freedom. Swami Satia Nanda, an Indian leader for the past twenty-eight years, exposed the British deceit to the Indian people. He warned the Indians that they should not be deceived. In a speech on the radio he added that only Britain dislikes India. It will be dangerous for India if she is controlled by the British any longer. If the Indians unite, they can throw off the shackles of slavery. The 400,000,000 people of India can produce an army which can be matchless. One can only achieve freedom by struggle and this is the best opportunity for India to achieve her freedom. We pray God that the Indian desire for freedom may be fulfilled in 1942.

2. India's hour of destiny (by Subhas Chandra Bose)   *28 February 1942*

Sisters and brothers. For about a year I have waited in silence and in patience for the march of events and now that the hour has struck I come forward to speak. The fall of Singapore means the collapse of the British Empire, the end of the iniquitous regime which it has symbolised, and the dawn of a new era in Indian history. The Indian people, who have long suffered from the humiliation of the foreign yoke and have been ruined spiritually, culturally, politically and economically while under British domination, must now offer their humble thanks to the Almighty for the auspicious event which bears for India the promise of life and freedom. British Imperialism has, in modern history, been the most diabolical enemy of freedom and the most formidable obstacle to progress. Because of it, a very large section of mankind has been kept enslaved and in India alone about one fifth of the human race has been ruthlessly suppressed and persecuted. For other nations British Imperialism may be the enemy of today, but for India it is the eternal foe. Between these two there can be neither peace nor compromise and the enemies of British imperialism are today our natural friends.

The outside world hears, from time to time, voices from India claiming to speak either in the name of the All India National Congress or of the Indian people, but these voices come through the channels of British propaganda and nobody should make the fatal mistake of regarding them as representative of free India. As is natural in a land that has been under foreign domination, the British oppressors have endeavoured to create divisions among the Indian people. As a consequence, we find in India some who openly support British Imperialism and who, whether intentionally or unintentionally, help the British cause, often camouflaging their real motives by talking of cooperation with Chungking China, Russia and other allies of England. There is, however, a vast majority of the Indian people who will have no compromise with British imperialism but will fight on till full independence is achieved. Owing to wartime conditions in India, the voice of these freedom-loving Indians cannot cross the frontiers of their country, but we, who have fought for more than two decades for our national emancipation, know exactly what the vast majority of our countrymen think and feel today.

Standing at one of the cross-roads of world history, I solemnly declare on behalf of all freedom-loving Indians in India and abroad, that we shall continue to fight British imperialism till India is once again the mistress of her own destiny. During this struggle, and in the reconstruction that will follow, we shall heartily cooperate with all those who help us to overthrow the common enemy. I am confident that, in this sacred struggle, the vast majority of the Indian people will be with us. No manoeuvre, intrigue or conspiracy on the part of the agents of Anglo-American imperialism, however prominent they may be and to whichever nationality they may belong, can throw dust in the eyes of the Indian people, or divert them from the path of patriotic duty. The hour of India's salvation is at hand. India will now rise and break the chains of servitude that have bound her so long. Through India's liberation Asia and the world will move forward towards the larger goal of human emancipation.

3. Free India Radio: BBC Nazi charges denied   *5 March 1942*

A cheap method of British propaganda is to describe any movement for the complete independence of India as either inopportune or inspired by foreign sources. The BBC has been accusing Free India Radio of being a Nazi broadcasting station. The intended implication is that through Free India Radio the Germans are trying to cause unrest in India and incite Indians against their own government. We should indeed welcome such a move if it were to succeed, because we, the uncompromising youth of India, are in fact preparing our people for revolution, in order to overthrow the foreign government which has been tyrannising over us for more than a century. We would remind the BBC that Free India Radio is the voice of freedom-loving India. It is the harbinger of the revolution which is fast approaching and which will soon strike a death blow at British power in India.

4. The formation of Greater East Asia (by Furst Urach)   *10 March 1942*

Every third inhabitant of this world is an East Asiatic. East Asia, in spite of its immense area, has the densest population in the world, and consequently one of the most precious raw materials, human labour. 'Asia for the Asiatics', under the strong leadership of Japan, is being fulfilled. Asia, with her old and highly cultured peoples will no more be exploited by pillaging foreign powers, but will be a co-prosperity sphere for its millions of inhabitants. This will be realised in a fantastically short time since the last fortresses of the foreign Powers in this area are breaking down. Everywhere the forces of reconstruction are starting to work. Japanese economic experts are entering the newly-occupied territories and starting to utilise the immense economic riches of the Southern Pacific for Japanese warfare and industries, as well as for the wealth of all the East Asiatic peoples. For too long Japan, so poor in raw materials, and whose population increases yearly by 1,000,000 has been kept by the Anglo-Saxon Powers, who held all the raw materials, from using a wealth which was lying on her doorstep. England and America hoped to be able to hold back the economic development of Japan in her own living-space, although such a development has become a necessity because of the increase in population and the lack of raw material. The Anglo-Saxons did not want to acknowledge the fact that such a development is a question of life and death for the 100 million Japanese and for the millions of other East Asiatic peoples.

Japan is the powerful spiritual motor driving the old East Asiatic peoples to a new fruition. Japan and the Asiatic peoples know that great successes cannot be achieved with guns and machines only, but that the human spirit is necessary for such achievements. Japan's recognised leadership is the best proof of this spirit in Asia. Never before in its thousand-year-old history has Japan led other nations. Only during the last few years Japan has entered victoriously into competition with other world Powers, not only because Japan is technically the most developed nation in East Asia, but mainly because her own spiritual values combined modern technique and old Asiatic cultural tradition. The peoples of East Asia are acknowledging Japan's leadership because they know it is in accordance with the spiritual laws of Asia. The Anglo-Saxons could hold their position in East Asia only with battleships, garrisons, plutocratic bank palaces whose profits went to London and New York, and by smuggling opium. After a century all these things are breaking down and an Asia which belongs to Asiatics is taking their place. The Japanese state religion contains the highest belief in human and social justice. Japan has always felt it to be a bitter injustice that the peoples of East Asia should be nothing but a colonial object of exploitation for the Western Powers. By the admirable victories of her armed forces, Japan has done away with this injustice, knowing she is doing a deed of equalisation and real justice which will come into effect not only in her own state, but also internationally.

Because of this sense of justice, Japan will never use the same methods in leading the East Asiatic peoples which have been hitherto used by the Anglo-Saxons for colonial exploitation of the East Asiatic. Instead of colonial exploitation and oppression Japan will work for the common prosperity of all the nations. All the millions of people will be able to work and to use the riches of the country for their own benefit. Every foreign possibility of disturbance will be excluded. Japan's entry into the war has brought about great confusion among our enemies and will soon make them realise the futility of their war against the young nations of the Tripartite Agreement. Churchill and Roosevelt do not know whether to use their main forces in the Pacific or the Atlantic, in North Africa or the Near East. On none of the fronts have they any prospect of success, and their armaments and shipping tonnage are not sufficient for a concentrated attack in any place on the world-wide front.

Today's fight for East Asia's liberation against our common enemies is closely connected with our fight in Europe and with our common victory. The economic resources of East Asia will not only satisfy the requirements of the East Asiatic peoples, but will also, after reconstruction of the great living spaces, be important commodities for export.

5. Quezon's assassination: Anglo-US Secret Service   *21 March 1942*

The assassination of Quezon is attributed to US fear that had he been left in the Philippines alive, he might come to cooperate fully with Japan and that the numerous cases of US brutality in the Philippines might be exposed. It might be recalled that the Hungarian Foreign Minister Teleki and the Greek Premier Metaxas lost their lives at the hands of the British Secret Service on 25th and 29th January, 1940. Faced with the imminent German invasion of the Balkans, the British succeeded in assassinating these leaders with policies inimical to British interests. Just before he was killed, Metaxas filed a strong protest with the British authorities that if Britain would not send more effective support, Greece would be forced to make peace with Italy and cooperate with the Axis. So, (?the equation can be turned) to the brutal assassination of Quezon by the (two words unintelligible) of the Anglo-US Powers who only think of their own selfish ends.

6. Britain looting India's wealth   *14 April 1942*

The BBC, that is, the Bluff and Bluster Corporation of London, has contradicted our report regarding the transhipment of India's gold reserve from India to England. People in India will laugh at the further assertion that, at the beginning of this war, part of India's gold, which was then in London, was sent back to India. We have not seen such generosity, and we remind the BBC that bluff and bluster beyond a certain degree becomes not only unbelievable, but laughable. Who does not know that Britain is on the verge of bankruptcy? Dollar-loving America is grabbing British assets all over the world. The process began with British assets in the USA, which were swallowed by the British Treasury in no time. Then the USA began to seize British credits in other parts of the American continent and in Asia. The USA have not forgotten the last world war when Britain took everything from America on loan and refused to pay when the war was over. That is why America, despite the Lease-Lend Bill, is making sure that British assets pass into her hands. To counteract this loss to a partial degree, Britain has assumed the role of beggar in relation to other parts of her Empire. This is particularly the case in India, where Britain is trying to get something out of the Indian people, under the name of war loan, or war funds, or so on. It is incredible, therefore, that Britain, when in such a desperate financial position, should hesitate to seize India's gold reserves. If the BBC continues with the ridiculous story that Britain has sent gold from London to India, Indians will realise that the Ministry of Information is really a Ministry of Lies. Our object in giving publicity to this transfer of gold reserves from India to England is to warn our countrymen about the robbing of India's wealth by Britain while the war is going on, and while Britain is talking about freedom and democracy. In the absence of gold reserves, India's paper currency is worth nothing today, and when the British are soon kicked out of India, nobody will look at British notes and Government securities, even when they are found lying in the streets of Delhi, Bombay and Calcutta.

7. Heydrich Revenge: 'Village Wiped Out:
   All Men Shot: Announcement' 10 June 1942

It is officially announced: The search and investigation for the murderers of
SS Obergruppenfuehrer Gen. Heydrich has established unimpeachable
indications (sic) that the population of the locality of Lidice, near Kladno,
supported and gave assistance to the circle (sic) of perpetrators in question. In
spite of the interrogation of the local inhabitants, the pertinent means of
evidence were secured without the help of the population. The attitude of the
inhabitants to the outrage thus manifested is emphasised also by other acts
hostile to the Reich, by the discoveries of printed matter hostile to the Reich,
of dumps of arms and ammunition, of an illegal wireless transmitter, and of
huge quantities of controlled goods, as well as by the fact that inhabitants of
the locality are in active enemy service abroad. Since the inhabitants of this
village (sic) have flagrantly violated the laws which have been issued, by their
activity and by the support given to the murderers of SS Obergruppenfuehrer
Heydrich, the male adults have been shot, the women have been sent to a
concentration camp and the children have been handed over to appropriate
educational authorities. The buildings of the locality have been levelled to the
ground, and the name of the community has been obliterated.

   (Monitor's note: This is an identical repetition, in German, of an
announcement made in Czech, from Prague at 19.00, when reception was
very bad.)

8. Message to Indians (by Subhas Chandra Bose) 20 July 1942

Recent happenings in the various theatres of war will have unavoidable
repercussions in India. It behoves Indians to forge ahead in the task of
achieving national emancipation. The British Empire has two lungs – Egypt
and India. Without Egypt that Empire would be reduced to one lung – India.
If that lung is also put out of action death will immediately follow. British
politicians and propagandists never visualised a situation such as that facing
them today. The reverses in Russia have been reacting on Britain and
seriously affecting public morale. The declaration of Egyptian independence
made by the Axis powers on entering Egypt had a profound affect on the
Egyptians who have now been seized with a desire to fight boldly for their
independence. Though the British have deprived the Egyptian army of its
modern equipment, it can still be hoped that the Egyptian army and people
will rise to the occasion and make the fullest use of the present opportunity for
winning complete independence. Our countrymen must have noticed that,
since the situation in North Africa became critical for the British Forces,
feelers for a compromise have been sent out to the Indian leaders, largely
through American and Chinese middlemen now living in India. On the other
hand, Conservatives who will hang on to their Empire to the very last, show
no signs of conciliation. The Indian people have fully understood the
imperialist role of Roosevelt and his desire to supplant the dying British

Empire. Consequently, there is no apprehension whatever that our countrymen will be turned from the path of national duty by the smiles or frowns of American politicians. Unfortunately, there are people still carried away by their sympathy for other nations. They do not seem to realise the great change which has taken place in the world situation during the last three years. It would be the height of folly to cling to a past which does not exist today.

For some time past I have been standing outside the circuit of British imperialism as the one (?dog) of Indian Nationalism. It is my duty to tell you what I see and hear and to advise you as to the best means of achieving our national liberation, and to do my utmost to further our national cause wherever I may happen to be. The only master I have served and shall serve, is India. Whatever I have done or may do, has been and will be in accordance with the wishes of the vast majority of my countrymen. Despite all obstacles, I remain in constant contact with my countrymen in India so that there may be the fullest accord between the policy followed by us at home and abroad. In spite of the efforts of British politicians to manufacture differences between the Indian people, and to exaggerate slight existing differences, and of all the bluff and bluster indulged in by the BBC, the whole world knows that the vast majority of the Indian people are determined to overthrow the British yoke. The bold stand taken by our countrymen at home, despite favours and threats, has enabled Indians abroad to hold their head erect with pride. Let me now tell you that the fundamental feature of the present World War is the tragic efforts of Britain and America to hold on to their imperialist tradition, and the equally determined efforts of some other powers to overthrow Britain and America. From the point of view of Indian Nationalism every other feature is secondary. Every Indian has to answer immediately: 'Do I want Britain and America to win this war?' If Britain had recognised the full independence of India there would have been some justification for desiring her to win; but the British have stubbornly refused to grant us our liberty. Perhaps they feel that if India is lost, their Empire will virtually cease to exist. The Indian people have refused to accept the empty promise of Dominion Status after the war and are convinced that an Anglo-American victory will mean the continued enslavement of India and several other nations. Consequently, I say that any Indian who wishes Britain to win this war must be branded as unpatriotic and dishonourable. It should be clear to every thinking man that only through the defeat and break-up of the British Empire can India obtain her liberty.

It is the duty of the Indian people to work for the destruction of that Empire. By a stroke of good luck we find today that several other Powers are striving to tear the British Empire to pieces. We should be grateful for the help given by Italy, Germany and Japan. It is for the Indian people to decide whether they should take any assistance in their struggle for liberty, but should they need such help, they will be perfectly justified in taking it. The less help India requires from outside, the better for her, however. No earthly calculation can offer the slightest hope of a British victory. Why, then, should there be regular attempts at compromise with Britain after every major military defeat suffered by her? They are a waste of time and probably do the Indian people infinite harm by side-tracking the revolutionary energy of the masses. There are three courses open to the Indian people at present – firstly, to side openly with Britain; secondly, to maintain strict neutrality; and thirdly, openly to enter the lists against Britain. To side with Britain will mean sharing her defeat and opening up a new chapter of slavery in India. To maintain neutrality would mean a wiser course of action, but it would not entitle us to liberty on our own merits. In that case, we should have to accept liberty as a gift from the victorious enemies of Britain. Actively to fight against Britain would entitle us to liberty, by virtue of our own efforts and sacrifice and not by the mercy of any power. Such liberty can be preserved in future through our own strength. If we do not play a dynamic role in the struggle against Britain, we shall either not secure our freedom at all, or, if we get it as a gift, we shall not be able to retain it. On the contrary, if we fight now, we shall not only win our freedom soon, but be able to preserve it for ever. Is it not a suicidal policy to think of compromise with a Power which will soon disappear from the face of the earth? If any Indian has not the strength to fight for his country's freedom, the least he can do is remain entirely passive, but refuse to enter into any compromise.

The height of folly for an Indian would be to offer to fight for Britain in return for a compromise. Such an agreement is altogether dishonourable. What interest has India in Europe or Africa or the British Empire, that she should go to war on the side of Britain? The only honourable course for Indians is to utilise the present crisis and fight for Indian independence, which is now within easy reach. It is my duty to draw your attention to the consequences that will follow if we enter into a compromise with Britain. There are people, including some Congressmen, who, in the event of a compromise, are prepared, not only to tolerate foreign troops in India, but also to permit India to be used as a military base by Britain. Such a policy is as pernicious as that of active participation in the war. No independent state will ever allow foreign troops to occupy its territory or to conduct military operations from bases within that territory. That would be the very negation of independence. It should be remembered that if British, American and Chinese troops are allowed to operate from Indian bases, the enemies of Britain will certainly attack them and India will become a theatre of war. It is a back-door method of dragging India into the war and submitting her to the inevitable horrors which will follow. Some of our countrymen are carrying on propaganda in favour of co-operating with Britain's war effort, but are camouflaging their real intentions by talking of helping China. Every Indian would like to help China, but the question is – does Chungking represent the real China? Did not Marshal Chiang Kai-Shek send troops to Burma to help the British retain their domination? Did not the Chungking Ambassador in London publicly declare the other day that Britain would try to reconquer Burma? It seems clear that Chungking is an Anglo-American puppet. A victory for the Allies would reduce China to a virtual colony. I am sure it is possible for Chungking to come to an honourable agreement with Tokyo. Britain's propaganda machinery has been trying to hoodwink the unsophisticated Indian people and to exploit their dire poverty, thereby recruiting them for the army, the police, civic guard and similar organisations. Your endeavour should be to keep them out of such organisations, but if you fail to do so, you should send nationalists and revolutionaries into all these bodies. They should receive all the training the British can give, and use it later for the benefit of the Indian revolution. It is indeed gratifying to know that, in the new Indian Army built up by the British since 1939, we have a fair percentage of friends and supporters. That percentage has to be increased still further in the days to come. This is how revolutions have been made all over the world, and history will repeat itself in India. To all those in internment and prison, I send once again my tribute of love and fraternal greetings. We who are outside India are continuing the battle, and know that the day of Indian liberation is at hand. Once again I pledge myself to carry on relentlessly the fight for India's independence until full success is achieved. Once again I assure you, that my co-operation with other Powers has been, and will always be, on the basis of a complete and unconditional independence of India. When the hour comes, I shall be at your side in order to lead the Indian revolution to its glorious conclusion.

Then it will be your task to take over the responsibility. As I told Mahatma Gandhi in my last talk with him in 1940, when my mission is over and India is liberated, I shall appear before him once again. Till then, let us all go on fighting each with his own weapons in his own place, but all agreed with the common cause and equally determined to bring about the speedy destruction of the British Empire!

9. British fomenting racial discord:
'The coffee-coloured nation'   *27 July 1942*

The July issue of 'Reader's Digest' publishes an article on the role played by American Negroes in the US war effort. These Negroes are determined to fight for a double victory, an external one against the enemy and an internal one against racial prejudice. The South African Minister, Roitz, said the time had not yet come for Kaffirs to receive the same rights as white men in the Union. Nevertheless, it was apparent that this time would come in due course. It is in the light of this declaration that we must understand the statement of Dr Louis Leopold. He said that, after the war, the race barrier must be eliminated. He declared that a coffee-coloured race must exist in the future South Africa just as Red Indian blood was added in the USA. It is very regrettable that a man who had created such true Boer poems as 'Om Gert vertel', had come so utterly under the influence of Smuts and his followers that he is now pleading for the adulteration of the white race, which so far has been kept clean in South Africa. In view of the abnormal character of this man, this is by no means surprising. We are anything but narrow-minded regarding the personal ideas of a man like Louis Leopold. When, however, such a man, with a well-known perverse attraction for Kaffir girls, leaves poetry and approaches the political sphere, then we can only utter a warning.

He has left the sphere in which he can be honoured. What is worse is that he stands side by side with Communists in South Africa. This also explains why the English have lifted the ban on the Communist Party in India. They did this, firstly, because of their alliance with Moscow, and, secondly, because they wished to do everything in their power to sow disunity among the Indian people. Exactly the same policy is applied to South Africa. Since, mainly at the instigation of the Boers, South Africa had succeeded in solving the native question, the present Smuts Government is doing its utmost to make the question so difficult that a final solution seems almost out of reach. This will certainly be the case unless a sound Government is soon placed in power in South Africa.

10. Uncensored news review *9 August 1942*

Rioting broke out in India today, following the arrest of Mahatma Gandhi, Pandit Nehru, Dr Azad and other leaders of the Congress Party. Fighting has been going on in Bombay all day long, a number of persons being killed and scores more injured. This evening, it was reported that the police had had to use tear gas and to open fire on the rebels. Orders were published this afternoon forbidding the carrying of weapons. Assemblies of five or more persons were also forbidden. Hundreds have been arrested and tonight a curfew is being imposed in the city and part of the Province of Bombay. At Allahabad, a curfew has also been imposed after fighting had continued for most of the day. Disorders have also been reported in Cawnpore, Lucknow and Calcutta. 'I pray to God it is not too late', said an expert on Indian affairs, when he heard of the measures taken against the Nationalist leaders. He said the Government should have taken vigorous action at an earlier date. Gandhi is said to be contemplating a fast until death. Meanwhile further arrests have taken place all over India.

11. General Gott shot by Indian N.C.O. *13 August 1942*

The British War Office recently reported that the British General Gott had been killed in action. The truth is that he was shot by Indian soldiers near Cairo. The greatest excitement was caused among Indian soldiers in Egypt when the arrest of Indian leaders and British terror in India became known. The Indian soldiers left their camp on the outskirts of Cairo and adopted a threatening attitude to British officers. When General Gott, who was returning to Cairo in his car from the El Alamein front, passed a group of excited Indian soldiers, an N.C.O. fired three shots at Gott, who was killed instantaneously.

12. Egypt: Indian troops 'unreliable' *26 August 1942*

Our Cairo correspondent informs us that 400 Indian soldiers who were court-martialled in Egypt for refusing to fight for Britain were sent to Suez.

For two days they were not given any food or drink, and, after that, only a starvation diet. The trouble among the Indian troops in Egypt is still spreading. There are now about three Indian divisions in Egypt, of whom there are about 7,000 Indian troops near Cairo. As they are not regarded as reliable they have been withdrawn from the El Alamein Front. This trouble is the aftermath of the murder of General Gott. To nip the trouble in the bud the Punjab Premier was commandeered from India; he has spent a long time in Egypt but has had little success. Mr Churchill did not dare to visit Indian troops when in Cairo.

13. Guerrilla war and plan of action
  (by Subhas Chandra Bose) 4 September 1942

Friends, I want to congratulate you most heartily on your achievements this fortnight. There is no doubt you did a lot of careful thinking and planning before the storm actually burst. There can also be no doubt that you set up in good time an underground organisation to carry on the campaign, even when the leading men were cast in prison. Perhaps most creditable of all was your setting up a transmitting radio station on behalf of the Indian National Congress, to direct and guide the whole movement from one centre. Your achievements have taken the enemy by surprise, and outwitted them completely. The prestige of India all over the world has gone up tremendously, and Indian nationals abroad can now hold their head erect with dignity and pride. This is the last and final struggle that we are waging against British imperialism, and it behoves us, therefore, to look out in advance for any dangers and pitfalls that may beset our path. If we are forewarned we shall also be forearmed, and if we are forearmed our success is guaranteed.

There are four dangers about which I should like to forewarn you. Firstly, the British Empire, which is now going through a process of voluntary liquidation and is in the hands of the auctioneers of Wall Street, may bring in more troops from America , from China and from Africa. We have already in India, American and Chinese troops, and we have in Ceylon African and negro troops, and these ... forces, ... of the India ..., have been growing more and more friendly towards us in recent months. Secondly, the British Government, in its desperation, may resort to more brutal measures for suppressing our movement in the days to come. Thirdly, there may be a gradual weakening of our forces from within, after some months, owing to a feeling that non-violent resistance cannot prevail against guns and bombs. Fourthly, in such a psychological moment, the agents of British imperialism may again put forward an offer or a compromise, and some of you may then be inclined to accept it as a lesser evil than failure.

Friends, it is my duty to warn you here that Britain will never surrender to India's demand for independence. India is the jewel of the British Empire. It is for preserving this jewel that Britain is now fighting. To this end she will fight till the very last. She will debase herself to any extent and stoop to any humiliation, so long as she can retain her hold over India. That is why Mr

Winston Churchill, the high priest of imperialism, the arch-enemy of Indian nationalism and the sworn opponent of all forms of Socialism, swallowed his imperialist pride and presented himself at the gates of the Kremlin. If the agents of British imperialism again put forward feelers for a compromise, it will not be for the purpose of granting India's national demands, but only for creating confusion within our own land and thereby sabotaging our movement morally. It will, therefore, be our solemn duty to prosecute the campaign without any sort of compromise, till the last Britisher is expelled from the soil of India.

I must tell you further that in this fight between nationalist India and imperialist Britain the latter does not depend exclusively on her own strength, nor do we. We know that today India does not stand isolated from the rest of the world. We, too, have powerful friends and allies who will gladly help us (?and contrive) to do so. Moreover, we are convinced that, as a result of the shattering defeats which Britain has been suffering in all the theatres of war, her Empire will soon collapse and break up. The next success in this direction will be the early expulsion of the British from Egypt. When the final dismemberment of the British Empire takes place, power will automatically come into the hands of the Indian people. Since our final victory will not come as a result of our effort alone, it does not matter in the least if we in India meet with temporary setbacks when confronted with machine-guns, bombs, tanks and aeroplanes. Our strategy should consist in sticking to our guns and continuing the campaign in spite of all obstacles and setbacks, to be firm in our belief that Britain will soon be overthrown, and, with the dissolution of her Empire, India will automatically win her freedom.

Friends, I have already assured that whatever I have been doing abroad is in accordance with the wishes of a very large section of my countrymen, and I shall never do anything which public opinion in India will not enthusiastically endorse. Ever since I left home I have remained in constant and intimate contact with my countrymen at home through more channels than one, in spite of all the efforts of the intelligence ... or of the British Secret Service to prevent it. During the last few months, you have had proof of my close contact with my countrymen in India, and many of you know by now how you can communicate with me whenever you so desire. It is no longer possible for the British to prevent my getting into India or out whenever I want to do so. If the British authorities think they know all about me I am glad, for I shall one day be able to give them the shock of their lives. If they had been as clever as they sometimes think they are, I should have been lying in a prison cell today, instead of fighting India's battle all over the world.

Friends, this is a time when all the countries suppressed or dominated by the satanic British Government are either in revolt or preparing for one. If the whole of India joins this fight we shall not only effect our emancipation speedily, but we shall also expedite the liberation of all the countries from Egypt to Iran. On the other hand, if Indian people were to remain inactive, the enemies of Britain would take the initiative in expelling the Britisher from India. The British Empire is in any case doomed, and the only question is as to what will happen to us when its final dissolution takes place. Shall we obtain our freedom as a gift from foreign Powers, or shall we win by our own effort? I would request Mr Jinnah, Mr (?Jayakay), and all those leaders who still think of a compromise with Britain, to realise for once that in the world of tomorrow there will be no British Empire. All those individuals, groups or parties who now participate in the fight of freedom will have an honoured place in free India, but those who still hang on to the coat-tails of our British rulers will naturally become nonentities in future.

You will be interested to know that British politicians are today terribly upset that the Indian people in general are not prepared to resist or oppose the civil disobedience campaign, even if they are not prepared to actively participate in it. It is but natural that the Indian people should take up this attitude. They know that the British are going to be driven out of India soon, as they have already been expelled from Burma. Consequently, all those who now oppose the Nationalist Movement will have to pay for it rather dearly at the end, when we come out victorious.

...

Friends, I appeal most earnestly to my countrymen who are in the British armed forces not to use weapons against their brothers and sisters fighting for the country's emancipation. I hope that in every crisis they will refuse to fire on the Indian people, and that, when a suitable opportunity comes, they will point their rifles at their alien oppressors. I also appeal to my countrymen who are seamen or Lascars not to risk their lives any longer in the service of the British. They know very well how badly they and their families are treated as compared with British seamen. When I was in Europe a few months ago I met some of the Indian seamen who had been rescued from torpedoed ships. Their experience had been horrible, and I was told many more Indian seamen had lost their lives at sea than could be rescued from the sinking ships. If Indian seamen now sacrifice themselves in the service of a Government that is going to disappear soon, nobody will look at them or care for them or their families in future.

In this connection I appeal also to all parties or groups who consider themselves to be Nationalists or anti-Imperialists to come forward and join in the epic struggle going on. I appeal to the progressive elements in the Moslem League, with some of whom I had the privilege of cooperating in the work of the Calcutta Municipal Corporation in 1940. I appeal to the brave Moslem ..., the Nationalist Moslem Party of India, that started in 1939 the civil disobedience against Britain's war effort long before any other party did so. I appeal to the Jamat Ulama, the only representative organisation of the Ulamas, or Muslim divines of India, led by that distinguished patriot, Mufti (?Gefit Ulla). I appeal to the Azad Moslem League. I appeal to the (?Asali Dull), the Nationalist Sikh Party of India and to its leader, (?Massa Parossi), and, last but not least, I appeal to the (?Predar) Party of Bengal, which commands the confidence of the Moslem Presidency of that province, and is led by a well known patriot. I have no doubt that if all these organisations plunged into the struggle, the day of India's salvation will be drawn nearer.

Friends, the campaign now going on in India may be described as a non-violent guerrilla war. In this guerrilla war, the tactics of dispersion have to be employed. We shall spread our activities all over the country, so that the British police and military will not be able to concentrate their attack on one point. In keeping with the principles of guerrilla warfare, we should also be as mobile as possible. The authorities should never be able to predict where our activities will emerge next. By continually harassing them in this manner, their nerves should be worn down, but to achieve this result the campaign has to be carried on for months without any break. Then, as you know already, I have been through all the campaigns between 1921 and 1940 and I know very well the causes of our failure in the past. Of late I have had the opportunity of taking expert advice with regard to the tactics of guerrilla warfare, and I am now in a position to offer you some suggestions as to how the present campaign should be (?brought) to a successful conclusion.

The object of this non-violent guerrilla campaign should be twofold: firstly, to destroy Britain's war production in India, and secondly, to paralyse British administration. Keeping this twofold object in view, every section of the community should participate in the struggle. First, peasants should stop paying all taxes and rents that directly or indirectly bring revenue to the Government. Second, workers in all war industries should either launch a stay-in strike on a demand for higher wages, or they should try to hamper production by conducting a go-slow campaign inside the factories. They should also carry out small acts of sabotage, like removing nuts and bolts from machines, reducing steam-pressure, throwing dust into delicate machines, etc. Third, students should give a fitting reply to the threat of expulsion held out by the provincial Governments and boycott schools and colleges with greater enthusiasm than before. They should organise secret guerrilla bands for carrying on sabotage in different parts of the country. They should also invent new ways of annoying the British authorities: for example burning stamps, etc. in post offices, shouting at Englishmen when they appear on the streets, creating noise and nuisance in Government offices, destroying British monuments, etc. Fourth, women and especially girl students should do underground work of all kinds, especially as secret messengers. They should also provide shelter for the men who fight. Fifth, Government officials prepared to help the campaign secretly should not think of resigning their posts at this stage. Clerks in Government offices and war industries should give all available secret information to the fighters outside and try to hamper war production by working inefficiently and slowly. Sixth, servants working in the houses of Britishers should be organised for the purpose of giving trouble and causing discomfort to their masters, for example by demanding higher salaries, cooking and serving bad food and drink, etc. Seventh, businessmen should give up all business with English firms, banks, insurance companies, etc.

For the general public I suggest the following additional plan for work. Boycott of British goods, including burning British stores and Government stores as well; total boycott of all Britishers in India and all Indians who are genuinely pro-British. Holding public meetings and demonstrations in spite of official prohibition. Publishing Secret bulletins and setting up secret radio stations. Burning Anglo-Indian and pro-British newspapers in public.

Marching to the houses of government officials and demanding their departure from India. Occupying government offices and institutions, like law courts, (?Secretariat) buildings, etc., with a view to dislocating the administration. Punishing police officers and prison officials who oppress or persecute the people. Erecting barricades in streets whenever there is likelihood of a clash with the police and the military. Setting fire to Government offices and factories working for war purposes. Travelling without tickets in railway trains in large numbers. Interrupting postal, telegraph and telephone communications as frequently as possible and in different places. Interrupting railway, bus or tram services, whenever there is a possibility of hampering the transport of soldiers or war materials. Storming and destroying police stations, railways and gaols in isolated places. Carrying on agitations for the release of political prisoners.

Friends, I can assure you that if only a part of this plan is put into operation all over the country, the administrative machinery can be brought to a standstill and war production ... In this direction, I must remind you that, in a non-violent guerrilla campaign, the peasantry always plays a decisive part. I am glad to notice that in several provinces, for example in Behar and the Central Provinces, the peasants are already in the forefront. I earnestly hope that ... and the peasant leaders, who, with the Forward Bloc, started the fight in April 1940, long before Mahatma Gandhi did, will now lead the campaign to a victorious conclusion. We want Swaraj for the masses, Swaraj for the peasants and workers. Consequently, the peasants and workers must be in the front-line of the struggle, for they who fight and win liberty always inherit power and responsibility. Then it is encouraging to hear that, for the first time, the people of the Indian States have begun to participate in an all-India national struggle. Reports to that effect have already come in from Baroda, Mysore, Hyderabad, and Kashmir, and I am confident that the day is not far off when the States in general will line up with the people in British India and form a common front against the combined strength of British imperialism and the Indian princes. Most gratifying of all is the news that the clarion call of liberty has reached the ears and the hearts of our soldiers at home and abroad. In Meerut and other places in India, and also in Egypt, Indian soldiers have revolted. They have no doubt been court-martialled and put down with characteristic imperialist brutality, but the fire is spreading from one place to another. A large number of Indian soldiers have voluntarily deserted to the Axis Forces in Egypt, and they have been welcomed with open arms by the latter. As a consequence all the Indian fighting units have been withdrawn from the El Alamein Front, as being unreliable. No wonder some Indian flunkeys of British imperialism have been hastily brought up from India in order to influence the Indian troops, but their efforts have so far failed. In fact, even the London radio announced on 2nd September – that is yesterday – that Sir Sikander Hyad Khan had received many complaints from Indian soldiers against the British officers, and that the soldiers wanted to go home on leave just as the British soldiers were allowed to do. In conclusion, I desire to draw your attention to the 6th September, 1942, on which day the Viceroy of India desires pro-British demonstrations to be organised. In accordance with the appeal of the National Congress Radio, I call upon you, friends, to organise from your side an all-India Day on the 6th September for opposing and, if necessary, breaking up all Governmental demonstrations, and for holding counter-demonstrations demanding that the Britishers should leave India at once. In other words, observe the 6th September as a National Quit India Day – not only British India but in the States as well. Let there be meetings and demonstrations from one end of India to the other. Let the sky be rent with the shouts of 'Go back, John Bull' ('Ungrez chalo jao') and write the words 'Go Back!' and (?'Chale jao') on every conceivable place, on the walls, on the trees, on the tram-cars, on the buses, on the trains, in fact, everywhere. And, last but not least, flood the whole country with the letters 'Q.I.' meaning 'Quit India', so that wherever the Britisher may turn his eyes, he will see these large letters 'Q.I.' staring him in the face. I am sure, friends, that if you organise properly a National Quit India Day on the 6th September, you will rouse such tremendous revolutionary enthusiasm among millions of our countrymen that, on that memorable day, you will also, sound the death-knell of British imperialism in India ...

14. Negro Soviet Republic for USA: secret plan discovered   *24 September 1942*

V(ölkische) B(eobachter) on Saturday morning. The paper publishes in facsimile a report of the French Ambassador to Moscow, Jean Herbette, dated 15th January 1931 which contains the guiding principles of the Comintern for dealing with the Negro problem in the USA. Herbette's report together with numerous other documents fell into German hands during the campaign in France. According to Herbette's report, the Comintern in 1930 issued detailed instructions as to how the Negro problem in the USA was to be dealt with. The following procedure was outlined and recommended by the Comintern. Firstly, the Negroes in the northern states of the Union, who are mostly industrial workers, are to fight for full equality rights, using for this purpose class warfare slogans, secondly nine million Negroes in the Black Belt of the South, where the Negroes are forming a majority of the population, are to demand the right of self-determination in order to secede from the Union and form an independent Negro Republic, as long as the USA remains a capitalistic state. If the Union should however become a Soviet Republic, the independent Negro Republic should again be incorporated in the American Union Soviet Republic. In the South, Communist propaganda was recommended to exploit for propaganda purpose the existing discrimination between Negroes and Whites. Demands of Negroes are to be realised at expense of the Whites. the programme prepared by the Communist International comprised the following three points: (several hundred words on the details of the proposed Negro Soviet Republic.)

15. Japanese heroes of Sydney harbour: Admiral Abo 7 *October 1942*

Four heroes of a special attack submarine flotilla which raided Sydney harbour on 31st May lived up to the best traditions of the Japanese Navy, Admiral Baron Abo, former Navy Minister and former member of Supreme War Council declared in Chugai. Once inside the enemy harbour the attacking Japanese submarines decided not to return unless duties discouraged, according to the traditional naval spirit, and the action symbolises the Japanese Navy, Abo said, adding: 'At their heroic act I cannot but bow in deep reverence.' Abo expressed the belief that the Australian Government in admiration of the noble self-sacrificing spirit of the naval heroes for Emperor and country, sent home the ashes of the war dead. He also revealed he visited Sydney in 1891 on a training cruise spending several days at the Australian port. He declared the mouth of the port was very narrow making it an ideal naval base.

16. Egypt: offensive reviewed
   (The Axis account of El Alamein) 1 *November 1942*

The High Command reports on the situation in North Africa: The large-scale British offensive in Egypt, continued in the past week, did not surprise the command of the German-Italian troops. When, on the evening of 23rd October, the artillery preparation was started and followed, at 23.00 by the infantry attack, the German-Italian defence was fully prepared. The position taken up by our troops covering approximately 50 to 60 kms between the sea and the Qattara depression, which is useless for large-scale movements and could not be encircled. The British were therefore compelled to make a frontal attack and deployed English troops over a breadth of 14 km leaving the remainder – in fact, the major part – to Dominion and Allied contingents. The main weight of the attack was at first directed against both wings of our positions, presumably so as to achieve penetration which could be developed into enveloping movements. In the offensive the British concentrated their strength on the Northern wing. Twice they also attempted to land in the rear of the defenders near Mersa Matruh. Both times, immediately during the first night and again on 29th October, the alertness of the covering forces frustrated the British attempt. The first attempt was foiled at sea by the interception of bombers. During the second attempt more effectively planned by landing at points, A.A. artillery was employed in the defence.
   The British continued the land offensive stubbornly, employing strong artillery and tank forces and bringing up more and more fresh reserves. At a few points they succeeded in making local penetrations, cleared up every time by German and Italian counter-attacks. The fighting swayed to and fro around important sectors but at no point were the British able to reach the main position, let alone pierce it. Up to 29th October they lost 345 armoured fighting vehicles and, as our troops succeeded repeatedly in cutting off the foremost spearheads of the attack, several hundred prisoners were taken.

The numerical superiority of the RAF could not alter these results. In the first four days of fighting it lost 60 planes, five by A.A., the remainder in air combat with Germans and Italians. On 30th October the British lost eight planes. From 25th to 30th October inclusive the Germans alone shot down 44 British planes, losing only 19. German and Italian bombers and fighter-bombers repeatedly reached assembly points and supply roads of the attackers, causing heavy losses.

17. *'Views on the News' by William Joyce, 'otherwise known as Lord Haw-Haw': Communist threat to Britain*   *14 February 1943*

As I have commented on other occasions, the offensives which Stalin has launched this winter have been costly in the extreme, and have – despite the gains of ground achieved – inflicted staggering blows on the Soviet war potential itself. Repeatedly I have pointed out that one day the order will be given to the German forces to resume the offensive; and when this day comes there will begin the period at which it will really be possible to pass reasoned judgments, supported by facts, upon Stalin's strategy.

In the meantime the German people are supremely and serenely confident of final victory. Let there be no doubt whatever on that point. On the other hand, they have taken to heart what the Fuehrer has told them more than once – that victory will not be presented as a free gift on a silver platter to those who merely hope for it and talk about it. Victory is a prize to be won only by sacrifice and in this case by whole-hearted, thorough, and radical sacrifice. The reverses the forces of European civilisation have suffered on the Front against Bolshevism only serve to emphasise the need for leaving nothing to chance, the need for a concentration of energy and will upon the goal of victory. I do not feel it necessary to describe in detail how that concentration is now being achieved here in Germany. I would only say that the whole nation has responded with a magnificent devotion to the Fuehrer's Proclamation of 30th January, in which he uttered the memorable words: 'This is a war, not of conquerors and conquered, but of the survivors and the annihilated.'

Throughout Germany today there is a new spirit, the spirit of total war, of grim determination to defeat Bolshevism by sacrificing all that does not pertain to the struggle – this struggle of life and death.

Now there may be some people in Britain who, misled by the present tenor of their official propaganda, will not only challenge my description of the fight against Bolshevism as a life-and-death struggle, but will even laugh in their folly and deride the warning. And yet it was only three years ago that Mr Winston Churchill said: 'We cannot predict the fate of Finland. But no sadder spectacle could be presented to what is left of civilised mankind than that this splendid Northern race should at last be worn down and reduced to a servitude worse than death by the dull, brutish force of overwhelming numbers.'

That was how Churchill described the danger of Bolshevism three years ago. Why should his views have undergone such a drastic revision in the meanwhile?

'A servitude worse than death' is not an inappropriate phrase to describe the fate of those who might physically survive, at least with their bare lives, the victory of Jewish-controlled Bolshevism. But if such a victory would have been, as Churchill argued, a terrible catastrophe for gallant little Finland, why should it be any lesser catastrophe for Germany, for France, for Norway, for Holland, for Spain, or, indeed, for England? I would recall the recent and very incisive aphorism used by Goebbels who pointed out that the Channel would in certain eventualities provide no barrier against Bolshevism. As he very wisely said, an idea is not dependent upon convoys for its propagation. And I think it was about 120 years ago that Metternich observed that fevers were no respectors of national boundaries.

Why then should there be such calm confidence in Britain today that Communism cannot rear its head in that land? The easy catchphrase 'It can't happen here' might prove to be very misleading in this connection. I see, for example, that in the Midlothian by-election the government candidate saved the seat by a narrow margin, less than 900 votes. He only just managed to defeat a person called Wintringham who, whatever label he may have adopted for the purpose of the by-election, is known throughout Britain as a rank Communist and one of those whose chief claims to notoriety is that he fought on the side of the Communists in the Spanish Civil War. That an individual with a record such as he possesses should have come within an ace of being elected to the House of Commons for what was considered a safe government seat, shows that there must be very profound changes taking place at the present time in British public opinion. It may be added that in another by-election the result of which was announced yesterday, the government candidate also had a narrow escape from defeat by Mr Wise, whose extreme left views are sufficiently well known to require no elaboration on my part.

No doubt in Conservative H.Q. there must be both anxiety and a certain amount of bewilderment at these results, which were not at all expected. The mystery, however, is not very hard to solve. Churchill in his attempts to please the Kremlin has given his agents carte blanche to allow the Communists to do as they please and to propagate their doctrines throughout the country. And to give Communism controlled from Moscow a free hand is to give an invitation to the Bolsheviks which they are very unlikely to reject. Even in peacetime the Soviet Embassy in London and the institution known as Arcos were hives of intrigue both against the Government and against British interests.

Of course Churchill's advisers may now tell him that this pro-Soviet agitation will subside as soon as the attempt is made to set up a Second Front in Europe or when the Bolsheviks profess themselves satisfied with the amount of supplies delivered to them by their allies. This, however, is a very dangerous argument. It is one thing to attempt an invasion of Europe and quite a different matter to attempt it with success. Nor is there any reason at all to believe that the Soviets will ever be satisfied with the quantity of food and raw materials which Britain and America can deliver in their harbours. It is a very dangerous fallacy to argue that people in Britain who now wish to support the Bolsheviks on military grounds will not later desire to support them on political grounds as well. It is also interesting to note that these election results, so unfavourable to the Government, followed Churchill's speech to the House on Thursday. I would repeat that it is not possible when an alliance has been concluded with the Soviets to shut out Bolshevik ideas with watertight bulkheads, and the ruling class of Britain does not as yet realise what hostages it gave to fortune in assenting to Churchill's pact with Moscow. But before long the members of that class may have reason to ponder on these words. 'The Bolsheviks despise such a mere commonplace as nationality. Their ideal is a world-wide proletarian revolution.' This is the verdict not of Goebbels but of Churchill, who uttered these words in the House on 5th November 1919. For the moment I will not attempt to outline what consequences a Soviet victory would produce for the Middle East and India. It is enough for me to remark that the greatest damage of which Bolshevism is capable has to do, not with the oil of the Middle East or the wealth of India – it has to do with the soul and the being of all that we prize in Western civilisation, those values which today are being defended and will be defended until victory or death by the armies that Hitler leads.

References for Appendix

1. SWB 898. Zeesen. IG(i)
2. SWB 957. Free India Radio. IG(ii)
3. SWB 962. Free India Radio. IG(ii)
4. SWB 967. Frankfurt (German Home Stations). IA(x-xi)
5. SWB 978. Tokyo. 9(ii)
6. SWB 971. Free India Radio. IG(i)
7. SWB 1,059. Prague (Czech Home Stations). ID(5 Protectorate) (ii)
8. SWB 1,099. Free India Radio. IG(i)
9. SWB 1,106. Zeesen (in Afrikaans). IJ(ii-iii)
10. SWB 1,119. New British Broadcasting Station (Axis Origin) IB(i)
11. SWB 1,122. German Home Service via Luxemburg. IA(xxi)
12. SWB 1,136. Free India Radio. IG(i)
13. SWB 1,145. Free India Radio. IG(i-iv)
14. SWB 1,165. Germany, Transocean. 0020
15. SWB 1,178. Japan, Domei. 0710
16. SWB 1,203. German Home Service via Friesland. IA(ix)
17. SWB 1,308. Calais, English Group. IB(vii)

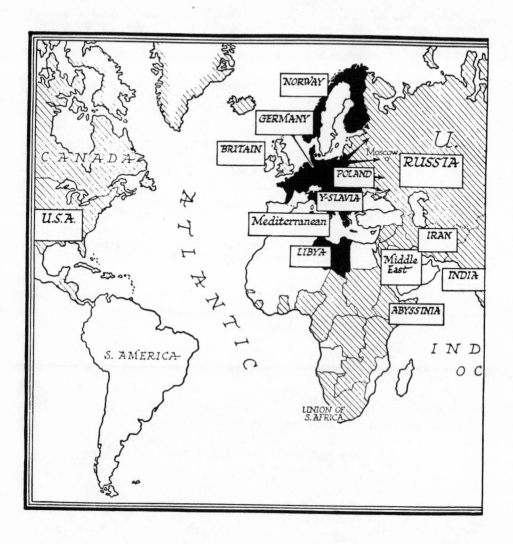

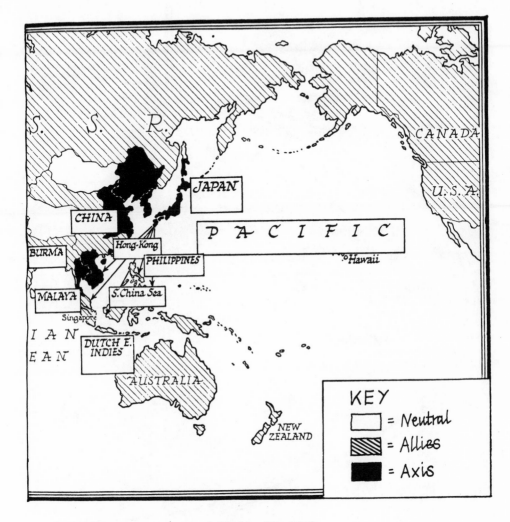

KEY

☐ = Neutral

▨ = Allies

■ = Axis

A World at War 1942

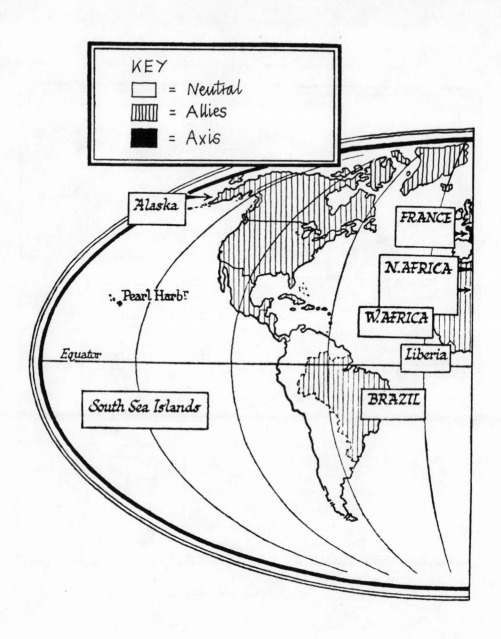

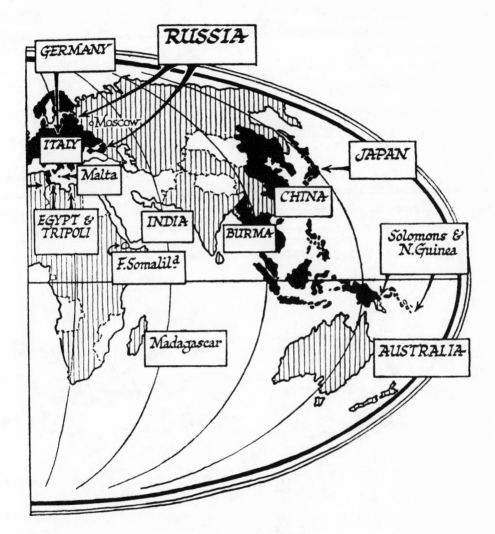

A World at War 1943

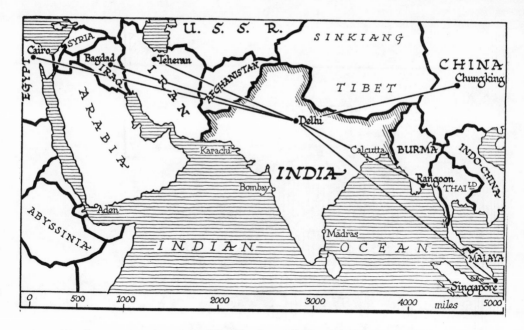

War Clouds over India

The Threat to Australia

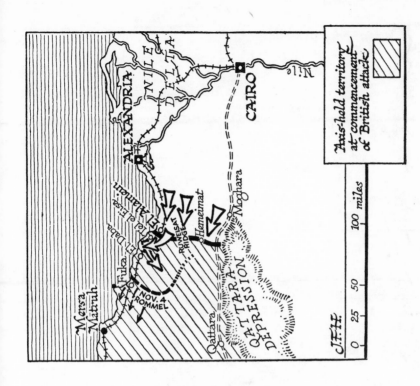

The Battle of El Alamein

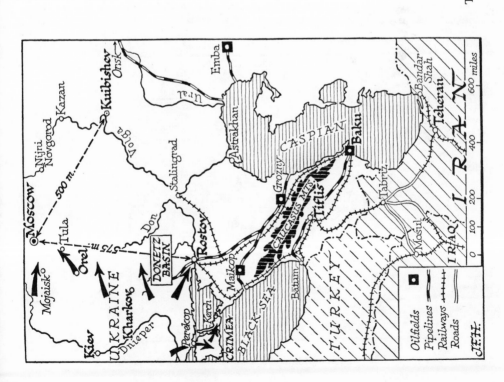

The Threat to the Caucasus

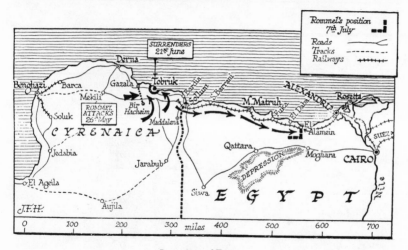

Invasion of Egypt

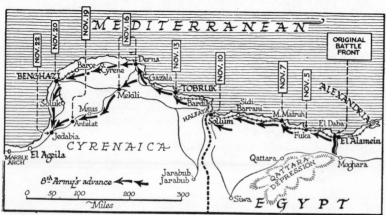

The Pursuit of Rommel I

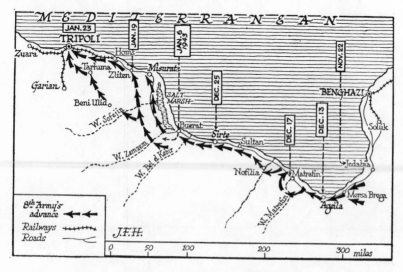

The Pursuit of Rommel II

Burma in the War Zone

The Conquest of Madagascar

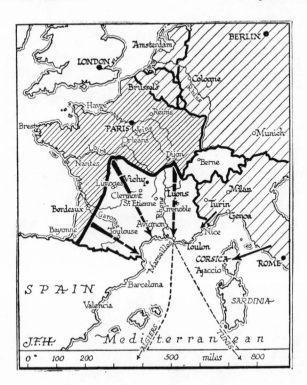

Hitler Occupies Vichy France

George Orwell (the pen name of Eric Blair) is best known for his shocking and cautionary tales of the future, *1984* and *Animal Farm*. He documented his experiences during the Spanish Civil War in *Homage to Catalonia* and has contributed such classics as *Down and Out in Paris and London* and the essay "Shooting an Elephant."